The Irish World Wide
History, Heritage, Identity

Volume 1 **Patterns of Migration**

The Irish World Wide
History, Heritage, Identity

Edited by Patrick O'Sullivan

The Irish World Wide
History, Heritage, Identity

Volume 1
Patterns of Migration

Edited by Patrick O'Sullivan

Leicester University Press
London and Washington

Leicester University Press
A Cassell imprint
Wellington House, 125 Strand, London WC2R 0BB, England
PO Box 605, Herndon, VA 20172

First published 1992
Reprinted in paperback 1997
© Editor and contributors 1992

British Library Cataloguing in Publication Data
A catalogue record for this book is available from the
British Library

ISBN 0 7185 0118 7

Typeset by Florencetype Ltd, Kewstoke, Avon
Printed and bound in Great Britain by Biddles Ltd, Guildford and King's Lynn

In memory of Michael O'Sullivan

Contents

List of illustrations

List of tables

List of contributors

Linda Dowling Almeida is a doctoral student in the history department at New York University. Her field of interest is late 19th and 20th century Irish migration to America. She lives in Upper Montclair, New Jersey.

Patrick Fitzgerald is Assistant Curator at the Ulster-American Folk Park in Northern Ireland. He is presently involved in the planning of a major exhibition on the subject of emigration from Ulster to America since 1700. He hopes to submit his Ph.D. thesis, 'Poverty and Vagrancy in early modern Ireland' to the Queen's University of Belfast in the autumn of 1992. He has a particular interest in the Irish in early modern Britain.

Seamus Grimes is a Geographer at University College, Galway. He specialises in a range of economic and social issues, among which is Australian immigration policy.

Gerard Hanlon is currently based at Trinity College, Dublin where he is completing his Ph.D. with the Sociology Department. His research interests include elite migration from peripheral societies, the social and economic development of the European periphery, and the future of professional work.

Joseph A. King of Lafayette, California, taught English at Diablo Valley College in Pleasant Hill, California, before his retirement. Specializing in Irish settlements in the New World, he is the author of several books and numerous articles in publications in Canada, Ireland, and the United States.

John McGurk is a writer with special interests in the study of early modern British and Irish history. He is Head of History at the Liverpool Institute of Higher Education and Visiting Lecturer at the Institute of Irish Studies, University of Liverpool and is a Fellow of the Royal Historical Society.

Patrick McKenna is a mature post-graduate Geography student in St

Patrick's College, Maynooth, Co. Kildare, Ireland. He is submitting a thesis entitled *Irish Migration to Argentina* for a Masters Degree in July 1992.

Alun Munslow is Principal Lecturer in the School of Arts, Staffordshire University, England. His published interests include the Irish experience in America, and he is author of the forthcoming *Discourse and Culture: the Creation of America, 1870–1920*.

T. D. Regehr is a Canadian business historian who has written extensively about Canadian railway, hydro-electric and other business undertakings. He is a Professor of History at the University of Saskatchewan.

James Sturgis is a co-director of the Centre of Canadian Studies at Birkbeck College, University of London and is a past President of the British Association for Canadian Studies. During 1991–92 he was Visiting Professor at the University of New Brunswick.

General introduction to the series

Patrick O'Sullivan

Here is an island. An island in the North Atlantic Ocean, a small island sitting next to a larger island, a little archipelago off the coast of Europe. An island the same size as Sri Lanka, for example – but with a much smaller population. Our island, Ireland, now has a population of about five million. Yet, throughout the world, many millions of people claim some Irish heritage or descent. At the same time migration is once again, or still, a major issue for present day Ireland. In a world characterized by population movement and flight, this is important. And this is interesting. How are we to study the Irish migrations, and their consequences? And how are we to share our experiences, and our understanding, with others?

A first chart

When I am asked to describe or explain *The Irish World Wide* I use a variety of images and expressions. The expression that comes most readily to my lips, just at the moment, is 'a good kick'. I wanted to give a good kick to the world-wide, interdisciplinary and comparative study of the Irish migrations.

But the best image, really, is that of a map or chart. The six volumes of *The Irish World Wide* map out an area of interdisciplinary academic study, one of those areas where, I feel, the interdisciplinary approach can bring genuine rewards and insights, and a more rounded understanding. We can call it, this new thing of ours, 'Irish Migration Studies'. And if I sometimes speak of 'Irish Migration Studies' as if it already exists, you will forgive me – for you will understand that, inside my head at least, it has already been in existence for some time. Irish Migration Studies is not quite the same thing as 'Irish Studies', as 'Irish Studies' has developed. Irish Migration Studies, it may be, is a response to the gaps, and distortions, found within 'Irish Studies'. In effect *The Irish World Wide* series asks: if there were an interdisciplinary academic area called Irish Migration Studies, what themes would it consider? What disciplines would it draw on?

Research is like coral – it builds on what is already there. It grows. And it leaves gaps. This first map of Irish Migration Studies will at times, necessarily, be somewhat crude – in places the map will be, if anything, over-detailed, in other places it will work through broad strokes, it will make suggestions. As you would expect with the first chart, in many areas the *Irish World Wide* series does not offer the authoritative last word on a subject – often it offers the first word. There will still be gaps, empty spaces in our chart – 'here be dragons'.

Such gaps are irritating to people who work from first principles. And it is worth spending some time looking at the pattern of gaps and seeing how and why they have arisen.[1] There is always the danger, not only within formal academic circles, that the research agenda is being decided for us – that, for example, we study what can easily be studied, rather than what needs to be studied for true understanding.

I have tracked the developing study of the Irish and their migrations. I have trawled the world. I found out what was being written about the Irish migrations, what was being studied and how it was being studied. What I found was an emotional and intellectual need to look at the Irish migrations, not simply as a sub-department of United States history, or of Canadian history, or of Australian history, or of English, Welsh and Scottish history – or of any country's history. There was a need to at least begin the study of the Irish migrations, for themselves, in a coherent and intellectually satisfying way. And I found an intellectual and emotional need to bring the migrations stage-centre to the study of Irish history.

In 1991, like Pangur Bán, I struck. I collected together the material to make the six volumes of *The Irish World Wide*. The series thus represents a report on 'the state of the art'. This is what world-wide Irish Migration-Studies looks like now. This series looks at the academic disciplines that are contributing to Irish Migration Studies. It does this in the simplest way possible, by placing before you chapters by practitioners of most of those disciplines. Most of those disciplines, but not all. Academic disciplines do have trouble in talking to each other. And the experience of talking to practitioners of some academic disciplines is like nothing more or less than that exercise we have experienced in therapeutic groups, where the group forms a ruck, and hugger-mugger, prevents any communication with outsiders.

We must try to sympathize with that attitude, for there are constant problems with an interdisciplinary approach. Each discipline, in turn finds its methodology not understood, its conclusions over-simplified, its vocabulary, or jargon, hijacked. Each discipline has its own methodologies and its own vocabularies, and the most dangerous moment is, perhaps, when a simple everyday word has one meaning within one discipline and a very different, or an exact opposite, meaning within another. I will try to alert you when that danger is present.

An academic discipline changes over time, often through fragmentation.[2] Or a discipline will be invaded by some general theory that a sister discipline abandoned ten years ago. One of the minor pleasures, and frustrations, of the interdisciplinary approach is to watch such theories wander, like some computer virus, from field to field.

But there are ground rules to the development of all disciplines. The way forward is quite simple: be conscious of methodology. Every methodology has its strengths and its limitations. There are perceptions that can only be arrived at by listening to a song in a pub, there are perceptions that can come only through the careful analysis of census material. Whatever methodology is used, the methodology must be clear, true to itself and know its own limitations.

My aim, then, is to bring you so much stuff, covering such a wide chronology, so many different themes and destinations, that you can make your own assessment of the present state of Irish Migration Studies. Then, without losing sight of the particular lived experience, you can make your own judgement about overall patterns.

Now, I do need to say something about my approach to the development of *The Irish World Wide* series, and about the selection of contributors and contributions. One of my aims of *The Irish World Wide* is to encourage you to undertake your own research. If your discipline, or your intended discipline, is broadly within history, the human sciences, or the study of culture generally, here is an area that offers intellectual rewards and insights. There is work to be done.

I must stress that the *Irish World Wide* series is an academic publishing project – that is its special contribution to the study of the Irish migrations. Other approaches have their place, their justifications and their agendas, and we can look at those. But here we are within the world of academic research, a rather formal world, with its own courtesies and rituals, its own feuds and vendettas. Coming into any academic debate, it has been said, is like coming into a cinema half-way through a gangster movie. Who are these people? Why are they shooting at each other? And who are the good guys?

Generally, of course, it is not a matter of good guys or bad guys. Though argument can be fierce, especially when a certain view of history is taken to support a certain view of politics.[3] Such arguments are not unusual, and are certainly not unique to the study of Irish history. It is in an effort to offer some sort of balance that I have brought you so many contributions, from many different disciplines, with many different research styles and approaches. One chapter will, indeed, work through a consideration of music in a pub, another will work through detailed analysis of census material. Interdisciplinary Irish Migration Studies puts the song next to the census, studies the individual and the masses. But, whether studying song or census, Irish Migration Studies must be thoughtful and thoroughly methodologically correct. We are teaching methodology by example.

All methodologies have their limitations, but the strength of the *Irish World Wide* series is the variety of methods and academic disciplines it calls upon. Each chapter is a thorough, sound piece of work within its writer's own discipline, whether that writer be historian, sociolinguist, ethnomusicologist, social geographer, sociologist, literary theorist ... You will appreciate that the contributors, as well as writing for you, are writing for their colleagues.

So, each chapter must stand alone, sound within its own discipline. But we know that the *Irish World Wide* series will now be the starting point for those who wish to study the Irish migrations. It will be used by beginners, in private reading and in seminars. Contributors have therefore made their chapters good starting points, using notes and comments to create, for you, jumping-off points into the literature and the thinking on that particular theme. In literary criticism, for example, I have sought out contributors who could guide students through easily available texts from an Irish Migration Studies perspective.

Throughout the series, I have sought to make telling points through simple juxtaposition – as an example, Volume 1, *Patterns of Migration*, begins with a study of the Irish poor in the sixteenth century and ends with a study of 'New Irish' 'illegals' in present day New York. It is for you to judge whether or not these juxtapositions work – whether the past can illuminate the present, or the present illuminate the past. What message can we give to the future?

Certainly I think that illuminating juxtapositions are created by the choice of contributors. 'The medium is the message': a point is made about Irish Migration Studies by our very diversity. The aim was to have, as much as possible, a good world-wide spread within each volume, to have a telling mix of academic disciplines, and a nice combination of well-known names, established academics, rising stars and freelancers. Sometimes you will find that a chapter within *The Irish World Wide* series is a contributor's first published work, or the first time that that a particular approach has been brought within the academic research fold. This is not a matter of your editor being kind and charitable, this is my attempt to draw the map, fill the gaps, to shape Irish Migration Studies, to give the good kick.

Generally, in my Introductions, I have tried to avoid jargon or technical vocabulary. As I have said, each discipline has its own jargon. Jargon is necessary, as a mode of analysis, if we are not to be trapped within the tyranny of common-sense language, and as a kind of shorthand within a discipline. But, in *The Irish World Wide*, we draw on so many disciplines and sub-disciplines, that there is a danger of getting bogged down in a quagmire of competing jargons. I have tried to control things.

I have not tried to impose an overview on the project. Contributors and chapters are not in *The Irish World Wide* series because I agree with them. You may find the approach of one chapter, in effect, contradicted by another. That is the state of the art, and we must acknowledge that there are different ways of analysing and understanding this complex of experiences.

Some of the editor's tasks have been, as it were, delegated – only sensible in a project of this size. You will notice that, at a number of points in the series, I stop the action and we have a more general chapter, a theoretical overview or a chapter of historiography – 'the story so far' – written by some eminent, and eminently brave, scholar. This generous support makes my task, in the Introductions to the individual volumes, an unusual, and unusually interesting, one. Yes, I must help place each chapter within a context, and I must also try to show how that chapter's discipline might link with other academic disciplines.

Stream and counterstream

Whilst I do not want to impose any particular overview, neither do I want to disguise my own theories and preconceptions. I think it right that I lay before you some of my own ground rules, as I developed this project. My first preconception – you might say, precondition – I laid down in the opening paragraphs of this General Introduction. There is something here to be studied. An interdisciplinary approach makes sense.

It does help, in an interdisciplinary area, if we have some over-arching structure. And I now want to outline two attempts of my own to develop some sort of structure, not in order to develop a 'thesis' but simply to find a way of ordering this diverse material, and, as I said in my opening paragraph, to find a way of sharing our experiences and understanding with others.[4]

Everett S. Lee's 'Theory of Migration' seems to have had very little direct influence on Irish Migration Studies, which is surprising given that so many researchers of other migrant groups go back to Lee, for perceptions and a basic structure.[5] Lee thus offers Irish Migration Studies a convenient window (to use more computer jargon) through which to get at and link studies of Irish migration with studies of other migrant groups. Lee's very short paper is like a checklist for future researchers; where and when does the Irish experience fit neatly within Lee's model, and where and why is there no tidy fit?

Lee's model identifies pluses and minuses for the migrant, in the place of origin and in the destination. The model also has places for 'intervening obstacles' and 'personal factors'. In other words it has a place for the journey, which figures so largely in the migrants' own accounts of their experiences. And it has a place for the study of the individual life.[6]

Amongst the perceptions I pick up from Lee are, for example, the importance of perception itself, and knowledge, the way migration itself operates to increase migration, and the patterns of 'stream and counterstream'. In Irish Migration Studies we have very good examples of 'stream'[7]

'Counterstream' has been less studied, partly, perhaps, because it does not figure so largely in Irish history. A study of such an absence would itself be significant, and would no doubt take us deep into Irish social and political history. But we might note that two key figures in twentieth-century Irish social and political history, James Larkin (born in Liverpool) and James Connolly (born in Edinburgh) are examples of 'counterstream'. Many of the key figures in Ireland's late nineteenth century and early twentieth century cultural history are examples of 'counterstream'. But the examination of cultural products and culture producers I want to leave to another volume of *The Irish World Wide*, Volume 3, *The Creative Migrant*.

Oppression, compensation, contribution

Is there any way we can categorize earlier research into the Irish migrations? What follows is based on Gerda Lerner's categorization of women's history. With some caution, and some modification, I have found it useful. The analogies are not exact, but the insights are fruitful. I think it appropriate to introduce Lerner here, remembering, of course, that an entire volume of *The Irish World Wide* series is devoted to *Irish Women*. I must add that this is not the first time that Lerner's insights have been thought helpful in the study of Irish themes – it was reassuring to find her quoted so appositely in Luddy and Murphy, *Women Surviving*.[8]

Often, Lerner feels, women's history starts from a position of seeing women as victims, continually oppressed; this focus keeps women within a conceptual framework shaped by the oppressor, and does not allow us to build up a history of women 'functioning in that male-defined world *on their own terms*. The question of oppression does not elicit that story, and is therefore a tool of limited usefulness to the historian.' Given this background of 'oppression history', women's history has moved in two directions: towards 'compensation history' and 'contribution history'. Compensation history would focus on 'famous' or 'extraordinary' women, for example, in Irish terms, Maud Gonne or Constance Markievicz. Contribution history would emphasise women's contribution to political or social movements: examination of the Ladies' Land League would revolve around women's contribution to the male-run Land League, and its success or failure judged entirely, or almost entirely, in those terms.[9]

Applying Lerner's insights to Irish Migration Studies, and to the study of Irish migrants, female and male, it is clear that large amounts of earlier work would fall into the broad categories: oppression history, compensation history, contribution history.

Some studies of Irish migration are 'oppression history' in its purest form. Now, let me make it clear that by acknowledging the existence of a category called 'oppression history' I am not saying that there was no oppression. Or that I am belittling that way of understanding the past, or the present. It is just that, like Gerda Lerner, I am aware of the limitations of that way of understanding – in particular that it conspires with the oppressor to let the oppressor shape our agenda. You will see that I offer you little in the way of studies of anti-Irish prejudice, for in my view that was not where the research gap lay. Prejudice itself certainly demands study, but a study of anti-Irish prejudice is not the same thing as a study of Irish migrants.[10] Yes, it is difficult to get past the prejudice, which so often fills our possible sources, get past and get through to the people themselves. Again, we are talking about methodology.

You can move on, to look at the ways that an oppressed people shape and use their history. To a great extent, to an extraordinary extent, the traditional history of the Irish migrations has been almost pure 'compensation history'. To an oppressed people the achievements of the Irish outside and inside Ireland in a glorified past, or outside Ireland in a tragic or difficult present, provide compensation – or perhaps, I could better say, evidence.

Evidence that 'failure', lack of achievement, or success, within Ireland, had not to do with some intrinsic inability within the group or the individual – as oppressors assert. Assertions about what those intrinsic inabilities might be are familiar to students of Irish history, and will become familiar to you as this series progresses.

The problems with a 'compensation history' approach to the study of Irish migrants are at once apparent. It tends to focus on 'famous', 'extra-ordinary', and successful people, usually people who are successful as a materialist world measures success. Hence the focus on Irish self-made millionaires – bless them all. And (here we are in the middle of that huge debate within the discipline of history itself) it reinforces history's tendency to focus on people who leave archives. It ignores 'the people whose sole historical accomplishment seems to have been that they lived.'[11] It can lead to certain sorts of Irish people becoming 'lost' to us.

The compensation history of an oppressed people will contain its own tensions and ambiguities. The simplest example is the focus on 'bandit' figures, of the sort analysed by Hobsbawm: there is always the suggestion that these are people of courage, organization and ingenuity, whose manifest abilities might have been better directed under a different political or social system.[12]

Then there is 'contribution history'. A massive amount of earlier work will fall into this category. Titles like *Australia's debt to the Irish nation-builders* come to mind.[13] But much recent scholarship is substantially 'contribution history' in action, and is valued as such, the Irish contribution to the American War of Independence, is an example.[14]

In fact, you can see at once that there is a continuum. An oppressed people produce compensation history as one way of countering oppression, and part of that compensation history will be contribution history. You can see this continuum in studies of the 'Wild Geese', Irish soldiers in the military forces of France, Spain or Austria in the eighteenth century. The Wild Geese are seen as driven out by oppression, their successes become a kind of compensation to the Irish in Ireland, and their contribution is such that the British government re-thinks its military recruitment policies. Battlefields have a simple and brutal way of measuring 'success'.[15]

A book like Davin's *The Irishman in Canada* moves through oppression, compensation and contribution histories in one coherent argument.[16] An excellent modern study of the Irish in San Francisco ends with an approving quote from one of its nineteenth century sources, in a plain statement of the historiographic pattern: oppression, compensation/success, contribution.[17]

That historiographic pattern (oppression, compensation and contri-bution) is, of course, particularly strong in studies of a migrant people, by a migrant people. They are often faced with prejudice and discrimination in their new communities, and need to prove that they can contribute, and have contributed, to the development of their new lands. Let me say again this sort of material, and this sort of approach, is not to be rejected. It is to be embraced, enfolded within Irish Migration Studies. It is an important part of what we are studying.

But there are problems. This entire historiographic pattern is, in one way or another, tendentious, out to prove a point, and therefore inclined to ignore certain sorts of evidence and remove certain sorts of people from study. There is, for example, a sort of tenderness, a raw nerve, a fear that an account of failure or of villainy gives ammunition to the oppressor. We are beyond that stage. We will embrace Typhoid Mary, and William Burke. For both experiences are central, not periphral, to the migration experience.[18] There is the tendency for any narrative to seek tidiness, a beginning and an end, to become a drama with plot and resolution, and clearly, though we may research the beginnings of the Irish migrations, we have not reached the end. Lastly, and rightly or wrongly, these approaches tend to fragment the Irish migration experience – they do not allow us to look at the inter-connectedness, over space and time, the world–wide–ness of the Irish migrations.

The lost Irish

You will have noticed throughout this General Introduction my concern that certain sorts of Irish people not be 'lost' to our study. Here I make what is, for me, a simple methodological point. People can get 'lost' for all sorts of reasons, not least because the material which might have allowed us to hear their voices, and which might have allowed us to study them, has not survived. Some people hide from us, lose themselves, or would not wish to be considered 'Irish' at all, or are somehow prevented from calling themselves 'Irish'.[19]

But consider Irish family names. In Irish Migration Studies, knowledge of the patterns of the Irish family names becomes in itself a research tool. We need, for example, to understand the processes whereby Norman and English names becames 'naturalized'. We find ourselves tracking the Irish family names across the centuries, across the world – tracking them first into their Anglicized forms or English translations, and then beyond. O'Brien becomes Aubriand in France, 'Prunty' or 'Brunty' becomes 'Brontë', as a red-haired mature student at Cambridge moves towards respectability and holy orders in the Church of England.[20] Again and again, our research takes us to graves, to stones bearing Irish family names, there to pay our respects.[21]

We even develop a sixth sense about the names, recognizing, for instance, when 'Flood' is that simple, everday English name, and when it is the over-literal translation of *Mac Tuile* or MacTully.[22] It is true that 'surnames are heirlooms – not mere words'.[23] But you will realize at once that there is a problem here. The current family-naming system within the English-speaking world means that a woman takes the husband's family name at marriage. Children of a marriage take the father's family name. Irish women who marry men without identifiable Irish names can become some of our 'lost Irish' – lost to our research, that is. So here is another area where our research methods must become more subtle and creative.[24]

Structure of this project

Let me now say something about the structure of the entire *Irish World Wide* series. This volume, Volume 1 of *The Irish World Wide* is called *Patterns of Migration*. It offers a series of case studies and is intended to be itself an introduction to the first tranche of themes and disciplines. I will say more about that later, in the Introduction to Volume 1. Volume 2, *The Irish in the New Communities*, is, like *Patterns of Migration* a 'broad theme' volume, but, as well as continuing our pattern of case studies, Volume 2 offers a series of more theoretical chapters, bringing out more clearly some of the theoretical under-pinnings of the case studies.

The other four volumes in *The Irish World Wide* series are more sharply focussed. And in the Introductions to each of those volumes I have more to say about their focussed themes. Volume 3, *The Creative Migrant*, is broadly the 'media studies' volume of our series, looking at cultural products and culture producers. Volume 4, *Irish Women* and *Irish Migration*, looks at one of the most extraordinary gaps in Irish Migration Studies. Volume 5 is called *Religion and Identity*. Volume 6 is called *The Meaning of the Famine*.

Let me stress that because there are volumes that look closely, and systematically, at issues around the arts, at women, at religion or at famine, this does not mean that those themes can be ignored, or are ignored, in other volumes. For example, Volumes 1 and 2 contain much material on Irish women as migrants, and throughout the series there are discussions of women's role in sustaining an Irish identity. The volume on religion contains a most illuminating chapter on a women's religious order. Both the *Religion and Identity* volume and the volume on *The Meaning of the Famine* contain 'media studies' chapters.

It is just that some decision had to be made about the shape of the project, and about putting the material in some sort of order. I think you can now begin to see why I chose this shape, rather than another. If a mistake has been made it was made by me, on the back of an envelope, in December 1990.

Acknowledgements

Lastly, let me acknowledge that a project like *The Irish World Wide* gathers new debts every day. I have decided to collect all the formal acknowledgements of debt and friendship in the last volume of the series.

Patrick O'Sullivan
Bradford
January 1992

Notes

1. This is the task of historiography and literature search, a task which I discuss more thoroughly in the Introduction to *The Irish in the New Communities*, Volume 2 of *The Irish World Wide*. See the chapters by Donald Harman Akenson and Roger Swift in that volume.

2. J. J. Lee, *Ireland 1912–1985: politics and society*, Cambridge University Press, Cambridge, 1989, begins, p. xi, by lamenting the fragmentation of history and goes on to lament 'the fragmentation of perspective characteristic of the contemporary mind'.

3. The debate within Irish history can be fierce. For a brief outline of the debate see, Seán Hutton and Paul Stewart, Introduction: perspectives on Irish history and social studies, pp 1–2, in Hutton and Stewart, eds, *Ireland's Histories: aspects of state, society and ideology*, Routledge, London and New York, 1991. They begin: 'Irish history has been, and continues to be, an area of debate and contestation. This is the case, partly, because of the abiding manner in which populist nationalist, and Unionist/loyalist, versions of Irish history continue to be used to legitimize current political positions and because of the suspicion and hostility with which academic historians regard populist versions of the past.' Brendan Bradshaw, 'Nationalism and historical scholarship in modern Ireland', *Irish Historical Studies*, 104, November 1989, has become a key text. The debate has become polarized around the reductionist labels 'traditional' versus 'revisionist' historian. But this debate is important to Irish Migration Studies because anecdotal evidence suggests that organized migrant communities have a special attachment to 'traditional' views of Irish history – see, for example, Jonathan Moore, 'Historical revisionism and the Irish in Britain', *Linen Hall Review*, 5, No. 3, Autumn 1988, pp. 14–15.

4. I must acknowledge here the influence, as I puzzled through these issues, of Austin E. Quigley, *The modern stage and other worlds*, Methuen, New York and London, 1985, especially pp. 59–62. His starting point is 'the absence of an active cycle of discovery in the field of modern drama criticism . . .', which he sees as as a consequence of 'the problematic impact of a characteristic use we make of generalizations'. But his insights are generalizable, outside drama criticism. 'Generalization is often regarded as the culminating goal of investigation, not as an instrument of subsequent investigation. As a result, we find ourselves repeatedly confronted with what the jargon of our trade has dubbed the premature generalization.' Quigley then develops a notion of generalization based, not upon a structure of common core features, but, following Wittgenstein, on a structure of continuity and discontinuity, 'family resemblance'. This is a discussion I want to continue in *The Irish in the New Communities*, Volume 2 of *The Irish World Wide*. But here I only want to stress that, following Quigley, behind my 'generalizations' is 'a commitment not to conclusions but to improved means of enquiry'.

5. Everett S. Lee, 'A theory of migration', *Demography*, 3 (1), 1966, pp. 47–57, Population Association of America. Lee's paper begins with a clarification of, and is a development of, two important papers by E. G. Ravenstein, The laws of migration, *Journal of the Statistical Society*, Vol. XLVIII, Part II, June 1885, pp. 167–227, and, 'The laws of migration, second paper', *Journal of the Statistical Society*, Vol. LII, June 1889, pp. 241–301. You will sometimes find that researchers have gone straight back to Ravenstein, for his perceptions, and Ravenstein is still worth reading. It is helpful to Irish Migration Studies that the theories of both Lee and Ravenstein encompass movement within a country as

well as between countries. That is, they attempt to develop theories of (just plain) 'migration', rather than 'emigration' or 'immigration', which focus on political boundaries.

6. Lee, 'A theory of migration', p. 50. On the individual life, consider: 'One of the most intriguing questions in the history of migration is this: what made some men and women leave their rural cottages and go to cities, sometimes foreign, to work for other men in factories, shipyards, offices, or railroads, while others did not?' Joel Mokyr, *Why Ireland Starved: A quantitative and analytical history of the Irish economy, 1800–1850*, George Allen and Unwin, London, 1983, p. 258

7. I would particularly recommend Patrick McKenna's study of Irish migration to Argentina, Chapter 3 in this volume, in itself an excellent one chapter introduction to 'the patterns of migration'.

8. Lerner, Gerda, *The majority finds its past: placing women in history*, Oxford University Press, Oxford & New York, 1979, pp. 145–8. The whole of Lerner's book, especially the last three chapters, is a challenge to rigid thinking about history. See, for example, p. 172, 'a challenge to traditional sources'. *Women surviving: studies in Irish women's history in the nineteenth and twentieth centuries*, edited by Maria Luddy and Cliona Murphy, Poolbeg, Swords, 1989, is generally a good starting point for an exploration of an emerging Ireland's women's history. See also Margaret Ward, 'Putting gender into Irish history', in *Irish Dimensions in British Education: Report on the Eighth National Conference, Saturday, February 9, 1991*, Irish Studies Workshop, Soar Valley College, Leicester, 1991.

9. Lerner, p. 148. The examples in this paragraph are the ones used by Luddy and Murphy, *Women Surviving*, p. 2.

10. For example, Dale T. Knobel, *Paddy and the Republic: ethnicity and nationality in antebellum America*, Wesleyan University Press, Middletown, 1986, is an excellent book, bringing nice methodologies to it subject matter. It is a study of the East Coast American mandarin cast of mind in that period – it is not a study of Irish people. Similarly with books like Richard Ned Lebow, *White Britain and Black Ireland: the influence of stereotypes on colonial policy*, Institute for the Study of Human Issues, Philadelphia, 1976.

11. Wlad Godzich and Nicolas Spadaccini, 'Foreword: the changing face of history', p. xiii, in José Antonio Maravall, *Culture of the Baroque: analysis of a historical structure*, translated by Terry Cochran, Manchester University Press, Manchester, 1986 (original Spanish edition 1975).

12. See the extensive discussion of this theme, below, in James Sturgis, 'Irish hooligans', Chapter 5 of this volume.

13. Patrick Scott Cleary, *Australia's debt to the Irish nation-builders*, Sydney, 1933.

14. David Noel Doyle, *Ireland, Irishmen and Revolutionary America, 1760–1820*. Mercier Press, Dublin, 1981. Doyle notes in passing that, for brevity's sake, he abandoned the 'peripheral and minor' topic of armed Irish Loyalism (p. x).

15. See John McGurk, 'Wild Geese: the Irish in European armies', in this volume.

16. Nicholas Flood Davin, *The Irishman in Canada* with an introduction by Daniel C. Lyne, Irish University Press, Shannon, 1969 (original edition 1877). I curb the urge to give Davin's title as 'The Irishman (sic) in Canada' – his title and his approach are very much of their time, and his book is indeed substantially a study of Irish men, saying little about Irish women, other than (p. 119) 'I could mention dozens of cases . . . where the woman inspired and helped, and was content that the husband should receive all the praise.'

17. R. A. Burchell, *The San Francisco Irish, 1848–1880*, Manchester University Press, Manchester, 1979, p. 185, quotes Hugh Quigley's 1878 *The Irish Race in California and on the Pacific Coast*.

18. J. F. Federspiel, *The Ballad of Typhoid Mary*, translated by Joel Agee, Penguin, Harmondsworth, is a hypnotic novelization of the life of Mary Mallon, hurriedly buried in St Raymond's Cemetary in the Bronx, in 1938. She was a typhoid carrier, herself immune to the disease but deadly to those for whom she worked as a cook. Owen Dudley Edwards, *Burke & Hare*, Polygon, Edinburgh, no date, has, particularly in Chapter 6, 'Burke, Hare and the Immigrant Enterprise', the courage to put the two murderers in that context: 'They were, in fact, excellent examples of immigrant enterprise whose ultimate business diligently answered the needs of the host culture and who adapted their own skills to meet the demands which the host culture let them know existed.' (p. 78). It will be recalled that William Burke and William Hare murdered their fellow Irish migrants to provide bodies for dissection in the medical schools of Edinburgh.

19. 'Complete the following sentence: you cannot really be Irish unless you . . .' There is no right answer, of course, and no complete answer. It is part of an exercise that I sometimes run for culture-shocked Irish students at English universities. Generally, my definition of 'Irish' is inclusive rather than exclusive – we are exploring 'family resemblances'.

20. John Cannon, *The road to Haworth: the story of the Brontës Irish ancestry*, Weidenfeld and Nicolson, London, 1980, pp 89–90. Brontë melancholia: Irish heritage or Yorkshire weather? Discuss.

21. As my research into the recruitment, and the destruction in battle, of the Tyneside Irish Regiment took me to the battlefields around Albert, in northern France, and to the orderly rows of stones in the military cemetaries there – see Rose E. B Coombs, *Before Endeavours Fade: a guide to the battlefields of the First World War*, An *After the Battle* publication, London, 1976, p. 80.

22. Edward MacLysaght, *The surnames of Ireland*, Irish University Press, Shannon, 1969, p. 92. This volume summarizes and adds to the material in the same author's *Irish families, their names, arms and origins*, Hodge, Figgis & Co., Dublin, 1957; *More Irish families*, O'Gorman, Galway, 1970; Supplement to Irish families, Helicon, Dublin, 1964. *More Irish families, a new and revised edition*, Irish Academic Press, Dublin, 1982, is effectively an integration of the 1964 and 1970 volumes, and a companion volume to the original 1957 *Irish families*, which has been reprinted many times. MacLysaght, Edward, *Guide to Irish surnames*, Helicon, Dublin, 1963, covers much the same ground as MacLysaght *The surnames of Ireland*. (You really need this whole MacLysaght family of volumes to have, within your grasp, all of MacLysaght's research advice and kind good sense.)

23. MacLysaght, *The surnames of Ireland*, p. 221.

24. It is worth stressing that, though the problem presents itself in this form within most English-speaking cultures, it is much modified by Irish naming traditions and by American patterns. Again, in Spanish-speaking cultures the traditions are quite different. Spanish naming traditions alert us to the Irish (and the Italian) heritage of the eighteenth century Madrid woman of letters Doña Margarita Hickey y Pellizzoni. My thanks to Philip Deacon for this example – see Philip Deacon, Vicente García de la Huerta y el círculo de Montiano: La amistad entre Huerta y Margarita Hickey, *Revista de Estudios Extremeños*, 44 (1988), pp 395–421, and Manuel Serrano y Sanz, *Apuntes para una biblioteca de escritoras españolas*, Atlas, Madrid, 1975, I, pp 503–522.

Introduction: Patterns of Migration

Patrick O'Sullivan

This volume offers a strenuous introduction to key themes, and basic methods and disciplines. Ten chapters plunge you into ten different, but linked debates. There is a good world-wide spread. There is a wide chronological spread – in part, to counteract a preoccupation in the existing literature with the mass migrations of the nineteenth century. The earlier migrations were proportionately very great. But we are also looking at the ways through which, in preparation for the nineteenth century, a culture of migration was created within Ireland. And, of course, it looks as if migration will continue to be an issue for Irish people well into the twenty-first century.

The ten chapters introduce you, not only to ten ways of thinking and researching, but to ten ways of writing. If, at times, you find a writer's way of presenting the material difficult, or hard to follow, do persevere. Think methodology, understand jargon. What is gained, or lost, by this way of presenting material?

In my Introductions to the separate volumes I am not going to belabour you with the structures, or organizing ideas, outlined in my General Introduction. But my hope is that you will bear those organizing ideas in mind, and that they will help you place each chapter, each approach, each methodology, in a pattern – so that you are not overwhelmed by detail. My task now here is to show you why I find these ten chapters so interesting. And I am also going to try to make interdisciplinary connections. Some chapters I will touch on fairly briefly at this stage – though later in The Irish World Wide series I will be asking you to look back again, with new perceptions, at the chapters in this volume.

I have said that, generally, I want to avoid jargon in these Introductions. But the development of a project like *The Irish World Wide* inevitably leads to the creation of a private jargon, if only inside my own head. Let me give you one piece of private jargon. In the study of the Irish migrations we will come across certain 'icons' – iconic figures who immediately spring to mind in any pub discussion of the Irish, the 'Wild Geese', Ned Kelly, any Irish millionaire and John Fitzgerald Kennedy. I am sure you can add to the list. These 'icons' attract the popularizing historian, and are certainly an important part of the Irish migrants' perceptions of self. For that very reason the academic historian may be cautious about studying them. But they must be studied, and placed in a context, placed within the patterns of migration. This volume does that with a number of our 'icons'.

Wild Geese and masterless men

The wandering Irish poor in England in the sixteenth and seventeenth centuries are often acknowledged in earlier studies of the Irish in Britain, though there is difficulty integrating them into some long-term structure.[1] These same Irish poor enter English social histories – but here again, there is a problem fitting them into a systematic overview. They are seen as an intrusion into England, as they are an intrusion into Beier's excellent study of the English poor in that period, *Masterless Men*.[2]

Our first contributor, Patrick Fitzgerald, is a social historian, whose work at the Ulster-American Folk Park involves an attempt to make the past physically present. What Fitzgerald has done, for *The Irish World Wide*, is to gather anew the evidence about the Irish poor, look at it, mull it over. You will see how he uses his knowledge of the patterns, as they were in that period, of Irish family names to let us look more closely at the origins of these 'Irish'.

There are two parts to the story. These people were, in the straight-forward sense of the words, 'displaced persons'. They were most probably in the strict definition 'migrants' – making a permanent or semi-permanent change of residence – not the seasonal workers of later movement to England. As Fitzgerald shows, wars, famine, expropriation of land and population movements in Ireland meant that people could be displaced west, or east. This archipelago behaves like a peninsula – poor people, like the soldiers on their way to Flanders, entered England.

Once on the move the wanderers become, for the English authorities, part of another, wider, English problem. Population movement within England caused great anxiety to the English ruling classes and they countered it with one of their periodic assaults on the rights of the English poor – what Beier calls 'the de-sanctification of the poor'. Beier's title encapsulates the perception of the problem, 'masterless men', and he chronicles the series of laws that attempted to tie the poor, and responsibility for the poor, to their place of origin.[3]

The wandering Irish poor thus entered a country where wandering was itself a crime. They entered a world of definitions – 'Vagrancy is perhaps the classic crime of status, the social crime *par excellence*. Offenders were arrested not because of their actions, but because of their position in society.'[4] They entered a 'catch zone', where the more or less random action of the authorities trapped some, punished some, sent some back to Ireland, fed others – and formed a written record for our historian. And he is as intrigued as we all are by the reported proto-nationalist statement, in 1630, of that wetback smuggler, Maurice Keysons or Curry: '. . . as long as there were English in Ireland, he would bring Irishmen into England, for if Englishmen would depart from Ireland, then the Irish had no need to come into England.'[5]

Fitzgerald's title quotation, 'like crickets to the crevice of a brew-house' from the play by Thomas Dekker, recalls all those comic Irishmen in the plays of the period, and the extraordinary frequency with which, in the plays, Englishmen masquerade as Irish. There is even the suggestion that some English criminals attempted to escape justice by pretending to be Irish.[6]

Like our next contributor, John McGurk, I am reminded of Shakespeare's only Irishman, 'Mackmorrice', in the 'four nations' scene in *Henry V*[7]. 'Mackmorrice' is an Irish soldier, who expects his nation to be insulted and gets angry beforehand – 'What is my Nation? Ish a Villaine, and a Basterd, and a Knaue, and a Rascall. What ish my Nation? Who talkes of my Nation?'[8]

Irish soldiers walk through Fitzgerald's pages, on their way to the armies of the Archduke in Flanders. And they bring us to the first work of historiography in *The Irish World Wide*, John McGurk's, 'Wild Geese: the Irish in European armies'. What John McGurk was asked to do – and what he has done marvellously well – is to bring us up to date, to tell the story and to tell us how the story has been told, so that we can understand the limitations of our thinking and so that we can plan further research.

My own thinking about the study of the Wild Geese is very influenced by Cynthia Enloe's *Ethnic Soldiers*, her exploration of the utility, to widespread empires and to the military mind, of the concept of a 'martial race'. 'Almost every multi-ethnic society has one or two groups that have been stereotyped as being prone to, and adept at, soldiering. They include some of the most popular subjects in romanticized military history: Gurkhas, Bedouin, Scots, Sikhs, Ibans, Berbers, Cossacks, Maori, Mongols, Kurds, Zulus, Irish, Montenegrins.'[9] Indeed, a list to ponder.

Enloe allows us to see the earlier involvement of the Irish in the armies of Europe, usually in the armies of Britain's enemies, and the later involvement in the armies of the British Empire as a continuum. It allows us to bring all this involvement in military forces into the study of the patterns of migration. So, here, I particularly value a recent paper by Louis M. Cullen, which asks severely prosaic questions about the 'Wild Geese' in the latter part of the eighteenth century. Mass involvement in military service is another question – what we are looking at, by this stage, are élite careers, occupations for gentlemen. How many military commissions were available in continental Europe to young Irish Catholic gentlemen? The answer is 'roughly 500'. How much did it cost to set up a young man in a military career? '£200 or £300'. 'Those already established in Europe were expected to contribute to the costs of educating or sending nephews abroad. This was in effect a form of levy to repay the assistance they had received at the outset of their own career.' Families invested in costly education to prepare their sons for military service abroad. 'Army service perforce turned families towards education and acted as a window on the outside world . . . The experiences of catholics abroad also made them and their families at home aware of what personal liberty really meant.'[10]

Enloe also gives special theoretical importance to the subject of mutiny, as a grievance procedure and as a potentially political process – and, of course these 'ethnic soldiers' are typically used to subdue peoples whose relationship with the employing empire is very like that of their own people at home.[11]

But what my approach does not quite get at is the 'romance' of the 'Wild Geese', their importance, as I suggested in my General Introduction, in the history of an oppressed people, the way that military exploits abroad assuaged pride, and sacrifice conferred legitimacy. Note the continuity of that appeal to exploits and sacrifice. In September, 1988, before the House subcommittee on immigration, a representative of the Irish Immigration Reform Movement commented on the fact that only 800 Irish people per year were allowed to legally enter the United States: 'That number is less by 120 the number of Irishmen who died storming Marye's Heights in Fredericksburg on December 13, 1862, in defense of this union.'[12] And the New York recruiting posters for that American Civil War Irish Brigade had said 'Irishmen, you are now training to meet your English enemies', and 'Remember Fontenoy!'.[13] The importance of Fontenoy, the evidence of Fontenoy, to the defeated and the oppressed, was that when a well-equipped and well-led Irish force met the English on equal terms, the Irish won the day. 'But hanging over the battlefield was that ever-present Irish ghost – Irish fighting Irish – for on the British side were many thousands of Irishmen.'[14]

Why were they called 'Wild Geese'? Maurice N. Hennessy approvingly quotes Seán O'Faoláin's 'beautiful prose': 'The Wild Geese come in their thousands with the October moon. They blacken the sky and they cry the coming of autumn. Where there are low marshlands, or sloblands, they settle down, and then the cabins are cooking them with much butter or grease in the bastables all the Winter. About the estuary of the Shannon, and all up the River into Limerick, they must have whizzed and moaned, that Winter of 1691 . . . The flying Irish, down the Shannon or down the Lee with Sarsfield, looked up at the skies, and took the name, The Wild Geese.'[15]

There are many differing accounts of the origins of the nickname, some more romantic than others. The Oxford English Dictionary quotes the 1845 M. J. Barry poem, with its footnote: 'The recruits for the Irish Brigade . . . were entered on the ship's books as "wild geese".' My own instinct is to look to the polemic English language prose and to the poetry of the seventeenth century, with its instinctive reaching to the natural world for its imagery. We have already seen an example in this volume, in Thomas Dekker's, 'like crickets to the crevice of a brewhouse'.

Thus, in the 1689 *Irish Hudibras*, you will find this line, spoken by a 'Dear-Joy' or comic Irishman: 'And Culleens flee, like flocks of Wild-gees.' And it would seem, from an extraordinary leaflet now in the library of Trinity College, Dublin, *THE PRETENDERS EXERCISE To his Irish Dragoons, and his Wild Geese*, that by 1727 the term 'Wild Geese' was established, in Dublin, as a joking, almost abusive, term for the Jacobite Irish soldiers.[16] The processes through which such terms of abuse become badges of honour are well established. But, whatever the origins of the nickname, it is an image with power – the threat, or the promise, is there in

O'Faoláin's poetic prose, and in the natural history: the wild geese return.

Self-made men

It is true that 'Almost all the Irish emigrants of the nineteenth century sought their fortunes in the English-speaking world, and very few settled in continental Europe.'[17] And certainly the Irish relationship with the English-speaking world is something we will want to consider in the other volumes of *The Irish World Wide*. But we will approach the study of the Irish in the English-speaking countries of the nineteenth century tangentially, as it were, with a chapter on Argentina, and the development of the only major nineteenth century Irish community in a non-English-speaking country.

It is clear, when you speak to those interested in research, that language itself is one of the obstacles to research into the experiences of the Irish outside the English-speaking countries. I speak as someone who is not himself an able or confident linguist, aware that this creates one of the research gaps I spoke of in my General Introduction. We must not forget the daunting financial cost of foreign archive research, and the amount of pure life a researcher must put into learning new languages. But to see the intellectual rewards you need only look at the work of a European-minded scholar like Marianne Elliott, who has made so much plain that was previously only guessed at in the history of the United Irishmen.[18]

Our contributor, Patrick McKenna, is to be congratulated on overcoming the language barrier and for recovering, for Irish Migration Studies, the story of the Irish in Argentina. A rural people, people of the frontier – they make us look again, with a quizzical eye, at some generalizations about the Irish in North America. Most of the patterns of Irish migration are made manifest in his chapter, which is a good introduction to the study of the more complex, larger migrations later in the century. And McKenna makes nice use of present day Argentinian recollections of the migration, discovering an ironic Irish-Argentinian version of that bitter north of Ireland quip about expropriation: the Protestants got the good land and the Catholics got the view. In Argentina, the English settlers wanted the view, and the Irish were happy with the good land.

I did not find any way of bringing family history, pure and simple, into the volumes of *The Irish World Wide*. But I do want to acknowledge the strength of the genealogical impulse, and the special insights it can bring to history. Joseph A. King is a historian and a genealogist. What he brings us is a tale of two families, the Murphys and the Breens. It is also a tale of two wagon trains. So perhaps this chapter can stand as homage to Sean O'Feeney, an Irish-American whose work name, John Ford, might have disguised his Irish heritage – if that heritage were not such a feature of his movies.[19]

We are going to spend much time looking at the historiography of the Irish in the nineteenth century cities, in *The Irish in the new communities*, Volume 2 of *The Irish World Wide*, and at *Religion and Identity*, in Volume 5. Ideally I would have liked you to have immersed yourself in those debates, before returning, with head buzzing, to the linked stories of the Murphys and the Breens. But that would be unfair to our contributor. For this chapter is deeply subversive.

Let me bring out at least some of King's themes. Traditional Irish historigraphy is obsessed with contrasts, Catholic/Protestant, traditional/ modern, Irish/English – and it inter-relates these dyads, often uncritically. For example, there is the equation: what happened in England = modern; therefore, where Ireland is unlike England, Ireland is 'unmodern'. Consider the Catholic/Protestant contrast. This mode of analysis has a considerable literature – the name of Weber will be familiar – outside Irish issues. And some analysis of Irish issues looks to that particular Weberian tradition for support.[20]

What King does is to drive a coach and horses – or rather, an ox team and wagon – right through these debates. In effect, he says, let us take these Catholic or traditional or Irish characteristics, and let us look at them in action, in the real world, in a real project, in a real crisis. By telling a story, by comparing the fates of the two wagon trains, the Stevens/Murphy party of 1844 and the Donner party of 1846, he shows that the disasters which struck the Donner party were predictable and avoidable. What was needed, he suggests, was an Irish sense of family and of community. Within the Donner party it was the Irish families, the Catholic Breens and the Protestant Reeds, that survived intact. The story is closed, tidily, with the marriage of Virginia Backenstoe Reed to John Murphy.

How do you even begin to absorb into Irish migration studies that supremely 'iconic' figure, Ned Kelly? The paintings of Sidney Nolan give us our veritable icon, hieratic, armour-clad. So much Irishry clings to Kelly, like magnets to iron-plating.[21] A massive popular literature energeti- cally recycles the basic story.[22] Approaches based on Hobsbawm's 'social bandit' have a calming effect, and have the merit of linking perennial nineteenth century Irish issues, like rural violence and access to land, with the Australian experience.[23]

Our contributor, James Sturgis, takes this discussion a step further, and from his base within the Centre of Canadian Studies, London, with its commitment to the inter-disciplinary approach, bravely brings us a com- parative perspective. This comparative study of the Kellys of Australia and the Donnellys of Canada really does throw a new light on those two family sagas. Ned Kelly and William Donnelly are separated by space, but linked in time and heritage. Their two stories become one – a story of Irish family pride, strong mothers, and 'intensity of living'.

If we want to give a strong narrative line to the history of the Irish migrations, or, at the very least, to the history of Irish America, our narrative would build, logically, dramatically, to that cold day in Washington, in January 1961, when John Fitzgerald Kennedy took the oath that made him the thirty-fifth President of the United States. Or would our narrative take us on, to another day, cold in a different way, in November 1963 – and the assassination?[24] We come now to one of those areas where, to go back to the image I used in my General Introduction, the chart is very detailed indeed. There is no easy way to introduce you to such a massive literature, and what I have asked Alun Munslow to do is simply to give you some flavour of the ways that America's political Irish are studied. And, as ever, this contributor has given you some hints about further reading.

In her autobiography, Rose Fitzgerald Kennedy, the daughter of John Francis Fitzgerald ('Honey Fitz') and the mother of President John Fitzgerald Kennedy, recalls her father's bid to circumvent the party machine and become the Democratic nominee in the election for Mayor of Boston – '. . . my father adroitly turned events to his advantage by making the main issue of the campaign "Down with the bosses! The people, not the bosses, must rule! I want a Bigger, Better, Busier Boston!" ' Honey Fitz won the nomination, and the election – 'I am the first son of foreign parents to become Mayor of Boston.'[25]

Munslow gives us another perspective on Rose Fitzgerald Kennedy's recollections. Whatever the fine detail about the Irish in rural North America, it was in the cities that the networks were created, and the fortunes made, that would eventually put an Irish-American Catholic in the White House. Munslow offers a framework for broader analysis whilst suggesting that Honey Fitz was a key figure in laying the foundations of Irish cultural and political power in the United States.[26]

Continuing our study of the Irish rich of North America, we now want our iconic millionaire. The 'Irishtocracy', the 'First Irish Families' of the United States, appear in an entertaining book by Stephen Birmingham.[27] Canada too has its 'First Irish Families'.

T.D. Regehr is a historian of Canadian business – his best known book is a study of the Canadian Northern Railway.[28] Historians of business are necessarily interested in psychology, indeed in developmental psychology. A need to understand the behaviour of the Irish-born Canadian capitalist, Herbert Holt, led Regehr to explore that Irish background. This child is father to the man – many features link the Irish childhood and youth with the subsequent career, not least the way that the name of the lost family farm, 'Ballycrystal', repeatedly resurfaces, like 'Rosebud' in the Orson Welles' movie, *Citizen Kane*. Regehr has managed to penetrate below the manicured surface. Who, for example, made the decision that this young man should emigrate?

Networks

The last three chapters in this volume take us up to the present day, with studies of Irish people living and working in Sydney, Australia, graduate emigrants aiming at careers in London and Manhattan, and 'New Irish' 'illegals' working as nannies and bar staff, in another part of New York. These three case studies come together to give you some impression of the patterns of present day migration, in preparation for the more general analyses offered in *The Irish in the New Communities*, Volume 2 of *The Irish World Wide*. But I would also ask you to look at the academic disciplines of these three chapters, and the methodologies used. Notice, for example, how in all three studies there are Irish people that the researcher has not been able to reach – we might want to think about the reasons for this, and its consequences.

We are now in the present, able to talk to the people we are studying, if they will allow us to. Their knowledge and experience are available to us. Steve Bruce has said, '. . . if you want to know what people are doing and why they are doing it, you go and ask them. They might not always know, or they might know and not tell you. But all other sources are inferior. This is a simple point but one sadly often neglected by social scientists.'[28] That is a good starting point, and it is my own starting point. However, as a starting point, it can lead to the setting up of many, loosely called, 'oral history projects'. The expression usually used to describe the ensuing methodological débâcle is 're-inventing the wheel'. I would be happy if something as readily identifiable as a wheel emerged from the process. Such confusion dishonours the people who have given their time and their memories. This is an area where academic disciplines must learn from one another. The methodological difficulties of 'oral history' research have been well explored and well pondered, and the strengths and limitations of research techniques are well known.[29] The methodological problem, the philosophical problem, is one of finding a theory of mediations, between the one and the many, the individual and those wider forces whose existence you may postulate.

Seamus Grimes, the author of Chapter 8, is a social geographer, based at University College, Galway. A fascinating feature of the present development of Irish Migration Studies is that again and again it is the social geographers and the historical geographers who are coming to us with new methodologies and new perceptions. Grimes has made his social geographer's framework very plain. And he has helpfully placed his study of friendship patterns in Sydney within the overall study, by geographers, of the Irish in Australia. Because he is studying 'network', rather than 'community', his 'snowballing' methodology is exactly right.

Earlier in this Introduction I spoke of the Irish involvement in the armies of continental Europe as forming an élite career structure. Who, then, are our latter day 'Wild Geese'? It would seem that they are, typically, the accountants. Or, as our next contributor shows, any graduate group with internationally transferrable skills.

Gerard Hanlon is a sociologist, based at Trinity College, Dublin. His study of graduate migration puts it within the pattern of 'core and periphery', an analysis which we look at in more detail in *The Irish in the New Communites* Volume 2 of *The Irish World Wide*. His study method is a nice combination of survey and semi-structured interview.

The title of the last chapter in this volume of *The Irish World Wide* is based on a song. The contributor thought that you would all instantly recognise the song. I was not so sure. I wonder which one of us is right.[30]

Linda Dowling Almeida's background discipline is history – but she is a historian of the present. Her earlier study of the nineteenth and early twentieth century Irish migrations to North America, and her work in oral history, had made her realise that there was, here in her very own New York, an immigrant group as significant as any in the history of those migrations. And she saw that, if she did not act soon, this ephemeral community would vanish from history, like so many other groups in the past, unstudied, unheard, the subject only of historical speculation. These 'New Irish' 'illegals' are our Irish icons for the last decade of the twentieth century.

Here, in New York, we enter that place of power, with all its ambiguities, the Irish migrants' pub. Almeida describes it well, a place of conviviality, yes, but also a place of business, job-hunting, contacts, rumours, cheque-cashing. And there is a darker side. There have been many similar descriptions, over the years, and over the centuries.[31]

Almeida has the same problems, in studying a population of unknown size, outlined by Grimes in his study of friendship networks, Chapter 8 of this volume. But she has the further problem of studying people living and working illegally in the United States, semi-hidden, often fearing to speak – yet wanting their voices to be heard. This is the sort of methodological problem I am used to from my past work with illicit drug users. The comparison is illuminating. In this case the oral historian has chosen a short cut – the survey, whose methodological imperfections Almeida is quite clear about. It is quite legitimate to use this sort of survey to explore, find pointers, identify typologies – it is as if Almeida's 247 New Irish illegals had written her a personal letter, giving her much information, which she can then arrange, codify, put in a context for us – and for them.

Let us hear what they have to say.

Patrick O'Sullivan
Bradford
March 1992

Notes

1. Kevin O'Connor, *The Irish in Britain*, Sidgwick & Jackson, London, 1972, pp. 2–3.
2. A. L. Beier, *Masterless Men: the vagrancy problem in England, 1560–1640*, Methuen, London, 1985, pp 62–5.
3. Population movement within England is shown by the extraordinary growth of London in this period, Beier p. 40. For 'the de-sanctification of the poor' see Beier, p. 4. For a study of a later, similar process, linked mainly with the name of Malthus, see Gertrude Himmelfarb, *The Idea of Poverty: England in the early industrial age*, Faber and Faber, London and Boston, 1984. Himmelfarb does not index 'the Irish', but the Irish poor intrude into the discussion and, of course, the discussion has consequences for poor people within Ireland – see, for example, p. 157 and p. 371.
4. Beier, p. xxii
5. Also quoted in Beier, p. 63
6. In the play *Sir John Oldcastle* (1599/1600) the genuinely Irish servant, 'Mack Chane of Vlster' is taken before a judge, who is determined not to be taken in: 'You cannot blind us with your broken Irish.' See, Alan Bliss, *Spoken English in Ireland, 1600–1740: representative texts assembled and analysed*, Dolmen, Dublin, 1979, p. 181.

7. A scene analysed by Bliss, pp. 34–6, who suggests, citing a similar 'four nations' scene in a play by Thomas Randolph, that there might have been a fashion for such scenes.

8. Bliss, p. 83. Or is Mackmorrice Shakespeare's only Irishman? A recurring typographical error in the First Folio renders the name of Caliban as 'Calihan', lending support to the intuition that, at one level of topical interest, Prospero's island is Ireland. (I am grateful to James. P. Myers, Jr., for bringing this point to my attention.) *The Tempest's* general connection with the colonialist project has often been noted. See, Paul Brown, ' "This thing of darkness I acknowledge mine": *The Tempest* and the discourse of colonialism', in Jonathan Dollimore and Alan Sinfield, eds., *Political Shakespeare: new essays in cultural materialism*, Manchester University Press, Manchester, 1985. Brown (pp. 54–8) links the English ruling classes' anxiety about vagrants, 'masterless men', with the colonial venture in Ireland. We, who love the lyric verse of the English language, love in particular the poetry of the Elizabethan and Jacobean periods. It is a sadness, and an irony, that these English poets so despised their fellows, the bards of Ireland, 'a breed of poets occupying precisely that position of respect and honour as counsellor and friend at a king's court so eagerly sought by the Elizabethans Lyly, Spenser, Jonson' – Philip Edwards, *Threshold of a Nation: a study in English and Irish drama*, Cambridge University Press, Cambridge, 1979, p. 10.

9. Cynthia H. Enloe, *State Security in Divided Societies*, Penguin, Harmondsworth, 1980, p. 26. Enloe offers only a few pages (pp 46–8) specifically about the Irish – it is the general value of her thesis that I call attention to here.

10. L. M. Cullen, 'Catholic social classes under the Penal Laws', in Power and Whelan, eds., *Endurance and Emergence*, Irish Academic Press, Blackrock, 1990, p. 71, p. 74, p. 75.

11. Enloe, pp 33–8. Enloe mentions Irish involvement in the naval mutinies of the 1790s and, of course, the mutiny of the Connaught Rangers in the Punjab in 1920. On the first, see Chapter 5, 'The Naval Mutinies of 1797', in Roger Wells, *Insurrection: the British experience, 1795–1803*. On the second see Sam Pollock, *Mutiny for the cause*, Sphere, London, 1971, original edition 1969. For a fascinating, but limited, account of a group of Irish soldiers who decided they were on the wrong side see Robert Ryal Miller *Shamrock and Sword: the Saint Patrick's Battalion in the U.S.–Mexican War*, University of Oklahoma Press, Tulsa, 1989. The 'San Patricios' were (mainly Irish) deserters from General Zachary Scott's U.S. Army, who fought in defence of Mexico, in the war of 1846–8, and who are still honoured as heroes in Mexico.

12. Quoted in Linda Dowling Almeida, 'The Lost Generation: the undocumented Irish in New York City in the 1980s', *New York Irish History*, 4, 1989, p. 49.

13. Hennessy, Maurice N., *The Wild Geese: the Irish soldier in exile*, Sidgwick & Jackson, London, 1973, p. 178.

14. Hennessy, p. 71.

15. Hennessy, p. 19. The quote comes originally from Seán O'Faoláin, *King of the Beggars: a life of Daniel O'Connell*, New York, Viking, 1938, p. 11.

16. Bliss, *Spoken English in Ireland*, p. 126, p. 335, note 14, pp. 68–9. Bliss deduces the date 1727, and deduces that this leaflet was a Trinity student 'lucubration'. A metropolitan wit making fun of yokels, the leaflet offers a little playlet whose basic joke is that, though the native language of the Jacobite sergeant and his recruits is obviously Irish, they must conduct their drilling in English, a language with which they are not well acquainted. The leaflet, therefore, is unlikely to tell us anything about the reality of service in France or Spain – it

tells us of Dublin perceptions. There is evidence that Irish was the language of command amongst the Wild Geese regiments in France. See, for example, J. G. Simms, 'The Irish on the Continent, 1691–1800', p. 645, in T. W. Moody and W. E. Vaughhan, *A New History of Ireland: IV Eighteenth-Century Ireland, 1691–1800*, Clarendon Press, Oxford, 1986.

17. Simms, p. 656.
18. Marianne Elliott, *Partners in Revolution: the United Irishmen and France*, Yale University Press, New Haven & London, 1982, and *Wolfe Tone: prophet of Irish independence*, Yale University Press, New Haven & London, 1989.
19. See Andrew Sinclair, *John Ford*, George Allen & Unwin, London, 1979, p. 15. Cumulatively, John Ford's films chart those elements of personality and culture that Irish-Americans see as distinctively 'Irish' – J. A. Place, *The non-western films of John Ford*, Citadel Press, Secaucus, 1979.
20. There is now a quite massive literature, ultimately deriving from Weber's thesis that there are *Wahlverwandtschaften* (the term comes from the title of a novel by Goethe), 'elective affinities' between the Protestant ethic and the rise of capitalism. See, for example, the sociologist's perspective in Robert Towler, *Homo Religiosus: sociological problems in the study of religion*, Constable, London, 1974, Chapter 5, and the psychologists' approach in Michael Argyle and Benjamin Beit-Hallahmi, *The Social Psychology of Religion*, Routledge & Kegan Paul, London, 1975 (revised edition). For a critique of the ways in which such perspectives are applied to Irish history and to Irish migration history see Donald Harman Akenson, *Small Differences: Irish Catholics and Irish Protestants, 1815–1922, an international perspective*, McGill-Queen's University Press, Montreal & Kingston, 1988, especially pp. 16–19. The place for fuller discussion is quite obviously in *Religion and Identity*, Volume 5 of *The Irish World Wide*. At this stage all that is necessary is that we be aware of this mode of analysis, which is often based on a simplistic reading of Weber.
21. See, for example the ballads collected in Charles Osborne, *Ned Kelly*, Anthony Blond, London, 1970, Appendix II.
22. I particularly enjoyed Frank Clune, *Ned Kelly's last stand*, Mayflower-Dell, London, 1964.
23. On the first see Edith Mary Johnston, 'Violence transported: aspects of Irish peasant society', in Oliver MacDonagh and W. F. Mandle, *Ireland and Irish-Australia: studies in cultural and political history*, Croom Helm, London, 1986. On the second see John McQuilton, *The Kelly Outbreak, 1878–1880: the geographical dimension of social banditry*, Melbourne University Press, Melbourne, 1979.
24. Richard J. Whalen, *The Founding Father: the story of Joseph P. Kennedy*, Signet, New York, 1966, p. 452, p. 470.
25. Rose Fitzgerald Kennedy, *Times to Remember: an autobiography*, Collins, London, 1974, p. 30, p. 32.
26. Munslow explores Fitzgerald's negotiation of the 'boss' system. For a highly critical study of an Irish-American city 'boss' see Mike Royko, *Boss: Richard J. Daley of Chicago*, Barrie & Jenkins, London, 1971. I always enjoy the John Ford movie, *The Last Hurrah* (1958), starring Spencer Tracy, and based on the career of James Michael Curley, a Mayor of Boston whose career, and reputation, contrast somewhat with that of Honey Fitz.
27. Stephen Birmingham, *Real Lace: America's Irish Rich*, Hamish Hamilton, London, 1974.
28. Steve Bruce, *God save Ulster: the religion and politics of Paisleyism*, Oxford University Press, Oxford, 1986, p. ix. This book is an excellent introduction to the sociology of religion.

29. There is, of course, a quite massive literature on these themes in the literatures of the social sciences. But see, for example, Anthony Seldon and Joanna Pappworth, *By Word of Mouth: élite oral history*, Methuen, London, 1983. I particularly value the approach of French sociologist, Daniel Bertaux – see Daniel Bertaux, ed, *Biography and Society: the life history approach and the social sciences*, Sage, Beverley Hills, 1981.
30. Almeida's title quotation is adapted from a song by U2, 'I still haven't found what I'm looking for', *The Joshua Tree*, produced by Daniel Lanois and Brian Eno, Island Records, 1987.
31. The 'Irish-run public houses . . . awash with alcoholic nostalgia . . . an atmosphere of cigarette smog and sullen faces . . .', in Kevin O'Connor's 1972 *The Irish in Britain*, pp 131–2. Or the 1848 Liverpool Irish pub – 'the continuum of convivial and bibulous associational culture extended from "Hibernian" burial and friendly societies, . . . sanctioned by the Catholic Church, to secret Ribbon branches linked to networks across the Irish sea': John Belchem, 'Liverpool in the year of revolution: the political and associational culture of the Irish immigrant community in 1848', p. 76, in John Belchem, ed., *Popular Politics, Riot and Labour: Essays in Liverpool History, 1790–1940*, Liverpool University Press, Liverpool, 1992.

1 'Like Crickets to the crevice of a Brew-house'[1] Poor Irish migrants in England, 1560–1640

Patrick Fitzgerald

During the course of the last two decades the historical study of the Irish in Britain has been transformed. Research and publication, however, have been concentrated to a very marked extent upon the period after 1800.[2] Whilst it is indisputable that the volume of migration from Ireland to England during the nineteenth century outstripped anything which had occurred previously, the flow of migrants during the early modern period should not be neglected. Consideration of Irish movement into pre-industrial England allows one to place the influx of the mid–nineteenth century in a more meaningful historical context. For example, the notorious Irish rookeries which so perplexed the municipal authorities of Victorian London had precedents not only in the Georgian but also the early Stuart capital.[3] Furthermore, it may help to provide a corrective to the view that migration across the Irish Sea during the sixteenth and seventeenth centuries operated exclusively in one direction or that migration from Ireland in the seventeenth and eighteenth centuries was directed solely towards continental Europe or the New World.

In this chapter I shall confine myself to the study of migration from Ireland to England during the period between 1560 and 1640, focusing upon the most visible and, from an official perspective, alarming manifestation of this migration: the wandering Irish poor.

Those Irish poor travelling in England during this period are recorded principally in three bodies of source material, the records of individual parishes, of municipal authorities and of county quarter sessions. By the mid-sixteenth century the English parish had emerged as the primary unit of local civil administration, and parish officers, such as the churchwarden, generally oversaw the relief of the deserving migrant poor. Both before and after the major legislation of 1598 and 1601, which effectively defined the Old Poor Law, churchwardens recorded payments made to passing migrants whom they deemed to be deserving cases. Individuals and groups from Ireland appear among these annual lists throughout the period, but with greatest frequency in the 1620s and 1630s. Generally such entries yield scant information about the subjects relieved. Churchwardens tended to refer to the relief of an Irish person or persons rather than recording names. Although other details are occasionally noted, the sum disbursed is the only other information systematically recorded. The other parish source which intermittently records Irish migrants is the register of births and burials. Irish burials are more common than christenings, and tend to be concentrated in those years when famine and disease stimulated migration from Ireland. Here again supplementary evidence is limited.

A more promising source for the construction of a meaningful profile of poor Irish migrants is the records of the arrest and examination of those Irish taken as vagrants in England. A. L. Beier's study of the problem of vagrancy in England 1560–1640 illustrates the use which can be made of such source material.[4] Yet it is by no means flawless. As Colin Pooley and Ian Whyte recently observed of the sources for the historical study of migrations in general, 'they shed light on the process incidentally, incompletely and often obliquely'.[5] In discussing the evidence below I shall attempt to identify some of the more specific difficulties associated with its use.[6]

A migrant profile

Geographical origins

The authorities in England were, unfortunately, less concerned with establishing the precise place of origin of those Irish arrested than was the case with regard to native English vagrants. A statute of 1536 demanded that arresting officials should establish a vagrant's place of birth or last residence, in order that they might be returned there to be dealt with by their own parish. A further vagrancy statute, of 1572, mentioned the Irish specifically, ordering that they be punished and returned to Ireland.[7] Thereafter, constables and justices of the peace were primarily concerned with determining the port of entry rather than their origins in Ireland. The priority was to ensure departure from England. Once they had disembarked in Ireland the subjects were deemed to be the responsibility of local governors in port towns such as Waterford, or ultimately the administration in Dublin.

In this context it is, perhaps, surprising that some reference to a vagrant's place of origin within Ireland occurs as frequently as it does. Undoubtedly many local officials, accustomed to seeking this information, simply recorded it as a matter of form. Some indication of place of origin is recorded in the case of fifty-nine individuals arrested in England during this period.

As a representative sample from which one may confidently infer patterns of movement on a national scale, however, this data set is of limited use. The source material from which the data are drawn, for reasons of both variable enforcement and uneven survival, is concentrated in the south and particularly the south-west of England. None of the fifty-nine subjects in the sample was arrested farther north than Leicester, whilst all but six were taken in the south-western counties of Cornwall, Devon, Somerset and Wiltshire. Given this distribution, one would expect the sample to be skewed towards those drawn from the south of Ireland.

This, indeed, is the pattern which emerges. Of the fifty-nine Irish arrested, no fewer than fifty-four originated in the southern province of Munster, whilst four were drawn from Leinster and one from Connacht. Of those who came from Munster, twenty-eight were from County Cork, eighteen from County Waterford, three each from counties Kerry and Limerick and a single subject each from both Clare and Tipperary. The remainder of the sample were distributed as follows: two from Dublin, one each from counties Kilkenny and Carlow in Leinster and one from Leitrim in Connacht.[8]

Whilst the distribution which emerges from this sample undoubtedly exaggerates the dominance of Munster in the traffic of vagrants across the Irish Sea, the broader picture, based upon a wider spectrum of evidence, tends to confirm the primacy of the movement between Munster and the Severn estuary. For example, letters to the Privy Council during this period concerning the influx of Irish vagrants come from counties such as Somerset, Middlesex and Essex in the south of England and Pembrokeshire in south-western Wales.[9] Bristol and London were also in correspondence with the council on this subject, whilst the municipal records of the two cities, unlike those of northern ports such as Chester and Liverpool, illustrate that the Irish constituted a particular problem.[10] In addition, the research of A. L. Beier and Paul Slack into the regional origins of vagrants arrested in England confirms the association between Irish vagrancy and the south-western counties, on the basis of more comprehensive sampling.[11] There is some evidence to suggest that vagrants also crossed the North Channel to Scotland. In 1629, for example, the Scottish Privy Council issued a proclamation ordering the removal of 'great nombers of strong and sturdie Yrish beggars' that were reported 'wandering the country in troops extorting alms'. In Scotland, as in England, it was very probably the south-west of the country which encountered these itinerant Irish beggars most frequently. In 1602, for example, the Kirk sessions of the parish of Dundonald, in Ayrshire, examined a number of parishioners who stood accused of entertaining and lodging one John Burg, described as a 'maisterful beggar' and 'Yrland man' who also had 'one harlot with him'. Whilst the lack of detailed evidence precludes any assessment of the volume of such migration, it would seem likely that the overwhelming majority of these migrants were drawn from the province of Ulster.[12]

Although the data relating to place of origin are insufficient to allow one to draw firm conclusions, closer analysis of the origins of those who were drawn from counties Cork and Waterford may, at least, suggest some pattern to the distribution of migrants. Of those from County Cork whose specific place of origin was stated, at least six came from Cork itself, five from Mallow, five from Mitchelstown, three from Youghal and one from Bandonbridge. From County Waterford at least five individuals gave Waterford town as their place of origin, whilst seven listed Dungarvan.[13] It is also worth noting that the one subject from County Tipperary hailed from Clonmel, on the banks of the river Suir, which formed the border with County Waterford.

From the pattern which emerges from this breakdown two features stand out. Firstly, the fact that all these migrants were of urban origin. This predominance may have been accentuated by a tendency for subjects, under examination in England, simply to refer to their nearest major settlement but it is nonetheless probable that a disproportionate number of migrants had urban origins. A similar pattern has been discerned in relation to vagrants of native birth in contemporary England.[14] The second notable feature is that migrants from the interior of County Cork and the single migrant from Clonmel, on the Waterford/Tipperary border, were drawn from settlements in the river valleys of the Suir, Bandon and Blackwater. The significance of the river valleys during the early modern period as both channels for in-migration and source regions of out-migration is now well established, and the outline pattern discernible here is thus unsurprising. These river valleys, along with the coastal lowland, represent the most fertile, economically developed and populous regions in the province. From the 1580s on, English plantation and settlement were carried on most intensively here.[15] The port towns were relatively accessible, and information about shipping and the south-west of England, in general, undoubtedly circulated readily. That towns such as Bandon and Mallow were experiencing a vagrancy problem by the 1630s is reflected in the efforts of both towns to establish houses of correction. When, in the mid-1630s, it appears that Mallow took over from Bandon as the site of the county assizes, and a bridewell was finally constructed at Doneraile, some five miles north of Mallow, Bandon reported an influx of beggars from the north of the county.[16]

Ethnic origins

The correlation, noted above, between the geographical origins of Cork and Waterford migrants arrested in England and areas of recent intensive English settlement obviously provokes the question of ethnicity. To what extent can those crossing the Irish sea be characterized as returning planters rather than members of either the native Gaelic or the 'Old English' communities? Assessing the ethnic origin of migrants is a far from straightforward task. Only in a small minority of cases is any explicit reference made to a subject's ethnic identity. In addition, little is known about English attitudes towards those who returned from the plantations in Ireland during this period. How long was it, for example, before an individual identified as a member of the 'New English' community in Ireland might be seen as Irish in England? Let us look, initially, at that evidence which exists concerning the ethnicity of Irish migrants in England before considering the use which may be made of name analysis for this purpose.

Whilst the vast majority of migrants were simply referred to as Irish, or as being from or born in a particular place in Ireland, others had their relationship to the country described in a somewhat different form – for example, 'a poor man who liveth in Ireland which had losses by fire' relieved at Broad Blumsden, in Wiltshire, in 1630; 'a poor woman driven out of Ireland' relieved at Dunwich, in Suffolk, two years later; 'Ellin, a poor woman that came out of Ireland' buried in the parish of St Augustine the Less, Bristol, in the winter of 1598; 'a gentlewoman that came out of Ireland' relieved at Windsor, in Berkshire, in 1635,[17] and finally 'a poor man that came out of Ireland' in 1640 and received 6*d* from churchwardens in Minehead, Somerset. Such subtle variations as these cannot be regarded as conclusive, but a later reference from 1664 in the same parish, in Minehead, lends credence to the view that they may signify members of the settler community. Then, a poor man that 'came out of Ireland' was positively identified as being Welsh.[18] Very occasionally the religion of subjects is recorded, and may be taken as a firm indicator of ethnicity. An 'Irish woman' who received 2*s* 6*d* 'by the consent of the parish' at Warfield, in Shropshire, during 1629–30 was recorded as being a Protestant. When Barbara and Robert Cluett were examined at Dover in January 1636, the latter confessed that 'he was married by a Masse priest in the night' at Youghal, in County Cork, three years before. Nicholas Farles, a messenger in the service of the Countess of Westmeath, was arrested in May 1635 by the watch at Ottery St Mary in Devon. Travelling on foot from Cornwall to London, but without any pass to authorize his journey, he was taken before Sir Peter Prideaux, a local justice of the peace. When examined, he confessed he was a Roman Catholic and had never taken the Oath of Supremacy and Allegiance.[19]

Similar expressions of suspicion concerning the loyalty of migrants from Ireland were recorded and point strongly to the subjects being natives rather than newcomers. McDonagh O'Sullivan from County Kerry refused to take the Oath of Allegiance when it was proffered him by the mayor of Barnstaple in Devon in 1624. This in spite of his claims that he had borne arms in defence of the Queen during Elizabeth's reign. A companion, Philip Russell, an unemployed tailor from County Limerick, was imprisoned when he also refused the oath, despite his protestations that he could not understand it.[20] Two of those suspected of operating ships which transported migrants across the Irish sea were also noted as having made statements of dubious loyalty to the English Crown. Edmond Walshe, master of a barque which sailed out of Dublin, was said to have spoken in 'irreverent and undutiful' terms about the King when examined at Bristol in 1629. He was nonetheless willing to take the Oath of Allegiance. Maurice Keysons, alias Curry, was arrested the following year after depositing a sizeable group of Irish migrants at Portishead Point on the Somerset coast. William Welsh, his servant, told the local justices that his master defended the trade by stating that 'as long as there were English in Ireland, he would bring Irishmen into England, for if Englishmen would depart from Ireland, then the Irish had no need to come into England'. Christopher Roche, like Keysons and Welsh, from County Waterford, was put in the stocks in

London in 1582 'for speaking seditious words against the Queen's Majesty'.[21]

Another factor which would identify the native Irish migrant was the use of the Gaelic language or ignorance of English. Conversely, however, one certainly cannot accept a knowledge of written or spoken English as an indication of settler origins. Familiarity with the English language was widespread among urban dwellers in Munster and Leinster by the mid-sixteenth century and increased with the expansion of British settlement from the last quarter of the sixteenth century on. Witness, for example, the testimony of George Owen, a Pembrokeshire landowner, who in the 1590s complained of a major Irish influx into the county. Noting that many of those who had settled in the coastal parishes came from County Wexford, he recorded that by their own admission 'they understood no Irish'.[22] There is little doubt that a couple arrested at Sutton, in Kent, in 1639 were native Irish, as it was recorded that neither could speak any English. Unfamiliarity with English may also account for those cases where justices or constables examined Irish vagrants but could not discover their names or where they were from or had landed. This occurred with a group taken in 1629 within the hundred of Swanborough, in Wiltshire, and a similar troop that came before the Essex bench the same year.[23]

On occasion circumstantial evidence might come together to indicate a migrant's ethnic origins. Such a case is that of Thomas Taylour, arrested and imprisoned at Reading in Berkshire in August 1629. Taylour, denying the charge of stealing a purse in the town's market place, informed his examiners that he had come from London the previous day, where he had been to visit his uncle, a tapster at the White Hart, an alehouse in Holborn. The strength of this evidence as a sign of settler status is enhanced by the additional information that Taylour was employed as a ship's carpenter in Dublin. In the early seventeenth century Dublin had a substantial Protestant population, and the skilled trades were likely to be dominated by British settlers.[24] John Smart, a labourer from Youghal, in County Cork, who was ordered out of Exeter in May 1638, claimed in his deposition that he had come to the city to see his sister. Whilst the probability is that Smart, like Taylour, was of British stock, there is evidence that the Irish also obtained employment and resided in England.[25]

On the surface it might appear that the names of individuals offer the surest and simplest means of identifying ethnic origin. Such a method has been adopted by historians seeking to isolate ethnic minorities in early modern London and colonial America.[26] However, at least one historian has concluded that 'the extraordinarily high rate of internal migration within the British Isles during the early modern period prevents any methodology premised upon nomenclatural frequencies from identifying regional origins with any assurance of accuracy'.[27] In Ireland, and particularly in Leinster and Munster, migration from across the Irish sea had been under way since the twelfth century and sustained Anglo-Norman settlement left a profound imprint upon the nomenclature of the island. In spite of the vulnerability of such an approach it may still be of use as a general guide to the ethnic composition of migrants. At very least, it may serve to demonstrate that the traffic in poor migrants from Ireland to England between 1560 and 1640 was not uniformly a movement of the native Irish.

Appendices 1.1–2 lists the names of 188 individuals from Ireland who were recorded in contemporary England, either as suspected vagrants or criminals, or as migrants in need of relief or the more elementary services of the parish church. Beside each name is listed the year in which their presence was recorded in England. In the final column I have indicated my own assessment of the subject's likely ethnic identity. This has been restricted, simply, to native or settler. I define a native as one whose family had been settled in Ireland for at least two generations, whilst settlers are regarded as those who had either been born to parents whose origins lay outside Ireland, or who had moved to Ireland themselves. This assessment of ethnicity is based primarily upon an interpretation of the derivation of an individual's surname. Christian names have been taken to offer slight corroboration only.[28] Where subjects are unclassified the origin of their name has been deemed sufficiently ambiguous to prevent identification with any degree of confidence. This reservation occurs almost exclusively with regard to those names which may be associated either with British settlement in the century after the Reformation or with the old English community which had established itself in Ireland during the preceding centuries. In addition, it should be borne in mind that local officials in England were unlikely to translate names with consistent precision. Thus where I have felt it to be appropriate I have added, in brackets, a recognizable contemporary name, when it is phonetically close to the literal translation. Letters whose transcription is doubtful have, likewise, been placed in brackets.

As stated above, the purpose of the appendices is to provide a general impression of the ethnic composition of the traffic in poor migrants between Ireland and England. Obviously the identity imposed upon individuals might be questioned. I would suggest, however, that the overall impression which these names convey is of a movement which included persons from a wide spectrum of Irish society and certainly not just a migration of the native Irish.

Occupational/social profile

Some indication of occupation or social status is recorded in the case of fifty-six individuals arrested or relieved in England during this period. In addition, one should take account of the large group of over 100 soldiers who were recorded in London in October 1605.[29] The flow of mercenaries between Ireland and the continent accounted for some of the Irish migrants found in England. From the 1580s on, many of those whom the government in Ireland dubbed 'Idle Swordsmen' crossed to Spain, France and particularly Flanders to seek relief or find military employment. For those destined for Flanders and northern France the journey might entail a passage through the southern counties of England. Kent, the bridgehead to Europe, appears to have seen many such migrants *en route* for the continent. Among those recorded in the county were a party of seven or eight Irishmen lodged in prison at Deal in 1623 when the ship they sought to take them to Flanders was delayed. They admitted, under examination, that they were intending to seek service in the army of the Archduke, but had been forced to eat grass and roots when the weather deteriorated and prevented any sailings. In 1631 four Irishmen were arrested on board a frigate off the county's coast. Between them they had seen military service in Flanders, Denmark, Germany and Holland. There is a strong possibility that the three or four Irishmen accused of murdering a family at Hartlip in the same county, on New Year's Eve 1632, were also mercenaries heading for, or returning from, Flanders. The only other migrant whose occupation was recorded as a soldier was Robert Griffin, who was apprehended as a 'wandering and vagrant rogue' at Someston, in Somerset, in May 1627.[30]

Not surprisingly, those involved in the maritime trades are also noted. An Irish sailor with a forged pass was arrested begging at Maldon, in Essex, in 1573. Thomas Taylour of Dublin, as noted above, declared himself to be employed as a ship's carpenter when arrested at Reading market in 1629.[31] Employment in fishing, the maritime trades or the merchant marine, and the less legitimate profits to be made from piracy, brought many Englishmen to the ports of the Munster coast. It is thus not surprising to find an individual such as William Barbour, who came originally from Wiltshire, being decribed as a 'seafaring man who came forth of Ireland' when punished as a vagrant in his native county in January 1632. Also in this category were the two ship's masters, Maurice Keysons, alias Curry, and Edmund Walshe, who were detained in England for questioning about this illicit trade.[32]

Some migrants from Ireland, whilst not having their exact occupation or position noted, were described as gentlemen or gentlewomen. It is impossible to assess exactly how the term was defined in this context, but it is clear that such people's social status was evident to the churchwardens or municipal officials who encountered them. Of the eight subjects who were acknowledged to be of gentle birth, only two were examined as suspicious persons. James MacDonnell, described as a gent. of twenty-one was detained in Dover in 1624 and explained to the mayor of the town that he had been born in Ireland but was studying in Paris. The other was McDonagh O'Sullivan, arrested in Barnstaple, Devon, in 1624. He appears to have declared his own gentility and the leadership of a force of 100 men in support of the Crown during the wars of Elizabeth's reign.[33] There were only two references to migrants connected with the Church of Ireland. Both of these appear among the churchwardens' accounts for the parish of St Mary le Strand, Westminister, in the year 1638–9. A minister's wife, who claimed her husband and children had been taken to Algiers by Turkish pirates, received 6d. Some months later a minister's son from near Limerick was given 1s 6d when he recounted how his father, all his neighbours, their children and servants had, likewise, been seized by Turkish pirates.[34]

Servants, of one form or another, were an occupational group that was also regularly noted. Personal servants might accompany their master or mistress whilst travelling in, or through, England. Thus we find that in 1636 an Irish woman relieved in the parish of Biddenden, in Kent, had with her a nurse, to tend her child. Others were travelling in the service of their employer. Nicholas Farles, whom we have encountered previously, was halted whilst travelling on foot to London in order to deliver a message on behalf of the Countess of Westmeath.[35] Examining different aspects of the experience of women in early modern Ireland, Mary O'Dowd and David Dickson have both drawn attention to the number of household servants revealed in the notices served on Catholic landowners, ordered to transplant to Connacht, during the 1650s.[36] There is no reason to suspect that domestic staff were any less frequent in the decades before the outbreak of the rebellion. England may well have served as an alternative market place for those who were unable to find employment in an Irish household, or who were inclined, or forced for other reasons, to leave the country. Such was the experience of Daniel Cartlee (probably McCarthy), of Mallow, in County Cork. He was compelled to leave Ireland and sail to Minehead, in Somerset, because of debts he had accumulated at home. When appearing at the quarter sessions held at Devizes, in Wiltshire, in September 1631 he told the justices of the peace that he had been retained in the service of Sir John Foxton in Lancashire for the space of a year. Thereafter he travelled south in search of his English wife, who had deserted him, and sought, unsuccessfully, to gain a position in the household of the Earl of Clanricarde at Somerhill, in Kent.[37]

Female servants were as ready to make the crossing to England as men. No fewer than three Irish maids were buried in the parish of St Augustine the Less in Bristol during this period. Alice Gallowhill, another Irish maid, was punished as a vagrant at Salisbury, in Wiltshire, two days before Christmas 1633. Katherine Morgan, whose father was a shoemaker in Christchurch parish, in the town of Cork, was taken with Gallowhill and may well have been hoping to find similar employment.[38] That Irish servants were highly regarded in England is suggested by the anonymous author of a 1599 pamphlet promoting English plantation in Ireland and the employment of the native Irish in England. Detached from the malign influence of their chieftains and priests, he suggested, the Irish were 'very faithful and loving', and he went on to claim that they 'be here industrious and commonly our best gardeners, fruiters and keepers of horses'.[39] Interestingly, three men from Ireland who were recorded in Exeter's strangers book during the 1630s described themselves as grooms, whilst another, Barnaby Clements, of Waterford, was a blacksmith.[40] Irish grooms and footmen also appear as characters in a number of Jacobean dramas. Furthermore, English soldiers and officials serving in Ireland employed native Irish entertainers in their personal retinues. Sir John Perrot, even whilst leading a vigorous campaign of persecution against the wandering bards and rhymers of Munster, could be found patronizing an Irish harper. In the wake of his notorious campaign against O'Neill, Mountjoy returned to England with an addition to his personal staff in the form, perhaps prophetically, of an Irish fool.[41]

The other principal occupation represented amongst migrants whose occupation or social position was recorded was the manufacture of shoes. Besides the two cordwainers ordered out of Exeter in 1637 and 1638 there was Robert Cluett, a shoemaker from Youghal, in County Cork, arrested at Dover, in Kent, in 1636.[42] Other migrants whose status or trade was noted included two tailors, a miller and a labourer.[43] Finally there was the case of John Campen, who returned to his native county of Dorset during the famine year of 1629. He was sent to the house of correction in Dorchester when he revealed himself to be an itinerant healer.[44]

Age and sex profile

Officials in England rarely recorded the specific age of migrants from Ireland. Indeed, only in the case of seven individuals examined during this period was any reference made to a subject's age. James MacDonnell, arrested at Dover in 1624, was aged twenty-one years. An Irish couple, arrested at Alderbury in Wiltshire in 1632, were recorded as being '20 years or thereabouts' in the case of the man and '30 years or thereabouts' in the case of his partner. Four soldiers, examined on board a frigate off the coast of Kent in 1631, turned out to be aged twenty-six, thirty-one, thirty-six and forty years.[45] Fortunately, however, there are many more general references to the age of migrants. From the full range of source material it is evident that both young and old were encountered wandering in England. Many of the individuals arrested or relieved were accompanied by children or, indeed, expecting a child. In addition, the registers of the church of St Augustine the Less, in Bristol, record in 1629 the christenings of two children whose parents had come from Ireland and the burial of a 'poor Irish child'.[46] Irish juveniles were not always recorded in the company of their parents. The court books of Bridewell, in London, contain several references to Irish boys and girls arrested in the city as vagrants. In the first six months of 1630 alone, eight Irish boys and an Irish girl came before the court. Whilst Irish migrants appear to have travelled with their siblings more commonly than their English counterparts, the number of Irish youths in the capital was not exceptional. In his study of vagrancy in England A. L. Beier calculated that 54 per cent of all Bridewell inmates in 1602 were under sixteen years of age. At the opposite end of the spectrum the records of Bridewell also document the arrest of a handful of Irish who were described as being old.[47]

The great majority of Irish migrants would appear to have been aged between fifteen and forty-five, and the majority of these were very probably under thirty. The number of migrants on the move with young families suggests this, but, since the young comprised such a huge proportion of early modern society, it is unsurprising. Young adults were also more likely to respond to poverty by migrating. Ireland had no statute-based, national system of poor relief to compare with that of early seventeenth-century England. Such alms or charitable support as was available within the family, neighbourhood or local community was likely to be concentrated upon those perceived as the deserving elderly.

Of 360 migrants from Ireland whose gender was recorded or is implicit in their christian name, 224 (62 per cent) were male and 136 (38 per cent) female. These figures may, if anything, underestimate the number of female migrants. Almost all the complaints that made their way to the Privy Council relating to the influx of the Irish mentioned the presence of women and children. The authorities in England may also have been more inclined to take male vagrants into custody because they were perceived to pose a greater threat. Some women, as we have seen, may have come to England in search of employment but many more arrived in families or larger groups which were uprooted in Ireland through the ravages of war or agricultural crisis. It would also be a mistake to assume that the movement of mercenaries through England to the continent was an exclusively male migration. A number of the groups of military men recorded in England were accompanied by women and children. Furthermore, Gráinne Henry's study of the Irish community in Flanders between 1586 and 1610 concludes that 'family migration was common amongst the lower ranks of the military'.[48]

Motives for migration

Specific information concerning the reasons why migrants left Ireland is again at a premium within the sources in England. Local officials there were more concerned with ensuring a speedy departure than understanding the motives of migrants. Naturally every individual had a personal story to tell, and some of the examinations of Irish vagrants in England reveal specific reasons for the subject's being in England. Among these were those migrants seeking work, others *en route* to the royal court to seek relief or redress, and some who claimed to be visiting friends or relatives.[49] However, two broad factors emerge as the key stimuli to migration from Ireland in this period, military conflict and subsistence crises. Although a stark division between war and dearth is somewhat arbitrary, both factors will be considered separately below.

The impact of war

The connection between war and Irish migration in this period expressed itself principally in two ways. First there were those members of the civilian population in combat zones, uprooted by the physical disruption and devastation. Second were the large numbers of military personnel who came to depend upon war as a way of life. From the 1580s on, but particularly from the end of the Nine Years War in 1603, the continental armies acted as a magnet to those who could not adjust to the new civil society being promoted in Ireland.

That victims of internecine warfare in Ireland sought solace in England is suggested by Thomas Harman, one of the most successful authors of the popular contemporary genre of 'rogue literature'. Harman claimed in 1566 that over 100 Irish refugees had entered England during the previous two years. These, he claims, were supporters of the Earl of Ormand, whose holdings had been burned and spoiled by the rival Geraldine forces.[50] More reliable evidence of the stimulus which war gave to migration comes from the final quarter of the sixteenth century, when the military struggle in Ireland intensified. In December 1583 the Privy Council informed the Lord Mayor of London of the 'great numbers of poor Irish people . . . begging in and about this city'.[51] Although no mention was made of where in Ireland these beggars emanated from or why they had come to England, it may be significant that Lord Grey of Wilton, the English commander in Munster, had spent the previous two years laying waste large tracts of the province. The presence of Irish beggars continued to be noted in London, and the council was forced to renew its complaints in May 1587. Hooker's *Chronicle* described a scene of devastation in Munster at this time and suggested that the only survivors were those who 'dwelled in cities and towns and such as were fled over into England'. By the end of 1587 the government in London was seeking to stem the flow of poor migrants at source, ordering the corporate towns of Munster to prepare to receive those transported back and advising the Lord Deputy in Ireland to ensure that no more took ship.[52]

The outbreak of the Nine Years War in 1593 ushered in a period of enormous flux in Irish society; military conflict upon an unprecedented scale coincided with a run of bad harvests that brought crisis conditions to much of northern Europe. The desolation brought fresh waves of refugees across the Irish sea. In 1603 a prominent landowner in Pembrokeshire, in south-west Wales, noted how the coastal parishes of the county had been inundated with settlers from Ireland and concluded that most had fled from the 'late wars in Ireland'.[53] Bristol was also affected. The Crown ordered the port's authorities to punish ships' masters importing Irish migrants. Such directives, however, were difficult to enforce, and by the mid-1590s the Irish were reported to be coming over to Bristol 'bag and baggage'. In the winter of 1601 the city's common council was forced to appoint a special 'beadle of beggars' whom it authorized to ship Irish beggars home.[54]

The treaty of Mellifont in March 1603 may have secured peace in Ireland but it brought no immediate end to the exodus from the country. After the battle of Kinsale in 1601 thousands of men whose life revolved around war were left effectively unemployed in Munster. Many, along with substantial numbers of women and children, found their way to England and the continent. In June 1605 the Privy Council alerted the Lord Warden of the Cinque Ports to the entry of 'base people' from Ireland who, after begging in France, were deported to England, where they dispersed, often ending up in London. Some months later William Waad, the lieutenant of the Tower of London, wrote to the Earl of Salisbury to complain about the 'great offence taken by the occasion of the great number of Irish people' in the vicinity of the tower. When a handful of these migrants were examined it became clear that they were part of a body of 200 men, accompanied by many women, who had been recruited in Ireland by a Captain De la Hide for the Archduke's army in Flanders. Having departed from the port of Waterford and landed at Penwin (the modern Penrhyn) in Cornwall, the group travelled to London. Allowed only 2s a head, many of the company had been forced to sell their armour in order to defray their costs.

It would appear from Waad's letter that not all the Irish begging in

London at this time were transitory. He went on to inform Salisbury of 'a new built lane called Hoge Lane' in the eastern suburbs, where there existed 'a cluster of base tenements, termed Knockfergus, peopled with Irish of very base sort'. Here, in these rapidly constructed tenements, Waad suggested, the Irish, with their numerous illegitimate children, lodged at night, only to descend upon the city by day to try and make a living by begging in the streets or in petty crime.[55]

Military men from Ireland continued to be drawn towards service in Europe during the decades before 1640. A body of 250 mercenaries experienced a tense and turbulent journey through England in 1634, and the following year, after a riot in London involving Irish soldiers, the government banned continental agents from recruiting in Ireland. It should not be assumed, however, that all soldiers from Ireland ended up serving abroad. There is evidence to suggest that some found employment in the army of Charles I during the war of 1627–9, as was later the case during the Civil War.[56]

Subsistence crises

Assessing the relationship between periods of dearth and the scale of migration between Ireland and England is hampered by the lack of detailed and unambiguous evidence. Identifying periods of crisis and measuring their intensity is a difficult task in itself, and based largely upon contemporary comment rather than firm evidence of fluctuations in the price of basic foodstuffs. Furthermore, the coincidence of military conflict and naturally induced dearth during the sixteenth century makes it difficult to isolate the effect of subsistence crises from the wider impact of war.[57]

The years between 1585 and 1587, for example, were clearly regarded by contemporaries as a crisis period in Munster. Yet chroniclers and commentators seemed divided in determining whether the distress was due primarily to an unseasonable harvest or to the military campaign to suppress the Desmond rebellion. The balance of the evidence would suggest that, whilst the military campaign took its toll of the civilian population, it was the ensuing famine that caused the greater devastation. There is certainly evidence to suggest that Gaelic society in the sixteenth century was more dependent upon arable crops than was once believed.[58]

The opening years of the seventeenth century saw recurrent harvest failure in Ireland. Both Cork and Dublin saw grain prices rise sharply in 1601 and 1602, and shortages, combined with plague, continued for several years.[59] There is clear evidence of a simultaneous increase in the numbers of poor Irish migrants in England. Bristol and the Severn estuary, London and the ports of the south coast were all affected. Occasional evidence from Ireland would suggest that towns were experiencing an increase in the numbers of vagrant begging poor at this time. Where the opportunity arose, such individuals were likely to try their luck in England.[60]

By the 1620s, when the next period of serious dearth hit Ireland, the evidence of specific subsistence migration is firmer. Between 1621 and 1624

Ireland experienced its first significant harvest failure and grain shortage for almost two decades. Whilst the records of central government in England remain silent, documentation at a local level does indicate an upturn in the flow of poor migrants from Ireland. Parish records from Wiltshire illustrate that in 1622 and 1624 an unusually large number of Irish people were relieved or noticed in parish business. In the parish of East Knoyle, in Wiltshire, groups of 'Irish folk' were relieved on seven separate occasions during 1624, and in the parish of Wylye, in the same county, the previous year, a poor Irishman was cited as the father in a case of prenuptial incontinence. In 1622 the Somerset quarter sessions heard a petition from the inhabitants of Porlock, who had paid out almost 50*s* for the relief and transportation of Irish people landed on a local beach.[61]

In the years between 1627 and 1632 Ireland suffered a further run of bad harvests which appears, at its peak, to have approached famine proportions. With fairly sustained population growth during the previous two decades, this crisis, no doubt, came as something of a jolt, particularly to the settler communtiy in Ireland. Grain seed, needed for the following year's harvest, was consumed through want, jeopardizing the next season's yield and the means to pay rent. There is firm evidence of increasing pauperization and vagrancy in Ireland during the later 1620s and early 1630s. In 1628 the government issued a proclamation which dealt with both the sale of corn and the regulation of begging, and in the Parliament of 1634–5 a statute was passed which obliged every county in Ireland to erect a house of correction.[62]

In the five years following the harvest failure of 1627 reports of poor Irish migrants in England increased dramatically. The coastline of the Severn estuary was particularly affected, and Bristol, Minehead and Barnstaple were all kept busy funding and organizing shipping to return migrants to Ireland. The scale of the influx is evidenced by the fact that in 1629 Bristol corporation was forced to hire seven ships and raise £30 to cover victuals and accommodation for migrants being transported to Ireland. In autumn the same year the city's parishes record the burial of several Irish people, including a man and his child whose bodies were 'taken out of the park'.[63] The Privy Council's proclamation attempting to stem the tide of wandering Irish poor had limited impact. In July 1629 Patrick Comerford, the Bishop of Waterford, noted that 'in our country there was some dearth of corn . . . wherefore our countrymen rushed into England'.[64]

Despite the fact that conditions slowly improved from the peak of the crisis in 1629–30, the food supply in Ireland seems to have remained unreliable throughout the 1630s. Dublin's municipal records give the clear impression that Ireland's capital was experiencing many of the social problems afflicting contemporary English towns. In 1634 separate action was taken to clear the city streets of beggars and pull down the shanty dwellings erected rapidly in the extramural suburbs by impoverished migrants.[65] For Munster people forced into subsistence migration, Bristol, only a day's sail away, was as convenient a destination as Dublin. Many continued to gain a passage on the numerous small craft trading between Munster and the ports of south-western England. In the south-east division of Devon, for example, forty-five Irish persons were arrested as vagrants, apparently together, in 1637. Two years later the parish of Steeple Ashton, in Wiltshire, decreed that no more Irish people were to be relieved from the church rates.[66]

Conclusion

In the wake of the 1641 rising in Ireland, England and Scotland experienced a large influx of refugees. Although the scale of this movement and the virtual hysteria which accompanied it were novel, there was a degree of continuity with the migration which had been under way during the preceding decades, particularly in the south-western counties. As suggested above, English settlers were among those who crossed the Irish Sea during periods of crisis in the early seventeenth century, and Catholic Irish migrants continued to enter England during the 1640s and 1650s. After the Act of Settlement in 1662 the problem of vagrancy in England declined, but there is little sign that the wandering Irish poor disappeared. It may well have been that they actually became more visible as the overall number of English tramping poor declined. Thus the itinerant Irish poor wandering England's roads during the Great Famine, immortalized in a contemporary painting by Walter Howell Deverell, were more of a perennial phenomenon than either the artist or the governors of the period, perhaps, assumed.[67]

Appendix 1.1
Irish migrants in England arrested and examined as vagrants and for other offences, 1560–1640

Name	Date	Ethnic identity
Christopher Roche	1592	N
Philip Maicroft	1601	S
Richard Couran	1600	N
Harry Harden	1609	
Toby Roch(e)	1637	N
William Browne	1637	
John Merri(cke)	1629	N
Mary How	1634	S
McDonagh O'Sullivan	1624	N
Philip Russell	1624	
Robert and Barbara Cluett	1636	N
James MacDonnell	1624	N
Robert, Mary and Honor Leigh	1634	S
Morris Thomas	1634	
Thomas and William Younge	1634	S
Margaret Waufeil(d)	1634	S
William Arley	1634	S

Name	Date	Ethnic identity
James Manfeild	1634	S
Edmund Wealsh	1629	N
Treolan MacBrean	1629	N
John Campen	1629	
John Hall	1598	
John Sellavand (Sullivan)	1605	N
George Persevall	1616	S
Honour Nuewater	1617	S
Daniel Murran	1629	N
John and Edmund Poore (Power)	1630	N
John Derman	1630	
James Brenar	1630	
Katherine Gawne	1630	
Mourne Trege	1633	N
Richard Whyte	1633	
Katherine Morgan	1633	
Alice Gallowhill	1633	
Daniel Micarte (McCarthy)	1635	N
Nicholas Farles	1635	
Agnes Courtney	1628	
William Skidmore	1630	N
Edmund Wyville	1630	
Daniel By(r)ne	1631	N
John Carr	1632	
Morishe Logan	1637	N
Mary Williams	1637	
Margaret Brown	1637	N
Morishe Mor Richard	1637	N
Margaret Thomas	1637	S
Philip Morerman	1637	N
Puchis Power	1637	N
Richard Gagon	1637	N
Richard Pauer (Power)	1637	N
Sheane Boyce	1637	
Tregomer Brise	1637	N
Thomas Felony	1637	
Tre(a)ely Carrell	1637	N
Teeg Marracke	1637	N
Roger Kells	1633	N
Edmund and Anne Flyde	1632	
George Broome	1634	N
Katherine Dodds	1626	
David Conne(y)	1623	N
Roger Maurice	1630	
Cornelius Daniel	1630	N
Jo Kelly	1630	N
Jo Foster	1630	S

Name	Date	Ethnic identity
Margaret Parr	1630	
Daniel Tacheane	1630	N
Miles Merry	1630	N
Mary Philips	1630	
Julyan K(u)orhan	1630	N
Toby Braine (Brahan)	1630	N
Morgan Daniel	1630	N
Edmund Crainley	1630	S
William Gay	1630	S
Bryan Furley	1630	N
John Bryan	1630	N
J. Carron	1630	N
Thomas Coggin	1630	N
B. Daniel	1630	N
Ma Henning	1630	
Sara Carey	1630	N
Katherine Vaughan	1630	N
James Toby	1629	N
Donner M(ac)Kersey	1628	N
Whilly Royle	1628	S
– Gabb	1635	S
George, Francis and Thomas Williams	1635	
Barnaby Clements	1637	S
Daniel Wilkinson	1637	S
Christopher Meme(we)	1638	S
Robert Browne	1639	N
Edmund Muirfield	1639	S
Ellen K(e)yes	1630	S
Jane Flyne	1631	N
Cornelius and William B(r)ian	1639	N
– Carter	1634	S
Robert Griffin	1627	N
John Atwood	1623	S
Thomas Taylour	1629	
Robert Hancocks	1604	
Walter Wall	1631	N
John, Johan and Thomas Mullis	1635	N
Johan Dawson	1638	S
John Malin	1637	N
Bryan Rea MacPhelyn	1637	N
Danniell Bri(s)e (Bryce)	1637	
Daniell Gardeine	1637	
David Bromacke	1637	
David Morfeh (Murphy)	1637	N
David Barry	1637	N
German MacPhills	1637	N
– Courant (Curran)	1637	N

Name	Date	Ethnic identity
Honor Alinge	1637	
James Cunday	1637	
John Courante (Curran)	1637	N
John Malin(okau)	1637	
John and Johan Downings	1637	
John Stone	1637	S
Johan Sym	1637	
John Earle	1637	
Jane Williams	1637	
John Alinge	1637	
Johane Alinge	1637	
Johane Eares	1637	
John Morris	1637	
John Hoggett	1637	
John Williams	1637	
Katherine Downings	1637	
John Smart	1638	
James Markjohn	1628	
Tara Donnett	1628	
Nicholas Donnett	1628	
Rayney McOrkney	1628	N
Anne Downly	1628	
Jane and Margaret Murreck	1628	N
John Chamberlyn	1628	S
Daniell Cartlee	1631	N
Thomas Heggard	1630	
Thomas Fintin	1630	
Marie Temple	1633	S
William Breach	1629	
Daniel Michart (McCarthy)	1631	N
Lynagh Colloquin	1631	N
Arthur Cormell	1631	N
Maurice Keyson (Curry)	1630	N
William Welch	1630	N
John (Cl)ath	1630	
Harris Mantell	1630	S
Roger, Maurice, William Jeffery	1630	S
Patrick Kelley	1606	N
Robert Rowe	1606	N
Edmund Roy	1606	
Daniel Mac-ashe	1598	N
Richard and John Rogers	1598	S

Appendix 1.2
Irish migrants in England who received relief or were noted in parish registers, 1560–1640

Name	Date	Ethnic identity
Margaret Welshe	1603	N
Thomas Cramell	1629	
John Dowse	1629	N
Kathren Gray	1629	S
Elynor Heal(ly)	1629	N
Morris (Healy)	1629	N
Charles Jolly	1634	N
J. Barry	1629	N
Teag Macholy	1629	N
Teag Sheon	1629	N
W. Cary	1629	N
Elizabeth Borcke	1631	
Daniel Norton (Naughton)	1639	N
John Courtney	1639	
John George	1638	S
– Love	1629	S
J. Flynne	1629	N
Richard Mulus	1629	N
John Groome	1629	
Michael Moore	1629	N
Robert Hait	1629	

Notes

1. In Act 1, Scene 1 of *The Honest Whore, Part 2*, by Thomas Dekker, Lodovico Sforza, a Knight, mocks the accent of 'Bryan the Footeman', and comments on the numbers of Irish found in England; 'Mary, England they count a warm chimney corner, and there they swarm like Crickets to the crevice of a Brewhouse.' The play was written around 1605 and first printed in 1630. See *The Dramatic Works of Thomas Dekker*, Volume 11, edited by Fredson Bowers, Cambridge University Press, Cambridge, 1964, p. 138.
2. M. Hartigan ed., *The History of the Irish in Britain: a Bibliography*, Irish in Britain History Centre, London, 1986.
3. L. H. Lees, *Exiles of Erin: Irish Migrants in Victorian London*, Manchester University Press, Manchester, 1979, chapter 3; M. D. George, *London Life in the Eighteenth Century*, Kegan Paul, London, 1925, chapter 3; Historical Manuscripts Commission, (hereafter H. M. C.), Salisbury MSS, XVII, pp. 448–9.
4. A. L. Beier, *Masterless Men: the Vagrancy Problem in England, 1560–1640*, Methuen, London and New York, 1985.
5. C. G. Pooley and I. D. Whyte, eds., *Migrants, Emigrants and Immigrants: a Social History of Migration*, Routledge, London and New York, 1991, p. 3.
6. The terms 'vagrant' and 'migrant' are both used throughout the chapter. Generally, the former is used in relation to those individuals arrested on suspicion of committing the offence of vagrancy, or where official sources

identify a vagrant problem. The term 'migrant' is used more comprehensively to include those noticed, relieved, buried, etc. The evidence would tend to suggest that the difference between these 'criminal' and 'legitimate' classes of migrant was not stark. Migrants relieved in one parish, if only on the understanding that they moved on, might be arrested and punished elsewhere.

7. 27 Henry VIII, c. 25; 14 Eliz. I c. 5.
8. Sources from which this sample is drawn: Wiltshire Record Office, QSR A1 110 1620–40; Somerset Record Office, Q/SR, 1–75, 1607–36; Devon Record Office, C5/102, Exeter Strangers Book 1621–68; Leicestershire Record Office, BRII/ 18/269; Kent Record Office, Dover Borough Records, Depositions before the mayor, 1630–59, f. 85v; E. Melling, *Kentish Sources: the Poor*, Maidstone, 1964, p. 19; H. M. C. Report, Various Collections, I, p. 197; Calendar of State Papers, Domestic (hereafter C. S. P. Dom.), 1623–5, p. 398; P. Slack, ed., Register of Passports for vagrants from Salisbury 1598–1668, *Wiltshire Record Society*, XXXI, 1975, pp. 17–65; J. M. Guilding, ed., *Reading Records*, II, London, 1895, p. 479; Public Record Office (London) (hereafter P.R.O.), S. P.16/289/15, 16/397/99.
9. P.R.O., S.P. 16/234/57; St Mary le Strand, churchwardens' accounts, 1586– 1650, vol. 22, Westminister City Archives; P.R.O., P.C. 2/43/463; H.M.C., Salisbury MSS, XXIV, pp. 254–5; C.S.P. Dom., 1628–9, p. 495.
10. P.R.O., S.P. 16/123/5, 16/144/62, 16/131/1; Bristol Record Office, Common Council Proceedings, No. 1, 1598–1608, f. 55, No. 3, 1627–42, f. 27; Mayor's Audits 04026 (12), f. 34; Corporation of London Record Office, Repertories of the Court of Aldermen, 21, ff. 119b, 429b, 430b, 456b, Journals, Court of Common Council, 21, f. 329b, 22, f. 101b; W. H. and H. C. Overall, ed., *Remembrancia Books, 1579–1664*, London, 1878, pp. 340, 362; Privy Council Registers, XI, 1968 (non-folio), 18 September 1640; M. J. Groombridge, ed., A Calendar of the Chester City Council Minutes, 1603–42, *Record Society of Lancashire and Cheshire*. 106, 1956; J. A. Tremlow, ed., *The Liverpool Town Books*, 1935.
11. Beier, *Masterless Men*; P. Slack, 'Vagrants and vagrancy in England, 1598–1664', *Economic History Review*, second series, XXVII, 1974.
12. Register of the Privy Council of Scotland, 1629–30, III, second series, p. 354; H. Paton, ed., *The Session Book of Dundonald, 1602–1731*, printed for private circulation, 1936, pp. 15–17.
13. As the towns of Cork and Waterford share their names with the counties in which they are situated it is possible that migrants listed simply as coming from Waterford or Cork came from the town. Here, however, I have counted only those migrants who were explicitly associated with the two towns.
14. Beier, *Masterless Men*, p. 39.
15. M. MacCarthy-Morrogh, *The Munster Plantation: English Migration to Southern Ireland, 1583–1641*, Oxford University Press, Oxford, 1986.
16. Chatsworth Devonshire Collections, Lismore MSS, 20/35, 36, 93, Cork Letter Book I, ff. 312–13; A. B. Grosart, ed., Lismore papers, series 1, London, 1886–8, I, p. 120, II, p. 257; National Library of Ireland MS 13237, No. 20, f. 17.
17. Broad Blumsdon churchwarden's accounts, 1606–54, Wiltshire Record Office, 1565/35; Records of the Corporation of Dunwich, Suffolk, H.M.C. Report, various collections, VII, 1914, pp. 95–7; A. Sabin, ed., Registers of the Church of St Augustine the Less, Bristol, 1577–1700, *Bristol and Gloucestershire Archaeological Society*, III, 1936, p. 17; R. R. Tighe and J. E. Davis, *Annals of Windsor: a History of the Castle and Town*, London, 1858, p. 17.
18. St Michael's, Minehead, churchwardens' accounts, Somerset Record Office, D/P/M St M. 4/1/1.

19. Worfield churchwardens' accounts 1603–48, *Shropshire Archaeological Society*, fourth series, II, 1912, pp. 48–9; Kent Record Office, Dover Borough Records,Depositions before the Mayor, 1630–59, f. 85v; J. Parkes, *Travel in England in the Seventeenth Century*, London, 1925, p. 257.
20. C.S.P. Dom., 1623, p. 398.
21. P.R.O., S.P., 16/144/62; Somerset Record Office, Q/SR, 62, ff. 38–42; D. B. Quinn, *The Elizabethans and the Irish*, Cornell University Press, New York, 1966, p. 157.
22. N. Canny, *Kingdom and Colony: Ireland in the Atlantic World, 1560–1800*, Baltimore, Md, 1988, pp. 44–5; B. E. Howells, ed., Elizabethan Pembrokeshire: the Evidence of George Owen, *Pembrokeshire Record Society*, second series, 1973, p. 3.
23. P.R.O., S.P. 16/426/87; Wiltshire Record Office, Q.S.R. A1 110, 1629 M, f. 102; C.S.P. Dom., 1628–9, p. 495.
24. J. M. Guilding, ed., *Reading Records*, II, London, 1895, p. 479; C. Lennon, *The Lords of Dublin in the Age of Reformation*, Irish Academic Press, Dublin, 1989, pp. 144, 215.
25. Devon Record Office, Exeter Strangers Book, 1621–68, C5/102, f. 135. For evidence of Irish native employment and residence see below and more generally Quinn, *The Elizabethans and the Irish*, chapter XI.
26. E. Jones, 'The Welsh in London in the seventeenth and eighteenth centuries', *Welsh History Review*, 10, 1981, pp. 461–79; F., and E. S. McDonald, 'The ethnic origins of the American people in 1790', *William and Mary Quarterly*, third series, XXXVII, 1980, pp. 179–99.
27. T. L. Purvis, 'The European ancestry of the United States population, 1790', *William and Mary Quarterly*, third series, XLI, 1984, p. 100.
28. This assessment is based largely upon E. MacLysaght, *The Surnames of Ireland*, Irish Academic Press, Dublin, 1978; D. O'Murchada, *Family Names of County Cork*, Glendale Press, Dublin, 1985.
29. H.M.C., Salisbury MSS, XVII, pp. 448–9.
30. P.R.O., S.P. 14/143/73; Kent Record Office, Fa/A2 No. 41, U570 01, f. 15; Somerset Record Office, Q/SR 59, examinations 1626–7, f. 60.
31. Essex Record Office, Q/SR 47/17; Guilding, *Reading Records*, II, p. 479.
32. Wiltshire Record Office, QSR A1 110, 1632 H, f. 155; Somerset Record Office, Q/SR 62/38–42; P.R.O., S.P. 16/144/62.
33. P.R.O., S.P. 14/170/4; C.S.P. Dom., 1623–5, p. 398.
34. St Mary le Strand Churchwardens' accounts, 1586–1650, vol. 22, Westminister City Archives.
35. Biddenden churchwardens' accounts, 1594–1778, Kent Record Office, P26/5/1; Parkes, *Travel in England*, p. 257.
36. M. O'Dowd, 'Women and war in Ireland in the 1640's', and D. Dickson, 'No Scythians here: women and marriage in seventeenth-century Ireland', in M. Mac Curtain and M. O'Dowd, eds., *Women in Early Modern Ireland*, Wolfhound Press, Dublin, 1991, pp. 106, 228–9.
37. Wiltshire Record Office, QSR A1 110, 1631 M.
38. Sabin, Registers of the Church of St Augustine the Less, pp. 23, 60; Slack, Register of Passports, p. 61.
39. D. B. Quinn, 'A discourse of Ireland: a sidelight on English colonial policy', *Proceedings of the Royal Irish Academy*, XLVII, section C, No. 3, 1942, p. 158.
40. Devon Record Office, C5/102, Exeter Strangers Book, 1621–68, ff. 80, 133, 140, 143.
41. J. O. Bartley, *Teague, Shenkin and Sawney: an Historical Study of the Earliest Irish. Welsh and Scots Characters in English Plays*, Cork University Press, Cork, 1954; B. Cunningham, 'Native culture and political change in Ireland, 1580–1640', in

C. Brady and R. Gillespie, eds., *Natives and Newcomers: the Making of Irish Colonial Society, 1534–1641*, Irish Academic Press, Dublin, 1986, p. 155; C. L. Falkiner, ed., *Illustrations of Irish History*, London, 1904, p. 315.

42. Devon Record Office, C5/102, Exeter Strangers Book, 1621–68, ff. 133, 137; Kent Record Office, Dover Borough Records, Depositions before the mayor, 1630–59, f. 85v.

43. C.S.P. Dom., 1623–5, p. 398; Somerset Record Office, Q/SR 62, f. 40; Devon Record Office, C5/102, Exeter Strangers Book, 1621–68, ff. 116, 135.

44. C. H. Mayo, ed., *Municipal Records of the Borough of Dorchester*, Exeter, 1908, p. 653.

45. P.R.O. S.P. 14/143/73; Wiltshire Record Office, QSR A1 110, 1633 H, f. 140; Kent Record Office, Fa/Az No. 41.

46. Sabin, Registers of the Church of St Augustine the Less, pp. 57, 60.

47. Guildhall Library, London, Bridewell Court Books, V, VII, MF 510–514; Beier, *Masterless Men*, p. 54.

48. G. Henry, ' "Wild Geese" in Spanish Flanders: the first generation, 1586–1610', *Irish Sword*, XVII, 68, 1989, pp. 189–202.

49. C.S.P. Dom., 1623–5, p. 398; Guilding, *Reading Records*, II, p. 479; Somerset Record Office, Q/SR 59, 1626–7, f. 60; Devon Record Office, C5/102, Exeter Strangers Book, 1621–68, f. 135.

50. A. V. Judges, ed., *The Elizabethan Underworld*, London, Routledge, 1930, p. 113.

51. Corporation of London Record Office, Repertories of the Court of Aldermen, 21, f. 429b.

52. H.M.C., Salisbury MSS, III, p. 113; Corporation of London Record Office, Journals of the Court of Common Council, 22, f. 329b; S. G. Ellis, *Tudor Ireland: Crown, Community and the Conflict of Cultures, 1470–1603*, Longman, London and New York, 1985, pp. 283–4; J. P. Harrington, ed., *The English Traveller in Ireland*, Wolfhound Press, Dublin, 1991, p. 47; Acts of the Privy Council, 1587–8, p. 109.

53. Howells, Elizabethan Pembrokeshire, p. 3.

54. Acts of the Privy Council, XV, pp. 109–10; C.S.P. Dom., 1598–1601, p. 121; J. Latimer, ed., *Annals of Bristol in the Seventeenth Century*, Bristol, 1900, p. 13; Bristol Record Office, Mayor's Audits, 1599–1604, ff. 31, 52, 66, 74, 77.

55. H.M.C. Report, Appendix 4, Rye Corporation MSS, p. 132; H.M.C. Salisbury MSS, XVII, pp. 448–9.

56. B. Jennings, *Wild Geese in Spanish Flanders, 1582–1700*, Irish Manuscripts Commission, Dublin, 1964, p. 30; G. E. Aylmer, 'St Patrick's Day, 1628, in Wiltham, Essex', *Past and Present*, 61, 1973, pp. 139–49; Somerset Record Office, Q/SR 59, Examinations, 1626–7, f. 60.

57. For a fuller discussion of subsistence crises see R. Gillespie, 'Harvest crises in early seventeenth-century Ireland', *Irish Economic and Social History*, XI, 1984, pp. 5–19; E. M. Crawford, ed., *Famine: the Irish Experience, 900–1900*, John Donald, Edinburgh, 1989.

58. J. Ware, ed., *Ancient Irish Histoires: the Works of Spenser, Campion, Hammer and Marleburrough*, Dublin, 1809, I, p. 166; J. Perrott, 'The Chronicle of Ireland, 1584–1608', J. Hooker, 'The Chronicles of Ireland, 1587', in Harrington, *The English Traveller in Ireland*, pp. 43–51, 71–81; Gillespie, 'Harvest crises', pp. 5–6.

59. Gillespie, 'Harvest crises', p. 8; J. T. Gilbert, ed., *Calendar of the Ancient Records of Dublin*. Dublin, 1889, II, p. 419.

60. Bristol Record Office, Common Council Proceedings, No. 1, 1598–1608, f. 55; British Library, Additional MS 11402, f. 101v.; H.M.C. Report, Appendix 4,

Rye Corporation MSS, p. 132; Guildhall Library, London, Bridewell Court Books, IV, V, MF 512, 513; H. F. Berry, ed., Minute Book of the Corporation of Dublin, Friday Book, 1567–1611, *Royal Irish Academy Proceedings*, XXX, section C, 1912–13, p. 500; 'Corporation Book of the Irish town of Kilkenny, 1539–1628', *Analecta Hibernica*, XXVIII, 1978, p. 48.

61. Bates, E. H., ed., Somerset Quarter Sessions Records, James I, *Somerset Record Society*, XXIII, p. 318; Hadow G R, ed., Registers of the parish of Wylye in the County of Wiltshire, Devizes, 1913 (I am grateful to Dr Martin Ingram for this reference); Wiltshire Record Office, 189/1, 536/45, 754/239; Swayne, H. J. F. ed., Churchwardens Accounts of St Edmonds and St Thomas, Sarum, 1443–1702, Wiltshire Record Society, 1896, p. 176.

62. R. R. Steele, ed., *Tudor and Stuart Proclamations, 1485–1714*, Oxford, 1910, II, 1, No. 279; 10 and 11 Car. I, c. 4.

63. E. H. Bates, ed., Somerset Quarter Sessions Records, Charles I, *Somerset Record Society*, XXIV, 1908, pp. 104, 131; T. Wainwright, ed., *Reprint of the Barnstaple Records*, II, Barnstaple, 1900, p. 135; Bristol Record Office, Common Council Proceedings, 1629, f. 27; Latimer, *Annals of Bristol in the Seventeenth Century*, p. 102; Sabin, Registers of the Church of St Augustine the Less, p. 60.

64. B. Jennings, ed., *Wadding Papers*, Irish Manuscripts Commission, Dublin, 1953, p. 298.

65. Gilbert, *Calendar of the Ancient Records of Dublin*, III, pp. 298–9; British Library, Harleian MS 2138, 28 November 1634.

66. P.R.O., S.P. 16/397/99; Steeple Ashton Churchwardens' accounts, *Wiltshire Notes and Queries*, VII, 1911–13, p. 76.

67. E. H. Bates, ed., Somerset Quarter Sessions Records, Commonwealth, *Somerset Record Society*, XXVIII, 1912, p. 115.

2 Wild Geese The Irish in European armies (sixteenth to eighteenth centuries)

John McGurk

I cannot too highly esteem those gentlemen of Ireland, who, with all the disadvantages of being exiles and strangers, have been able to distinguish themselves, in so many parts of Europe, by their valour and conduct above all other nations.

Jonathan Swift

This chapter is so broad in theme and geography that a special plea may be made for its impressionistic, and general chronological, treatment. The essay may be regarded as an exploratory contribution to the debate on the Irish as soldiers abroad. The bibliography, accompanying notes and references as well as pointers to case studies may also be regarded as a guide to further reading and research.

The plain facts of the achievements of Irishmen and Irish regiments in the armies of the continent are easy enough to come by in many of the standard histories of European warfare; their thoughts, their motives for becoming soldiers – in other words, the psychology and ideology of Irish military migration – are quite another and largely, and almost necessarily, an untold story. In this period it is more than probable that there is no such thing as a representative Irish soldier abroad; hence there are minefields to be eschewed should we rely too much on a series of case studies from which to draw general conclusions. Of its nature, the historical evidence is too selective for that. By culling out certain indicative themes in recent work and illustrating them by select evidence it is hoped to reach the spirit of the 'Wild Geese' without in any way suggesting that what is offered is conclusive or encyclopaedic of the topic. What is not treated is the Irish soldier in the Americas or the Irish in the British army; both themes need their own volumes, not chapters.

The weighty authority of Aristotle is sometimes brought to bear on the claim that the Celt is innately courageous and therefore militaristic. In his

Eudemian Ethics Aristotle wrote of the Keltoi living proximate to the Caspian Sea and so brave in their passion that they 'take arms and march against the waves'. However, it must be noted that the import of the passage cited is not so much that the Celts are particularly brave as that they are passionate as all barbarians are.[1]

It was the mature opinion of G. A. Hayes-McCoy, Ireland's foremost military historian of the sixteenth century, on the question of innate aggression in the Irish, that if as a nation they had been left to themselves they would not have been especially militaristic or defensive. Nonetheless we cannot fly in the face of the historical facts or indeed of the general impression that Irishmen have ever been attracted to military service at home and abroad, to such an extent that the very type and image of the traditional Irishman should and could well be a male in soldier's uniform. Likewise, the qualities of that distinctively Irish animal, the wolfhound, have long been accepted as symbolic of that vague entity, the Irish national character, epitomized in the motto of the United States 69th Regiment, 'the Fighting Irish' – 'Gentle when stroked; fierce when provoked.'[2]

Ever since the twelfth-century Anglo-Norman (strictly Cymru–Norman) conquest of Ireland, Irish soldiers can always be found fighting under the banners of the English monarchs.[3] At Crécy (1346) battle formations show Welsh and Irish contingents under the command of the Black Prince, Edward III's son. It is also more than likely that the Irish were at Agincourt under Henry V. William Shakespeare in his *Henry V* paints for posterity an inimitable pen portrait of an Irish captain, McMorris, who as a type must have been familiar enough in English arms by the sixteenth century for the national bard to have given him a place of importance at that historic victory.[4]

Origins of the 'Wild Geese' tradition

Apart from the perennial problem of nationalistic identities, the further problem for the historian of the Irish diaspora is how far to follow it around the globe and how to relate it to movements within the homeland of Ireland. In the case of some of the earlier migrants, the scholars, the seminarians and itinerant religious, but not those who sought a permanent exile, many did not necessarily intend to remain abroad but to return to strengthen and reform the Church within Ireland. It is, however, the departure from Ireland of mercenaries, soldiers of fortune, that military aristocratic class who, despairing of Ireland's future and their own fortunes, fled the country in the aftermath of the Elizabethan, Cromwellian and Williamite conquests of the sixteenth and seventeenth centuries which is the main burden of this chapter. From the glamorized 'Flight of the Earls' at the beginning of the seventeenth century to the even more romanticized flight of the Wild Geese at its end, Irish soldiers soon found that they could sell their swords and service to the Catholic monarchs of Europe, so that by the eighteenth century Irish soldiers and Irish brigades were familiar institutions in the armies of Spain, Austria and especially of France.

The term 'Wild Geese', certainly in romantic literature, came to signify those Irish soldiers who for at least three centuries died on the battlefields of Europe and whose souls, it was believed, returned to Ireland by a form of transmigration into the sounds and shapes of migrating wild geese. However, the more recent students of some of these Irish soldiers, notably Brendan Jennings, whose pioneering work in the 1960s on the Irish in Spanish Flanders, and the work of Micheline Kerney Walsh, especially on Irish aristocratic families in Spanish armies, and of the latest researcher, Gráinne Henry, who has taken up the theme afresh in very recent articles, all make the point that the term 'Wild Geese' must also be interpreted much more widely than in the anthropological or mythological sense. Simply, in the context of Irish history, the 'wild goose' or migrating soldier has to be interpreted as a victim either of fate or of the tyrannical behaviour of England, regarded as the wicked sister or cruel stepmother, depending on the century studied or on whether or not Ireland itself is regarded as a kingdom or a colony. 'Wild Geese', then, became an ideological term giving direct historical identity to groups of Irish military migrants into the armies of continental Europe specifically in the years that followed the Williamite conquest and the Treaty of Limerick in 1691. The very use of the term declares a particular interpretation of the Irish past *viz* that of a set of antagonisms between English and Irish, Catholic and Protestant, and which get exported abroad with the ever underlying hope that help will come from over the seas to shake off Protestant oppression and end English rule in Ireland. This view of Irish history hardened with every victory abroad over the English enemy, memorably at Fontenoy on 30 April 1745, and earlier with every returning Irish hero, such as the celebrated Owen Roe O'Neill and Thomas Preston when they returned to Ireland from service with Spain to intervene so dramatically in the events following the rebellion of 1641.

According to one historian, Gráinne Henry, this interpretation gets in the way of new approaches to studying 'the complex phenomenon of sixteenth and seventeenth century migration to European armies from Ireland'. In an important article in the *Irish Sword* Dr Henry, contrary to those who say the Wild Geese did not produce a concentrated Irish colony in any single place, sees the first generation of Irish who saw military service in Flanders in the period 1586–1610 as being such a unit and therefore perfectly identifiable. In what follows here the Irish in sixteenth-century Flanders may be seen as the precursors of the seventeenth-century 'Wild Geese' strictly speaking. Parallel with and in the wake of the various attempts during Elizabeth I's reign to reduce the island of Ireland to obedience to the Crown, Irishmen can be found fighting abroad; how far they can be regarded as the beginning of the Wild Geese tradition may still be regarded as a matter of unfinished historiography, needing a revaluation as further sources become available from the continental archives, and/or, as the genealogies of descendants of the continental dynasties of the Wild Geese themselves become better established. Probably the first Irishmen as a group to serve abroad militarily in any great number were those who sought refuge in Spain with their defeated chieftains from Munster when the last Desmond rebellion was crushed around 1583. In the 1580s and especially after the execution of Marie Queen of Scots (1587) relations between England and Spain hastened on towards open warfare with Drake's attack on Cadiz that same year.

Irish exiles in Spain aided, abetted and applauded the preparations for the Armada of 1588, for a Spanish victory would likely restore them to their confiscated lands and ensure the free practice of traditional Catholicism. It is certain that many Irish were engaged as guides, pilots, sailors and mariners in that disastrous expedition, and indeed there were many who volunteered to serve against the ancient enemy without pay. Those Irish who acted as guides and interpreters in the flight away from the Irish coast and across Scotland until they reached Spanish Flanders eventually made their way back to Spain, where they were re-employed in the navy and army; this movement is likely the origin too of some companies of Irish marines who remained in the Spanish service until the Anglo–Spanish peace of 1604 under James I.

However, the origins of Irish military service to Spain begin with the Army of Flanders, the name given the Spanish forces fighting the Dutch and their English allies. The first Irish regiment serving under the Spanish flag had been recruited in Ireland from both camps, the English forces in Ireland and native Gaelic forces, by Sir William Stanley of Hooton, in the Wirral, Cheshire, and initially transported to the Low Countries to fight under Leicester against the Spanish. In January 1587 Stanley surrendered his garrison to the Spanish and changed sides, bringing with him his regiment, then consisting of about a thousand English, Irish and Scottish troops. Though the Irish may well have been happier fighting for the Spaniard than against him difficulties soon arose within the regiment. Since it was officered by Englishmen, the Irish objected, on the grounds that they had no hope of promotion. Between 1596 and 1604 the Irish were allowed to serve in independent Irish companies under Irish captains. Stanley was regarded as a traitor and his extradition demanded, especially when it was discovered that Guy Fawkes had served in his regiment, the schemer and executor of the notorious Gunpowder Plot of 1605. Guy Fawkes remained under the protection of the King of Spain until the end of his days.

Between 1605 and 1610 all these independent Irish military companies, together with many of the soldier migrants who left Ireland after the defeat of the Irish and the Spanish at Kinsale in 1602, were consolidated into an Irish regiment in September 1605 under the command of Henry O'Neill, son of the Great O'Neill, Hugh, second Earl of Tyrone. Henry had been educated at Salamanca and was then at the court in Valladolid. After the Flight of the Earls in 1607, the number of Irish companies in Henry O'Neill's regiment in Flanders was fifteen, totalling between 1,600 and 1,700 men. Of Stanley's original expedition in 1586, 500 were described as Irish kerne, while 600 were discharged from the royal bands of Ireland, which, though English, always contained native Gaelic Irish.[11]

From a set of cautious calculations Gráinne Henry compares the number of Irish in Stanley's regiment with those in Henry O'Neill's, that is, over a twenty-five-year period, and concludes that there had been a decided growth of about a thousand Irish serving Spain between 1586 and 1609 in

Henry O'Neill's regiment alone. But her more significant calculation, allowing for the incompleteness of the records of the Army of Flanders, the rate of wastage in that army, and for comings and goings of the same soldiers to Flanders, is that over the twenty-five-year period between 1586 and 1611 a total of about 20,000 Irish soldiers saw service in Flanders; and, moreover, that Irish numbers 'were at their highest (about 900) during two of the most intense periods of fighting in Flanders, 1586–88 and 1600–02'.[12]

Mere statistics of Irish military personnel in Spanish Flanders in the late sixteenth century do less than justice to the detailed reconstruction of an emergent Irish community which Dr Henry has so painstakingly and excellently achieved, a veritable model for what might be possible for other Irish military communities in, say, France or in the imperial service of later centuries. Her study of marriage, baptismal and military records such as pensions indicates settlements of Irish families, their close interaction, their preoccupation with genealogy, ancestry, with land and lineage, especially in Bruges and Brussels, where 'Irish quarters' can be identified and in which the Irish language was almost certainly spoken. The officers among them, such as Maurice Fitzgibbon, Thomas Preston, Thomas Stanihurst and others in the upper circles of Irish military society, had Spanish or French or both languages, while the ordinary Irish foot soldier, as was said of him in the Deventer garrison of the 1580s, 'spoke an unintelligible language and could not have any intercourse with the inhabitants'.[13]

Despite its family cohesion and self-conscious links with Ireland this emergent Irish military community in Flanders through intermarriages forged links with the local Netherlands population. An army list of widows' pensions of 1635, which included wives of both rank and file and officers, indicates that one-third of the marriages were mixed; but highly selective evidence such as this might lead to an exaggerated conclusion about assimilation if we do not recall that the normal relations between soldier and civilian populations when pay was in arrears and food in short supply did not normally lead to the making of happy families. Moreover the normal sixteenth and seventeenth-century reputation of the Irish soldier abroad was one of wild barbarity, inhumanity and incivility.[14] When death, disease and disaster are the lot of the Irish soldier fighting abroad, and when transience and mobility are also necessary factors in military life, it might be safer to speak of a smaller first-generation Irish military presence rather than the temporary migrants into the army in the quarter of a century from 1586 to 1610.

Following the research of Brendan Jennings, Micheline Kerney Walsh and Gráinne Henry on the Irish in the Spanish service, and especially the overseas history of the O'Neills, it is no longer possible to assess the Irish soldier abroad simply as a mercenary selling his sword to the highest bidder, or as simply a militant nationalist abroad. On the contrary, these scholars have sufficiently proved how the Irish military community through their familial connections with the Irish colleges in Spain, the Netherlands and France were very much part of the new world of Counter-Reformation Europe and thereby necessarily part of the wider world of political and religious ambitions within Ireland itself.

The power and influence of Hugh O'Neill and of his son Henry in keeping the 'Regiment of Tirone' intact and ever under the command of an O'Neill is only one measure of their well established diplomatic network in Madrid and at Rome.[15] Again, Hugh O'Neill's plea to King Philip III on behalf of former soldiers of his and of O'Donnell's from the Nine Years War who had been dismissed by the King of Poland in 1613, that they be 'established as soldiers among those of their nation' in Flanders, is also indicative of his ambition to keep an all-powerful influence over the Irish regiment.[16] A celebrated 'Memorial of Hugh O'Neill to the King of Spain' in 1610 makes his wider vision of its eventual use perfectly clear; he requests King Philip 'to send an army secretly and in the name of His Holiness to Ireland' which with 'the help of the Irish in these parts and especially . . . the Irish regiment of 1,500 men serving your Majesty in Flanders . . . would be sufficient to take Ireland with speed'.[17] To the end of his days O'Neill in exile hoped for and planned the eventual military overthrow of the English administration in Ireland.[18] Counter-Reformation Catholicism and an Irish national consciousness were certainly beginning to coalesce and emerge as a political force in the early decades of the seventeenth century.

An astonishing range of evidence may be easily accumulated to demonstrate the close relationship between Counter-Reformation Catholicism and the Irish military groups on the continent. The calendars of state papers, domestic and Ireland, particularly in the years after the Spanish Armada, are full of English reports which indubitably stress the connection between priests and Irish soldiers.[19] Sir Ralph Sadler called Stanley's regiment, for example, 'a regiment of seminarie soldiers'. James Archer, the Irish Jesuit, was likely one of the chaplains to the Irish kerne in that regiment.[20] Sir George Carew, President of Munster, close friend of Sir Robert Cecil, frequently wrote from Ireland about the activities of the friars, Jesuits and popish priests as agents of rebellion or as spies for England's enemies.[21] Brendan Jennings's work on the registers of religious houses in the archdiocese of Malines, which includes Louvain, Douai and their daughter houses elsewhere, proves close ties between the Irish religious and military groups. In a list of twenty-eight Irish names of clerical students in that archdiocese between the years 1600 and 1610 only five did not have brothers or cousins serving in an Irish regiment.[22]

The appointment of Irish chaplains to the Irish companies in the Army of Flanders is also an obvious link, but the role of chaplain then did not stop at simply being 'preacher and ghostlie father' to the soldiers or their spiritual comforter when wounded or dying; being literate, the chaplain carried responsibility for a wide variety of financial and business transactions, and, of course, for the drawing up of wills and marriage certificates and the writing of testimonials.[23] Financial contributions for the upkeep of the Irish colleges were frequently collected by the chaplains. James Gernon, for example, collected 850 escudos from 122 soldiers in the regiment in 1616, most of the soldiers giving the equivalent of a month's pay.[24] Religious and military communities were also closely linked by the number of clerical students who, to finance their studies, served as soldiers in the Irish companies; Edmund O'Kelly, for instance, had permission to transfer his army grant to help him at St Anthony's College, Louvain. Though the evidence is patchy it is almost certain that by the first decade of the seventeenth century the Irish priest exercised much authority and influence over recruitment in Ireland itself for foreign armies.

In that vast collection of letters and reports from literate captains in Ireland to Sir Robert Cecil, namely the Cecil and Salisbury papers in Hatfield House, as well as throughout the calendars of state papers, Ireland, English captains like William Nuce complain of the difficulty of recruiting in Ireland for the United Provinces because the Irish 'under the influence of the priests will not serve against the King of Spain'. On the other hand, Nuce wrote, if he went recruiting for the Archduke, he would have 'not only choice of as many men as he desired, but the lords of the countries would arm them and give them cess till their embarking . . . at the procurement of the priests'.[25] Furthermore, when the two chief administrators of Ireland, Sir Arthur Chichester and Sir John Davies, in 1609 and 1610 tried to cleanse Ulster of idle swordsmen in a state-sponsored expedition to aid the King of Sweden, the expedition was opposed by the friars and the Jesuits, who tried to dissuade the soldiers from fighting for a heretic and usurper against a Catholic and rightful king.[26]

Strictly speaking, then, departure from Ireland to foreign military service was undoubtedly a form of migration, whether it was by direct recruitment under captains, or by means of a hastily got together expedition, or simply to get out of Ireland to avoid misery and starvation, on the part of many young men who were courageous, ambitious and desperate enough to do so, especially in those well documented periods following devastating war such as after the Desmond rising, the Baltinglas rebellion and, above all, when the highest numbers left Ireland, in the aftermath of the scorched earth policy of Mountjoy, Carew and Chichester at the end of the Nine Years War. This tragic view of military migration applied especially to the exoduses of 1601, 1652 and the best known of all, that of 1691;[27] the latter exodus, after the Treaty of Limerick (1691), was historically and properly known as 'the flight of the wild geese'.

The development of the tradition in the seventeenth and eighteenth centuries

Though not as consistently well documented as the Irish military migration to Spain and Spanish Flanders, there was steady recruitment in Ireland on the part of many European states from the outbreak of the Thirty Years War in 1618 until the rising in Ireland of 1641. The King of Poland, for example, through his ambassador in London, wanted a bodyguard of Irishmen in 1621. More than likely he had been impressed by the recruits one of his captains had already taken out of Ireland in 1618 for the Polish army. In Austria the first Irish regiment of many was formed by 1630 under Colonel James Butler. When it was virtually wiped out by the Swedish army the following year, Butler's brother, Walter, raised a regiment of Irish dragoons. This was the Butler notorious in history for his part in the murder of the imperial general Wallenstein. This presence in the imperial forces of Austria had been greatly augmented by a drift of Irish from the Polish army in 1638. After that date few Irish rank-and-file recruits are to be found in those regiments; on the other hand, there is a higher proportion of Irish officers 'eating the Emperor's bread' than of any other nationality. They are especially noted in the following century as the Irish tradition continued in those regiments to add lustre to Austrian battle honours. In general by the eighteenth century Irish brigades, Irish colonels, many of them proprietary colonels, and their regiments had become a familiar institution of continental military life, in Spain, in the imperial service and most outstandingly of all in France.

Ever since the end of the Elizabethan conquest and until 1641 it seems to have been English government policy to encourage able-bodied Irishmen to quit the country. Lord Mountjoy reckoned that in his day three out of four did not return from foreign service. In the repressive years after the Gunpowder Plot (1605) many Irish people, not all soldiers or the able-bodied, left for France, where they swelled the ranks of the Irish colonies already there, especially in Paris, Nantes, Rouen or Bordeaux. These migrants were mainly refugees, not the military elite from the old aristocracy, native Gaelic Irish and Anglo-Irish who continued in succeeding generations to win honours in their adopted countries, and not merely in the armies but at court and in the Church – the O'Neills, O'Donnells, MacCarthys, O'Driscolls, O'Sullivans, the Walshes, the Brownes, the Maguires and the Lallys and Dillons, to name the more ubiquitous in Europe. A brief analysis, for example, of the Irish names in the indexes to O'Callaghan's monumental work, *Irish Brigades in the Service of France* (1870), indicates that the names of indubitably Gaelic origin, the Macs and O's, are more predominant than those of Anglo-Irish provenance. The names of refugees, however, are but rarely recorded. And in the migration which took place after Gunpowder Plot the French government in 1606 ordered six boatloads of Irish refugees who had taken up station on the Ile de la Cité in the Seine to be sent back to Ireland.[28]

We have seen above that recruitment of Irish soldiers was actively encouraged, especially for the armies of the Protestant powers Denmark and Sweden; but that many of them never arrived. Recruitment by Catholic European powers was tolerated in periods of peace between England and those countries, except for clerical diplomats who sought help from foreign Catholic rulers in the conflict against the English Crown; indeed, a lineage of such diplomats and clerical leaders can be traced from the days of Silken Thomas's rebellion to Father Murphy of '98. Their names deserve notice in the history of a distinct class of migrants devoted to the politico-religious cause and include, to name a few, Anthony Daly, emissary to the King of France for James Fitzgerald, the eleventh Earl Desmond (1523), Alexander Lynch and Charles Reynolds at the time of Shane O'Neill's rebellion, three observant bishops, Patrick O'Hely of Mayo, Cornelius Ryan of Killaloe and Donat Og Ó Gallagher of Kilala; these as well as Fitzgibbon of Cashel, O'Herlihy of Ross, O'Brien of Emly, Tanner of Cork and Walsh of Meath all supplicated the cause of James Fitzmaurice Fitzgerald in the 1570s at the courts of Europe.[29]

Counter-Reformation militancy necessarily explains much of the ethos of the early Wild Geese before the end of the seventeenth century. Archbishop Edmund MacGauran of Armagh (1587–93) put much faith in the return of the Irish Flanders regiment; and after the sensational success of Hugh O'Neill at the Yellow Ford in 1598 he became importunate with Archduke Albert, the Governor of the Netherlands, to send back the Irish veterans; but few officers returned to help O'Neill lick his forces into professional shape.[30] Many of the hopes of the restoration of the Old Gaelic order and the power of the exiled Gaelic aristocracy centred on the O'Neill family on the continent in the early seventeenth century but the peace between Spain and England and between France and Spain did not help O'Neill's ambitions. Nonetheless, Irish regiments began to appear in France between 1635 and 1640, and, when war broke out again between France and Spain, Richelieu sought the consent of the English king, Charles I, to recruit men in Ireland to strengthen the French army. Within a five-year period seven regiments were raised for the French under Colonels O'Reilly, Cullen, Sinnott, Crosbie, Bellings, Wall and Fitzwilliam. Cardinal Richelieu thought a lot of Irish fighting men; in 1638, while actually at war with Spain, he wanted to get the two most distinguished Irish regiments in the Spanish army, those of Tyrone and Tyrconnell, then led by John O'Neill, son of Hugh, and Hugh Albert O'Donnell, son of Rory, Earl of Tyrconnell, to desert to the French service.[31]

The Irish rising of 1641 put an end to the recruiting activity for foreign service. Much was expected from the Irish soldiers in Flanders but in the event Eoghan Rua O'Neill (Owen Roe), already celebrated for his defence of Arras in 1640, and his nephew Hugh Dubh O'Neill, who would eventually distinguish himself at the siege of Clonmel against the Cromwellian forces, returned to Ireland to aid the insurgents, Owen Roe's victory at Benburb doing so much to redress the balance of Kinsale's defeat at the beginning of the century.[32] The only Irish regiment to remain in France during the confederate war was the regiment of Wall and, in Spain, the regiments of Tyrone and Tyrconnell; but in both countries there were many Irishmen serving in non-Irish regiments and, indeed, in opposing armies, a situation which repeated itself throughout the history of modern warfare: Irish fought Irish, for example, from the battle of Rocroi in 1643 to that of Waterloo. Recruitment for France and Spain went on during the confederate war in Ireland; the confederates hoping for arms, ammunition and money; and the king's men, under the Duke of Ormond, so that they could keep troops from joining the confederation's army. But, with the ending of the war in 1652–3 and the demise of the Confederation, movement out of Ireland began again. Irish soldiers left for Spain, France and Flanders on condition that they surrendered. Within two years about 25,000 were shipped to Spain and possibly 10,000 or even 15,000 to France; certainly eight regiments went to France. Of those who went to Spain, Clarendon reckoned that only half were fit to take up arms, and a smaller proportion returned to Ireland at the restoration of the monarchy in 1660.[33] Of the regiments recruited for Spain at this time, one was that of Colonel Walter Dongan, who arrived in San Sebastian with 3,000 men in 1652. In the following two years one Richard White was responsible for transporting 7,759 Irishmen to Spain, where they were formed into three regiments under Colonels Murtagh O'Brien, James Fitzgerald and John Fitzpatrick; and in February 1653 a Colonel Daniel MacCarthy arrived in Spain with 2,000 more. The eight Irish regiments in France augmented the armed forces, those of Inchiquin, Muskerry, Digby, Butler, Darcy, Wall and James Preston.[34]

A bewildering set of changes of allegiances is understandable at this period when we recall that the Irish had come through a war which caused, and emphasized, divisions among themselves; when France and Spain were still at war with one another; when France experienced its own civil war; and when both France and Spain attempted to recruit in Ireland. The Irish garrison at Bordeaux under the *condottiere* Condé went over to France. Lord Inchiquin, who held a French command in Catalonia, persuaded Irish soldiers to change sides. And, as a direct result of Oliver Cromwell's political alliance with France in 1655, the Stuart court in exile, Charles II and his brother James, Duke of York, were forced to move to Spanish Flanders, and with the Duke of York went many Irish, among whom were Cormac MacCarthy of Muskerry and his regiment as well as the duke's lieutenant – Colonel Richard Talbot, the future Tyrconnell. Again, as the French regular army was being reorganized, James Dillon, son of Theobold, first Viscount Dillon, became the *maréchal de camp*, or major-general, of a newly formed distinct Irish regiment which maintained its identity under the Dillons until 1793. In the upheaval of the French revolution the two remaining Irish regiments in France, the Dillon and the Berwick, became the 87th and 88th respectively. Though there was a reduction of armies to peacetime proportions after the Restoration in 1660 and following the peace between France and Spain, the recruitment of Irishmen for foreign service went on unabated. Sir George Hamilton, for example, raised an infantry regiment of 1,500 in 1671 and gave the French outstanding service under General Turenne in the wars against the Dutch and their allies for the next five years. Future distinguished Irish soldiers who served in that regiment included Patrick Sarsfield, later Earl of Lucan, Justin MacCarthy, later Lord Mountcashel, Morogh O'Brien, later major-general of Clare's regiment, and Andrew Lee, later lieutenant-general and colonel of his own regiment. When Sir George Hamilton was killed in 1676, Thomas Dongan, his lieutenant-general, commanded the regiment until the end of the war between France and Spain in 1678; he later became Governor of the Province of New York for King Charles II.[35] Clare's Irish regiment was first established in 1675 to fight under Spanish colours in Flanders. In 1681 and 1682 Colonel Denis O'Byrne and Sir Thomas Nugent recruited about a thousand in Ireland for Flanders. But it is also estimated that by 1672 about half those who had gone abroad during the Commonwealth had returned to Ireland.[36] And it must be remembered that at the beginning of the Jacobite/ Williamite war, 1688, many others of the Irish abroad returned home when the issues of land, religion and political power lay in the balance between

Catholics and Protestants, matters dearer to their hearts than either James II's throne or the European balance of power in favour of Louis XIV of France. On the other hand, as Dr John Childs points out in his *The Army, James II and the Glorious Revolution* (Manchester, 1980) one in three of the officers in James's army opted for service under William III.

With the defeat of James II, not ultimately at the Boyne but more definitively with 'Aughrim's grim disaster' (12 July 1691) and the subsequent surrender of Galway, Sligo and Limerick, military migration to Europe reached its peak. Since the 'usurpation' of William of Orange of the English throne it was the policy of Louis XIV to bring out Irish troops to France in exchange for French soldiers to be sent into Ireland.[37] In March 1690, for example, an exchange took place when the men of Mountcashel's brigade, between five and six thousand, were sent to France in the ships returning there, which had landed a somewhat greater number of French troops in Cork. In France, Mountcashel's force was divided into three regiments: Mountcashel's own (later known as Lee's and Bulkeley's, after subsequent commanders), Dillon's and Clare's. The war record of all three in the campaigns of the eighteenth century is one of the most distinguished in the annals of modern military history. An O'Brien always commanded the Clare regiment until its amalgamation with the regiment of Berwick in 1775. Dillon's absorbed Bulkeley's that same year and was led by successive Dillons up to the time of the French revolution.[38] The three regiments drew higher rates of pay than the French because they were treated as a foreign unit in the army. They wore red coats and their colours displayed the St George cross. The first foreign action they saw was in Savoy in 1690 under Charles Chalmont, Marquis de Saint-Ruth. In those operations against the Protestants of Savoy the general thought very highly of his Irish Catholic troops and they so appreciated the enthusiasm with which he fought the campaign that he became known as 'le missionaire botte', the missionary in top boots. He is, of course, the same Saint-Ruth who by his death at the battle of Aughrim likely cost the Jacobites a victory in the war, where many famous families lost their sons.[39]

In the articles of the Treaty of Limerick an essential condition for surrender and the conclusion of the war was the agreement made with Ginkel, William's general, to transport into France all of the Irish army who wished to go and to include women and children. Within two weeks of signing the Treaty of Limerick a French fleet arrived in the mouth of the Shannon to supplement Ginkel's transport vessels; it is estimated that about 12,000 soldiers and several hundred women and children set sail for France. How many of them under the command of Patrick Sarsfield, Earl of Lucan, is not certain. Sarsfield's wish to go to France was both personal and tactical but his departure certainly caused some ruptures on the Jacobite side. On the other hand many of William's officers were astonished that Ginkel had in effect given Louis XIV *gratis* a large army of 12,000 soldiers.[40] The arrangements which had been made at the Treaty of Limerick are yet another example of the Irish solution of exporting human resources to succeed famously elsewhere. However, this force, the Wild Geese properly so called, formed a separate army under James's control, with English colours

and uniforms but paid by Louis at French rates of pay. Such a force lent
credibility to James's ambition to regain his throne. Irish support of the
Stuarts in exile was given in the hope that the Irish soldiery would be able to
return home when the House of Stuart was restored. In the 1690s that was
not just a pious and romantic dream; in 1692 they were moved to
Cherbourg in preparation for an invasion of England, but the French naval
defeat of La Hogue extinguished that hope. In 1696 they were sent to Calais
to support the Jacobite rising of the Duke of Berwick, James's illegitimate
son, but that plan too was abortive. Later attempts in the eighteenth century
to restore the Stuarts gave encouragement to recruitment from Ireland.

When the peace of Ryswick was signed (1697) Louis XIV had to recog-
nize William as King of England, hence James was no longer permitted to
have his own army. The Irish regiments were reduced; many Irish then
were out of work. There were probably about 10,000 men and their families
without means of subsistence. Some joined the French regular army, others
went into the service of Spain or Austria, for as soldiers they could not
return to Ireland, where those who had fought against King William were
in fact outlawed.[41]

However, the Jacobite court at Saint-Germain remained a centre of
patronage for many Irish soldiers, ex-soldiers, clerics and courtiers. The
peace of Ryswick was short-lived. In 1700 the last Habsburg king of Spain
died without issue, but he nominated the Duke of Anjou, the grandson of
Louis XIV, as heir to the Spanish throne, a decision disputed by Austria.
The War of the Spanish Succession (1701–14) split Europe into two camps:
France and Spain allied in support of the duke, who was termed King Philip
V of Spain and Austria; England, Holland and Portugal backed the
Archduke Charles, the rival claimant to the Spanish throne.

Fresh opportunities for the Irish fighting men opened up. Louis XIV
wished to strengthen his army; a memoir submitted to him in 1702 mentioned the Irish as first-rate troops and proposed recruiting them in Spain,
Brittany and Ireland itself.[42] An additional reservoir of recruits was also
found in the deserters from the British army, in which there were numerous
Irish Catholics. The records of the French war archives show how local
governors had to return lists of Irishmen settled in the provinces who had
previously been discharged from the army; the officers among them state
their occupations as teachers of law, philosophy, rhetoric, mathematics and
the classics.[43] But in the lists at the other end of the social scale there were
Irishmen who had been condemned to the galleys and who were pardoned
by the king provided they joined one of the Irish regiments, which at that
stage in the history of the French army were Sheldon's cavalry [44] and the
infantry regiments of Dillon, Clare, Berwick, Lee, Dorrington, Burke,
Albemarle and Galmoy. These regiments often changed their names with a
bewildering change of colonels and whenever regiments amalgamated;
Clare's, for example, was always known as O'Brien's from 1706 to 1720,
then it reverted to its original name, but by 1775 it was incorporated with
Berwick's. Dorrington's became known as Rothe's from 1718 to 1766,
when it was commanded by Count Michael Rothe and by his son, Count
Charles Edward. In 1766 it took the name Roscommon from Robert

Dillon, Earl of Roscommon, who was succeeded in 1770 by Count Antoine Walsh de Serrant; it was then known as Walsh's until the time of the French revolution. Of these three Irish regiments which fought through the War of the Spanish Succession at the beginning of the century only three remained in 1775: Dillon's, Berwick's and Walsh's, the 87th, 88th and 92nd by the time of the revolution.[45] In 1702 Philip V began negotiations for the formation of the first Irish regiments which were to serve in the Spanish army under the Bourbon kings; they were the three dragoon regiments of Mahony, Crafton and Fitzharris and the infantry regiments of Castelar, MacAuliffe, Comerford, Vandoma and Bourke. Many of the officers of these new regiments had left Ireland after Limerick and had served France up to the peace of Ryswick. Sir Patrick Lawless, a Kilkenny man, is such an example; he sojourned at the Jacobite court in exile, and during the War of the Spanish Succession he became James III's (or the Old Pretender's) ambassador to Philip V. After the peace of Utrecht (1713) Lawless became an envoy from Spain to London. In the celebrated impeachment of Harley it was alleged that Harley had accepted Lawless as a minister, a man who was an Irish papist, who had fought against both King William in Ireland and Queen Anne in Spain, and, even more notoriously, that Harley had him granted an audience with the Queen under the name of Don Carlo Moro.[46]

As the many wars of the eighteenth century gave opportunities to Irish soldiers there was a fairly constant flow of recruits from Ireland to the regiments of their nation in France and Spain. To recruit in Ireland in these years was to risk imprisonment and execution, for to take men out of Ireland to England's enemies abroad was tantamount to treason. Nonetheless recruitment was successful, probably because of the penal code operating in Ireland to maintain the Protestant ascendancy. The general effects of the penal code are nowadays much revised in the new historiography but their intention was to keep the Catholic interest in the depressed condition in which the last confiscation, the Williamite, had left it.[47] With few exceptions it was the landless men, the 'vexed and troubled', who followed the well worn path of the Wild Geese. It is sometimes said that the penal laws were provoked by, if not modelled on, the anti-Protestant laws of Louis XIV but with this difference, that the French penal laws stopped at the Vosges; the Protestants of Alsace remained unharmed in pocket or in conscience by their foreign rulers but staying different in religion and language from France while at one with her in sentiment. In the same age the distinguished Irish officer, Count Taaffe, in the imperial service asserted that Protestantism was no bar to advancement under the empress Maria Teresa nor Catholicism a hindrance to promotion under her rival, Frederick the Great; Taaffe went on to conclude that it was not Ireland so much as England which was the loser by the restrictive penal laws in Ireland. In more pious and traditional mood Nicholas Taaffe spoke of his motives in taking up foreign service when he addressed a petition to the emperor Franz Stephen and Maria Theresa. He had left Ireland, he declared:

Because he was afraid that his descendants pressed by the penal laws would not resist the temptation of becoming protestants. He therefore took refuge to a catholic country where his ancestors were well known by the military service they had rendered at different intervals to the House of Austria. He had abandoned his relations and his estate and the rank and liberty he had in his own country to prevent his descendants from deserting a religion to which their Imperial Majesties so fervently adhered.[48]

Colonel O'Shee, from Kilkenny, who commanded 3,000 men in the Austrian army fighting Napoleon at the battle of Wagram, also made a similar point, stating that nowhere in the Austrian empire or in the various Germanic states would a man's creed exclude him from military command; in the British Isles alone it would bar him from the service of his lawful sovereign.[49]

The influence of the Irish in continental Europe in its military aspect, the armies, battles and wars of the eighteenth century would require multiple volumes to relate and assess; space here allows a mere sampling of their achievement. Their successful defence of Cremona early in 1702 against Prince Eugène of Savoy and an imperial army can be attributed to the regiments of Dillon and Burke as well as to the skill and bravery of Daniel O'Mahony's men, who foiled a surprise night attack. In the opposing Austrian army there were also Irish soldiers, who attempted to parley at Cremona with their compatriots. In his career advancement O'Mahony's son, General Count Dermico, Spanish ambassador to Vienna, was, perhaps, living proof of his father's oft cited remark that 'une campagne à la cour en vaut trois contre les ennemis'.[50] Throughout the pages of the *Irish Sword*, the excellent organ of the Military Society of Ireland, which is devoted to the study of Irishmen in warfare, there is evidence of many numbers of Irish generals, colonels and captains who became illustrious in the profession of arms in most countries of the world (other than Ireland), and in any century after the sixteenth it is noteworthy among high-ranking officers of Irish origin what an extraordinary number were chosen as governors of provinces, ambassadors and ministers of state.[51] A sample suffices. General Ricardo Wall was minister of foreign affairs in Spain under two monarchs successively from 1754 to 1763; in Austria at roughly the same time, Field Marshal Count Francis Maurice Lacy was president of the council of war; in France, Charles O'Brien, Earl of Thomond, was made *maréchal de France* in 1757. On St Patrick's Day 1766, in Vienna, Count O'Mahony, the Spanish ambassador at the Austrian court, gave a party at which the guests included Count Lacy, Generals O'Donnell, Maguire, O'Kelly, Browne, Plunkett and McElligott; four chiefs of the Grand Cross, two provincial governors, several knights military and four privy councillors, all claiming Irish descent.[52] The three brothers, Robert, James and Thomas Smith McGavan, natives of Longford, had their claims for recognition of nobility in Austria honoured in 1743 when the empress Maria Theresa knighted them because they had previously held titles of nobility in Ireland and, as additional justification in the case of James, because of his distinguished medical services to the University of Prague. And, because of the loyalty and gallant military services of the other two brothers, they were raised to baronial rank in the Austrian empire.[53] A veritable litany of the distinguished of Irish birth serving in the armies of Europe, including the British, might be easily enough compiled from the pages of the *Irish Sword*. But much more is known of individual officers and little of the Irish rank and file in the continental armies. In the archives of most European capitals records of Irish military elites turn up, their names often persisting in recognizably Irish forms, and in many cases their descendants proudly trace their ancestry to their Irish roots. This is particularly the case with the descendants of the Wild Geese in France. The recent work by Reneagh Holohan, *The Irish Châteaux*, the fruit of her travels in France among those Irish whose ancestors had settled, writes of them:

> . . . They are now French in all but name, but they retain a strong interest in their background. Genealogies and histories are all on hand to tell their 'romantic' story. Strangely they are almost as out of step with modern France as they are with modern Ireland and *ancien régime* in attitude; they are almost to a man solidly royalist and universally refer to the Old Pretender, their ancestors' Stuart leader and benefactor as Jacques Trois and in many cases have called their sons Charles Edouard after his son, Bonnie Prince Charlie.[54]

Archival materials such as we have seen used by Gráinne Henry to identify the emergent Irish community in Spanish Flanders also evince this emphasis on genealogy, 'roots' and heraldry, particularly on the part of those Irish who established families abroad. Once again the pages of the *Irish Sword* frequently publish family letters, memoirs, eye-witness accounts of military action and personnel – all necessary spadework for anyone in search of 'wild geese'. Here we can sample but a few from the eighteenth century alone.

The achievement of the Dillon regiment in a memoir compiled by its lieutenant-colonel, Richard Gaydon, in 1738 is translated in the *Irish Sword* by Liam O'Brian.[55] The number of Irish in the officer corps of the Bavarian army in the early eighteenth century is revealed by a manuscript list of 10 November 1705 in which Irish-born officers account for 8 per cent of the total. J. L. Garland has analysed the list in the *Irish Sword*.[56] V. H. Walsh has also followed up the theme of Irishmen in the imperial service by tracing his own family military history in the Austrian branches of the Walsh family tree.[57]

Much contemporary anxiety was expressed that the Irish soldiers abroad might be used to support the Jacobite cause. Charles Forman wrote a plea to the government to have the Irish regiments in France and Spain disbanded:

> They are British subjects, he wrote. 'They speak the same language with us, and are consequently the fittest troops to invade us with. They are seasoned to dangers and so perfected in the art of war that not only the sergeants and corporals, but even the private men, can make very good officers on occasion.'[58]

This letter and his defence in 1732 of the Irish fighting man is contemporary evidence of the excellent reputation that the Irish soldier had already earned in the wars.[59]

Charles Wogan, colleague of the second Duke of Ormond, from

Rathcoffey, Kildare, helped the duke to organize the 1715 Jacobite rising, was himself taken prisoner but escaped from Newgate in 1719. He has left his own account of the dramatic rescue he undertook of Princess Clementine Sobieski, the granddaughter of the former king of Poland, as a bride for James III, who rewarded him with a baronetcy, and the Pope made him a senator of Rome. The account, 'Mémoires sur l'enterprise d'Inspruck', is of the stuff of a Gothic drama.[60] Wogan's enthusiasm for the Jacobite cause drove him to transfer his service to Spain because France was then in alliance with Hanoverian England. He actually planned to bring James III from Elba to England in 1724. For his deeds against the Moors of North Africa he became the governor of La Mancha province. Wogan was no mere man of action but a linguist and correspondent with Jonathan Swift and friend of Alexander Pope. In a fifty-page letter to Swift he shows another side of foreign service. Wogan is bitter in complaints of how slow the French and Spanish were to give promotion to foreigners and how the only reward of the Irish was to be slaughtered. But Swift's reply is yet another piece of evidence of the facility of the Irish abroad to distinguish themselves; 'I cannot but highly esteem those gentlemen of Ireland who with all the disadvantages of being exiles and strangers have been able to distinguish themselves by their valour and conduct in so many parts of Europe.'[61]

The fears, realistic enough, of renewed Jacobite activity and deep Irish involvement, heightened in the years after the '15 and before the final attempt in the celebrated '45. Nor were these fears confined to the Irish in France and Spain. On the death of Owen O'Rourke, the Pretender's ambassador to Vienna in 1742, the imperial police seized all his correspondence. His letters to and from James Edward Stuart or James III are naturally full of international political intrigue, but in the cache of documents seized is O'Rourke's private letters from his kin in Ireland, O'Connor and O'Donnell cousins. They are still happily preserved in the Austrian state archives in Vienna and have now been published by his descendant, Brian de Breffny, in the *Irish Ancestor* as 'Letters from Connaught to a Wild Goose'; they were all written between 1736 and 1741. O'Rourke had fought at the Boyne and at Aughrim and had followed James II into France – a typical 'wild goose on clamorous wing following the flight of an alien king'.[62] Is he not more typical of the social advancement of the Irish soldier abroad when we recall that he had been in the Duke of Lorraine's Regiment of Guards at Nancy in 1697, then rose to noble status as Baron O'Rorke of Carrha in 1727 and was further ennobled to Viscount of Breffny by the emperor the year before his death? The military historian C. Duffy sees a kind of 'rule' in that Irishmen often approach greatness when turning outwards rather than in upon themselves. He goes on to suggest a parallel between the Irish officers, Taaffes, Butlers, Brownes, Nugents and Lacys, who were numbered among the most outstanding servants in the Austrian service 'eating the Emperor's bread'.[63] It was easier for the Irish to reach high rank in the imperial service than in France or Spain, but their reputation for courage, diplomacy and organization was well attested to: 'the more Irish officers in the Austrian service the better;

our troops will always be disciplined; an Irish coward is an uncommon character . . .' observed Emperor Francis I.[64] Before their most notable achievement, at Fontenoy in 1745, which preceded the last serious Jacobite attempt, Irish regiments had already gone into the annals of distinguished military service when three Irish regiments fought at Blenheim, when Mountcashel's – that is, Clare's – dragoons had captured not merely a colour but what is now thought to have been the royal standard taken at Ramillies; it was later presented to the Irish Benedictine nuns at Ypres.[65] Again no fewer than five infantry and one cavalry Irish regiments were heavily engaged at Malplacquet.[66]

It was, however, at Fontenoy that the Irish brigades made a most significant contribution to the French victory. There the six Irish regiments of foot – Bulkely, Dillon, Lally, Rothe, Berwick and Clare – were under the command of Viscount Clare, later *maréchal de France*. The single Irish cavalry regiment, the Fitzjames, held the centre. Dillon's was badly mauled but the French were saved from utter rout by the concerted charge of the Irish and the use of cannon at point-blank range, a tactic attributed to Thomas Arthur Lally de Tollendal, from Tullynadala, County Galway, who, after the French victory, visited the Scottish Highlands and his father's home in Connaught to prepare for a Jacobite rising. Fontenoy has long since been regarded as the highest of the Irish battle honours abroad; its folklore and traditions are much enshrined in the folk memory of the Irish kept green by the patriotic verse of the nationalist poet Thomas Davies:

> On through the camp the column trod – King Louis turns his rein;
> 'Not yet, my liege,' Saxe interposed, The Irish troops remain. . . .
> On Fontenoy, on Fontenoy, like eagles in the sun,
> With bloody plumes the Irish stand – the field is fought and won.[67]

Most military historians now agree that the Irish were the main cause of Marshal Saxe's victory against the English that day; it is said that the Irish fury was much enforced by the battle cries of 'Cuimhnigi ar Luimneach agus feall na Sasanach,' 'Remember Limerick and Saxon perfidy.' Two days after Fontenoy the French commander wrote in his report, '. . . we moved forward and the Irish brigade, which led the van, attacked with the greatest possible daring'. It was Lord Clare, Charles O'Brien, who commanded the Irish brigade that day. His uncle was killed at Marsaglea in 1693; his father was mortally wounded at Ramillies in 1706. And, is it not reliably reported that the Duke of Cumberland, the future 'butcher of Cullodon', said as he witnessed the Irish charge, 'God's curse on the laws that made those men our enemies.' Lally was singled out for honours and made a brigadier by Louis XV. Voltaire wrote a memoir of Lally's bravery at Fontenoy. Later, as the theatre of warfare in Anglo-French rivalry spread to India, Lally took his regiment there for the French, where he was opposed by another famous Irish commander, Eyre Coote. Lally's tragic end is well known; on his return to France he was executed as a scapegoat for the mismanagement that had frustrated his efforts on behalf of the French cause in India. His son later vindicated his name.[68]

It is also now recognized that Bonnie Prince Charlie's expedition to Scotland in 1745, following the great boost given to French morale by the victory at Fontenoy, would not have been feasible without Irish help. Pierre André O'Heuguerty, diplomat, man of ideas and of the pen, was also a wealthy ship owner at Nantes and Saint-Malo who with Antoine Walsh acted as intermediary between the English Jacobites and the French minister. His partner, Walsh, supplied the *Du Teillay* [Doutelle], which landed Prince Charles Edward Stuart at Loch nan Uamh in August. His plan to use the Irish brigades to make a diversionary landing in Ireland and its later use in either Scotland or England was taken seriously by the French foreign office. O'Heuguerty sincerely believed that the English Jacobites were a credible force and his optimism for the Stuart cause remained undiminished even after the news of the disastrous retreat from Derby. His myriad actions on behalf of the Jacobite cause are not well known in the history of the '45. Interestingly, his correspondence shows that he would have liked it to have been French policy to detach Ireland from England and to set the country up as an independent kingdom; he claimed that the interest of Ireland would never be served by union with England, no matter which royal dynasty occupied the Palace of St James. Heuguerty therefore had no time for the Stuart ambition to regain the three kingdoms.[69]

It is in Jacobite poetry and song that the theme of a return of the Irish exile recurs; in an Irish poem of the mid-eighteenth century the exiles are termed *geanna* (geese), and it is now thought that the English words 'wild geese' appear in poems of an earlier date.[70] Contemporary reactions in Ireland itself to heroic Irish deeds abroad are hard to come by; however, when news of Lally's success at Bergen-op-Zoom arrived in the west of Ireland bonfires and illuminations were lit in his honour. When the French planned an invasion of Ireland in 1759 with the aid of four or five Irish regiments, including Clare's, Lord Clare hoped to recover the ancestral estates which had been confiscated for the Burton family in the Williamite land transfer after Limerick.

The French naval defeat of Quiberon Bay put an end to such dreams. In the second half of the eighteenth century the Irish presence in continental armies was greatly reduced, partly owing to the fact that Irish Catholic recruitment into the British forces was going forward in an unauthorized way, until the new Oath of Allegiance changed that on the eve of the American war, which lasted eight years and which after 1778 became a European conflict.

Irish names remained in Europe among the officer class at large. In the Archives du Ministère de la Guerre in Paris that pioneer and relentless searcher for wild geese Micheline Kerney Walsh unearthed many certificates or testimonials given by the priests of the Irish college in favour of Irish soldiers, mainly officers seeking promotion or pensions. The strict army regulations of France made it necessary to produce written evidence of birth and baptism, and some of the earlier testimonials are simply of genealogy and Catholicity. The chronological span of the documents is from 1711 to 1791, and so they aid greater identification of the Irish officer cadre up to the time of the revolution.[71] On the other hand names of the lower rank and file gradually disappear from view in the Irish regiments in the late eighteenth century. It must be presumed that the descendants of the rank and file of Irish in the continental armies became assimilated, their Irish origins lost in oblivion. In France the revolution swept away the identity of the three remaining Irish regiments of Dillon, Walsh and Berwick. In Spain the last three surviving Irish regiments, the Hibernia, Irlanda and Ultonia, were disbanded in 1818. The last representatives of the 'Wild Geese in France' were bidden farewell by the future Louis XVIII in these memorable phrases:

> Gentlemen, we acknowledge the invaluable services that France has received from the Irish Brigade in the last hundred years, services that we shall never forget, though under an impossibility of requiting them. Receive this standard as a pledge of our remembrance, and a monument of our admiration, and of our respect; and in future, generous Irishmen, this shall be the motto of your spotless flag: '1692–1792, Semper et ubique Fideles'.[72]

Conclusion

Although this chapter has eschewed treating the Irish in the British army, it must be noted that by the end of the 1780s restrictions on the recruitment of the Catholic Irish were gradually eroded; from then on there was a veritable flood of the peasantry into the British army, so much so that the commander-in-chief in 1797 hesitated to send troops into Ireland on the eve of the 1798 rebellion, since in some cases entire regiments were composed of Irishmen. Of course the 1798 rebellion was the first rising in Ireland in which the leading Protestants as United Irishmen took up arms against the British government. And, it must be recalled, the French revolution altered the general strategic situation by once more turning Ireland into England's endangered back door, as in the days of Philip II and of Louis XIV. In the hard times before and after the Great Hunger, British army recruitment came to depend heavily upon the Irish. In 1830 the Irish accounted for 42·2 per cent of the noncommissioned ranks; this proportion gradually declined but it was still around 14 per cent in 1891; in precise figures the Irish in the army fluctuated between 55,000 in 1868 to around 25,000 in 1896.[73] The Irish in the American wars, i.e. of independence and the Civil War, need separate discussion; so too do the Irish in the British armed forces of the nineteenth and twentieth centuries. They have been excluded here on the maybe simple grounds that neither America nor Britain lay on the flight paths of the original Wild Geese even though Irishmen fighting for and against the British may well have been conscious of the glorious traditions of their military ancestors in the continental conflicts of the preceding centuries.

However, as we have seen, the tradition of Irish service in foreign armies, especially among the officer class, generally aristocratic and literate, was well established in Spain, France and Austria by the seventeenth century. By the eighteenth century military service had in any case become a normal career expectation for many younger sons. To what extent loss of land and status, not to speak of the prohibitions against Catholic and Dissenter under the penal laws following 1691, gave a confrontational bitterness to the world view of the Irish military exile is a question which largely remains to be addressed by historians and others. Likewise, how far were the Irish clerics in the colleges abroad responsible in their writings for an interpretation of the Irish past which stressed the conflict between Irish and English, Catholic and Protestant? Many of these writers, like Geoffrey Keating, Philip O'Sullivan Beare and Stephen White, conscious of the lack of apologists, were determined to stand up for Ireland and the Irish against the slanders and specious war propaganda from the English enemy, their vitriolic attacks beginning with the twelfth-century writer and reporter on Ireland Gerald of Wales, 'the lying bull of the herd', as Keating called him.[74] Modern historians with perhaps more objectivity and with less emphasis on the misery, banishment and military traumas would see the traditional interpretations of exile, hopes of return to redress ancient wrongs, revenge for injustices, and so forth, as all getting in the way of a wider visionary interpretation of the Irish military diaspora. In the most liberal sense of historical interpretation there has to be room for both views in any military history of the Irish overseas, even though visions, mentalities and attitudes are notoriously difficult for the historian to document with any degree of accuracy. It is understandable and historically justifiable to see the Irish migrant travelling with a sense of grievance in an age of persecution and listening eagerly to the words of his priest in support of his faith and fatherland. The love of family, the Catholic faith and the land of Ireland itself are clearly the dominant attitudes in the documents, artefacts, inscriptions and histories of the Irish military classes abroad. Matthew O'Conor, whose history of the Irish brigades antedates that of O'Callaghan, puts forward their defence in this way:

> Let no one asperse the character of the Irish because they fought so often under foreign colours. Exiled, persecuted and loyal they lent their value to the States which supported their dethroned kings, their outlawed religion, their denationalized country, their vow of vengeance, or their hopes of freedom . . . their varied services, examined in detail, with reference to the creed, politics and foreign relations of Ireland at each period . . . only prove the amount of patriotism, piety and valour which, concentrated at home to national service, would have made Ireland all we could wish her.[75]

O'Conor's tone and sentiments are understandable; he wrote in the wake of the famine and at a time when his fellow countrymen were dying in one of Queen Victoria's 'little wars', the Crimean. For many an Irish country lad the Queen's shilling offered the possibility of freedom from slavish conditions, farming hard and hungry hills on a mountainy farm. In the imperial wars of the nineteenth century Irishmen were found fighting round the globe so that their motto indeed from the days of the Wild Geese could very well have been *ubique*. But how very different from the high-flown sentiments of patriotic religion and politics so often foisted upon the Irish military migrant are these lines from a nineteenth-century ballad:

> Oh, I wish the Queen of England
> Would write to me a line
> And place me in a regiment
> All in my youth and prime;
> I'd fight for England's glory
> From the clear daylight of dawn
> And I never would return again
> To plough the rocks of Bawn.

We began with a comment on the pugnacity of the Irish, but have not poverty, politics or the patterns of economic, political and religious change between Ireland and Britain and continental Europe ever been the propelling and attracting forces to explain the ubiquity of Irish migrants, be they missionaries or military folk? Social and often geographical factors in Ireland itself indicated, in the main, that army service abroad would be the widest option open, especially for younger sons. Abroad, as we have seen, there were interrelated family groups to attract them, too, especially in the well established military families like the O'Tooles from Wexford – eight sons of that family served in the Irish Brigade. Histories and genealogies of such families, particularly in France, tend to glory in their Irishness, but whether sadness, regrets and lamentations are to be found in the mentalities of the soldiers who fled Ireland at various times from the late sixteenth century to the late nineteenth can be historically documented with convincing contemporary evidence remains a largely untilled field. Can it be called the 'fifth province' or that other Ireland overseas? Whatever is written about Irish military migration will have to be interpreted in a much wider sense than formerly, and certainly not in the simplistic and possibly racist terms of 'the bugle in the blood'.

Notes

1. Aristotle, *Eudemian ethics*, III, i, 26. The phrase is often taken out of context to give the Celt's legendary bravery a classical lineage. I am grateful to my colleague, Dr Helen King, for this reference and its context.
2. G. A. Hayes McCoy, *Irish Battles: a Military History of Ireland*, 1969, introduction, p. i.
3. The entire theme of Irishmen fighting for England and in the British imperial armies would need a volume to itself; a cursory but historiographical glance is given the theme at the end of this chapter.
4. Shakespeare, *Henry V*, Act III, scene 2, II, lines 116–17.
5. J. J. N. McGurk, 'The Recruitment and Transportation of Elizabethan Troops and their Service in Ireland, 1594–1603', Ph.D. thesis, University of Liverpool, 1982.
6. The relationship of the Irish soldier abroad and the Irish cleric, apart from being

frequently familial, is but one reflection of the close alliance of religion and politics in the era of the Counter-Reformation and need not surprise anyone with a fleeting knowledge of sixteenth and seventeenth century European history. For one set of family relationships between the Irish soldiers in the Netherlands and the Irish colleges see G. Henry, 'The emerging identity of an Irish military group in the Spanish Netherlands, 1586–1610', in *Religion, Conflict and Coexistence in Ireland*, 1991, pp. 66–73, and for some relations between the English clergy and the militia forces, illustrative of the general theme, see J. J. N. McGurk, 'The clergy and the militia, 1580–1610', *History*, LX, 1975, pp. 198–210.

7. G. Henry, 'Wild Geese in Spanish Flanders', M.A. thesis National University of Ireland (Maynooth), 1986.

8. The theme is developed further in her article, same title as her thesis, in *Irish Sword*, XVII, 68, 1989, pp. 189–193.

9. J. J. N. McGurk, 'Ireland and the Spanish Armada, September/October 1588', *Contemporary Review*, 254, 1477, 1989, pp. 98–103.

10. G. Parker, *The Army of Flanders and the Spanish Road, 1567–1659*, Cambridge University Press, Cambridge, 1972.

11. McGurk, thesis; see section on the employment of Irish and Scots in the Elizabethan forces, pp. 79–90.

12. Henry, 'The emerging identity', p. 55.

13. Henry, 'The emerging identity', p. 62.

14. The reputation was commonplace in Elizabethan war propaganda; many instances are found in the calendars of the state papers, Ireland, and in those of the Carew papers in Lambeth Palace Library for the late sixteenth and early seventeenth centuries. The heroic qualities of the Irish fighting man are frequently attested to by friend and foe alike in the histories of warfare throughout the English-speaking world.

15. M. Kerney Walsh, 'The O'Neills in Spain', the first O'Donnell lecture, April 1957, National University of Ireland.

16. There were seven of these Irish companies. Originally they were part of an expedition sent by Sir Arthur Chichester, Lord Deputy of Ireland after Mountjoy, 'to serve the heretics of Moscow and Sweden . . . against the King of Poland' but they in fact deserted to the Catholic army of the Archduke, who first refused O'Neill's request. See M. Kerney Walsh, 'The last years of Hugh O'Neill', *Irish Sword*, VIII, 1967–8, pp. 230–4.

17. The full document in translation may be found in M. Kerney Walsh, *Destruction by Peace: Hugh O'Neill after Kinsale*, Cumann Seanchais Ard Mhacha, Armagh, 1986, pp. 251–4.

18. The collection of letters, memorials and other documents from the continental archives, especially those in Madrid and Rome concerning the exile of Hugh O'Neill show him to have been no idle romancer, rather a frustrated realist about his genuine ambitions to regain his lost position in Ireland.

19. For an insight into the wealth of sources for the early modern period in Irish history and indeed as a critical guide to these sources see R. W. Dudley Edwards and M. O'Dowd, eds., *Sources for Early Modern Irish History, 1534–1641*, Cambridge University Press, Cambridge, 1985.

20. T. J. Morrissey, *James Archer of Kilkenny: first Rector of the Irish College at Salamanca and Ally of the Great Hugh O'Neill*, Dublin, 1979.

21. Calendar of Carew MSS, III, pp. 457–9 for one instance but for many see McGurk, thesis, pp. 50–7.

22. B. Jennings, 'Irish names in the Malines ordination registers, 1602–1794', *Irish*

Ecclesiastical Record, LXXV, 1951, LXXVI, 1952, LXXVII, 1952. Jennings's findings have been analysed by Henry, 'The emerging identity', p. 67.

23. For a list of chaplains' names see Henry, thesis, appendix IX.

24. B. Jennings, *Wild Geese in Spanish Flanders, 1582–1700*, Dublin, 1964, pp. 486–8.

25. Historical Manuscripts Commission (H.M.C.), Salisbury MSS, XVIII, p. 11, Captain Nuce to Sir Robert Cecil, 8 January 1606.

26. Calendar of State Papers, Ireland, 1608–1610, p. 300, 19 October 1609.

27. L. M. Cullen, 'Catholic social classes under the penal laws', in *Endurance and Emergence*, ed. Power and Whelan, Irish Academic Press, Dublin, 1990, p. 72, which sees the search for employment as the main driving force behind the military migration, 'which is far removed from the romantic picture of "wild geese" fleeing from Ireland'.

28. J. J. Silke, 'The Irish abroad, 1534–1691', in *A New History of Ireland*, III, ed. Moody, Martin and Byrne, Oxford, 1976, p. 593.

29. Silke, 'The Irish abroad', pp. 594–7.

30. J. Hagan, ed., 'Some papers relating to the Nine Years War from the Borghese collection of MSS in the Vatican archives', *Archivium Hibernicum*, III, 1914, pp. 274 ff.

31. M. Kerney Walsh, 'The Wild Goose tradition', *Irish Sword*, XVII, 66, summer 1987, p. 7, and, despite the lack of full references, R. Hayes, *A Biographical Dictionary of Irishmen in France*, Dublin, 1949, is a mine of information.

32. J. I. Casway, 'Owen Roe O'Neill's return to Ireland in 1642; the diplomatic background', *Studia Hibernica*, IX, 1969, pp. 48–64, and, for the latest biography of Owen Roe, the same author's *Owen Roe O'Neill and the Struggle for Catholic Ireland*, Philadelphia, 1984.

33. For three very different treatments of the period *c.* 1630 – *c.* 1660 of Irish history see T. C. Barnard, *Cromwellian Ireland: English Government and Reform in Ireland, 1649–1660*, Oxford, 1975; D. Stevenson, *Scottish Covenanters and Irish Confederates*, Belfast, 1981, and K. Bottigheimer, *English Money and Irish Land: the Adventurers in the Cromwellian Settlement of Ireland*, Oxford, 1971.

34. Kerney Walsh, 'The Wild Goose tradition', p. 7.

35. Kerney Walsh, 'The Wild Goose tradition', pp. 9–10.

36. Silke, 'The Irish abroad', p. 609.

37. For a historiographical overview of the significance of the Boyne see J. J. N. McGurk, 'The battle of the Boyne, 1st July 1690: "The Twelfth" 1990', *Contemporary Review*, 257, 1494, pp. 24–9.

38. J. G. Simms, 'The Irish on the Continent, 1691–1800', in *A New History of Ireland*, IV, ed. Moody and Vaughan, Oxford, 1986, pp. 629–30.

39. J. G. Simms, 'The battle of Aughrim: history and poetry', *Irish University Review*. But, as the author concluded, 'The course of history did not turn on one man's life', p. 43.

40. For a full and careful account of military and political events in the Jacobite/Williamite wars in Ireland see J. G. Simms, *Jacobite Ireland 1685–1691*, 1969.

41. The banishment Act of 1697 (9 Will. III, c. 1, 25 September 1697) specifically referred to religious, men and women and the secular clergy. The Jacobite court in exile became a generous patron of the Catholic clergy. The Stuarts could nominate bishops to Irish sees; but, to draw off the hostility of the government to such bishops, the Vatican issued double briefs of appointment, one referring to royal nomination was sent to the Jacobite court and the other to the bishop which made no mention of his nomination. See C. Giblin, 'Irish exiles in Catholic Europe', in P. Corish, *Irish Catholicism*, IV, Chapter 3, 1971, p. 50.

42. 'Memoire de M. de Chamlay to Louis XIV', 25 October 1702, cited in J. C. O'Callaghan, *History of the Irish Brigades in the Service of France*, Glasgow, 1870, p. 219.

43. Kerney Walsh, 'The Wild Goose tradition', p. 13.

44. Dominic Sheldon was colonel–proprietor of this cavalry regiment; he resigned it in 1706 when it became the Nugent, after its new colonel, Christopher Nugent, and continuing under his son Jacques Nugent until 1733. From then until its dissolution in 1766 it was known as Fitzjames's, its last colonel being Jean Charles, Marquis de Fitzjames, son of the Duke of Berwick. For this and for a brief history of the more famous Regiment of Lally, see O'Callaghan, *Irish Brigades*, throughout.

45. M. Kerney Walsh, 'Irish soldiers and Father O'Neill of the Irish college in Paris', *Seanchas Ard Mhacha*, 9, 1, 1978, p. 107, n. 1.

46. The example is given in full in Simms, *Jacobite Ireland*, p. 640.

47. For some of the latest research on these laws see T. Bartlett and D. W. Hayton, eds., *Penal Era and Golden Age*, Belfast, 1979.

48. *Memoires of the House of Taaffe*, Vienna, 1865, quoted in C. Duffy, *The Wild Goose and the Eagle: a Life of Marshal von Browne, 1705–1757*, 1964, p. 6. Nicholas Taaffe, sixth viscount, born in Sligo *c.* 1685, failed to get the Taaffe estates restored to the family; the English Parliament ordered their sale, a third to go to the viscount and the rest to the Protestant claimant.

49. The example is given in W. F. T. Butler, *Confiscation in Irish History*, 1917, p. 252.

50. 'One campaign at court is worth three against the enemy.' Count Daniel O'Mahony, the hero of Cremona, claimed descent from Brian Boru. With Louis XIV's consent he transferred his allegiance to Spain, where, after distinguished service at Almanza, Alcoy and in Sicily, he was made Count of Castile and promoted to lieutenant-general; one of his sons, James, reached the same rank, and the other was Dermod, or Dermico, the Spanish ambassador to Vienna.

51. To take a random instance, say volume XIV of the *Irish Sword*, the reader will find interesting material on the Dillons, MacMahons and Pierre André O'Heuguerty (1700–63), the Jacobite leader in the '45.

52. Quoted in Simms, 'The Irish on the Continent', p. 642. Count Francis Lacy was a protégé of Field Marshal Browne, and 'the confidant of the Emperor Joseph II, and the reformer of the Austrian army, and the very epitome of the spirit of eighteenth century warfare, especially in the science of supply, according to no less an authority than Clausewitz. See Duffy, *The Wild Goose and the Eagle*, p. 87.

53. V. H. Walsh, 'Some Irishmen in the imperial service', *Irish Sword*, V, p. 79.

54. R. Holohan, *The Irish Châteaux: in Search of Descendants of the Wild Geese*, Dublin, 1989. In the search the author travelled from the Pas de Calais, and the Château Noeux les Auxi, of the Butlers' to the southern chateaux of St Géry, owned by the O'Byrne family, and from Brittany to the Château du Verger, home of Comte Alberic de Walsh-Serrant, thence to the eastern region of Burgundy and the Château des Colombiers, owned by Comte Georges de Wall . . . and elsewhere.

55. L. O'Brian, 'The Chevalier Gaydon's memoir of the regiment of Dillon, 1738', *Irish Sword*, III–VI, 1958–64, translation.

56. J. L. Garland, *Irish Sword*, 56, 1981, pp. 240–55.

57. Walsh, 'Some Irishmen'.

58. Cited in Simms, 'The Irish on the Continent', p. 634.

59. Charles Forman, *Defence of the Courage, Honour and Loyalty of the Irish Nation*, 1732, cited in Simms. 'The Irish on the Continent', p. 634.
60. Included in J. T. Gilbert, ed., *Narratives of the Detention, Liberation and Marriage of Maria Clementina Stuart*, Dublin, 1984, pp. 31–108.
61. Cited in Simms, 'The Irish on the Continent', p. 639, nn. 1, 2.
62. Brian de Breffny, ed., 'Letters from Connaught to a Wild Goose', *Irish Ancestor*, X, 1978, pp. 81–98. The verse is cited in W. F. T. Butler in his *Confiscation in Irish History*, 1917.
63. Duffy, *The Wild Goose and the Eagle*, preface.
64. Found among the emperor's papers after his death and cited in O'Callaghan, *Irish Brigades*, pp. 601–2.
65. D.M.C. (Dame M. Columban), *The Irish Nuns at Ypres* ed. R. Barry O'Brien and with an introduction by John Redmond, 1915; see the note to chapter III on the flag and its capture, pp. 41–6.
66. W. S. Churchill, *Marlborough: his Life and Times*, Cassell, London, 1933–8. In Sir John Fortescue's *History of the British Army*, 1899, the battle of Ramillies is treated as the revenge for Landen, at which Sarsfield was mortally wounded, and Fontenoy. At Malplacquet (1709), two royal regiments, one in the British and the other in the French service, both in red coats, came into direct conflict in a famous clash.
67. A full bibliographical reference on Fontenoy cannot be given here because of its great wealth, but see O'Callaghan, *Irish Brigades*; Hayes, *Biographical Dictionary*; Simms, 'The Irish on the Continent'; P. Boyle, 'The Irish brigade at Fontenoy', *Irish Ecclesiastical Record*, fourth series, XVII, 1905, pp. 427–44. It must also be remembered that there were fewer than 4,000 Irish soldiers in the French army of approximately 50,000. The numbers who died in the service of France were exaggerated in Abbe MacGeoghegan's *History of Ireland* as more than 450,000 between the years 1691 and 1745. The dedication of that work to the Irish brigade by the author, chaplain to the Irish soldiers, is a magnificent example of nineteenth-century rhetoric.
68. J. C. O'Callaghan, R. Hayes and M. Hennessey (works listed in the bibliography) have much material on the Lally regiment.
69. *Irish Sword*, XIV, 55.
70. Simms, 'The Irish on the Continent', p. 637, n. 1.
71. One group of these documents has been published in L. Swords, ed., *The Irish French Connection, 1578–1978*, Paris, 1978, pp. 63–87, and a further group in *Seanchas Ard Mhacha*, 9, 1978, pp. 95–122, both sets ed. M. Kerney Walsh.
72. O'Callaghan, *Irish Brigades*, p. 634.
73. C. Barnett, *Britain and her Army*, London, 1970, p. 241, and more specifically for the Irish in the British armed forces see H. J. Hanham, 'Religion and nationality in the mid-Victorian Army', in *War and Society: Essays in Honour and Memory of J. R. Western*, ed. M. R. D. Foot, 1973.
74. For full bibliographical details of the authors here mentioned see Edwards and O'Dowd, *Sources for Early Modern Irish History*.
75. Cited from J. Carty, ed., *Ireland from the Flight of the Earls to Grattan's Parliament, 1607–1782*, Dublin, 1949, p. 172.
76. The example is cited from Cullen, 'Catholic social classes', p. 74.

A select bibliography
(In addition to works mentioned in the references)

Books

H. A. Boylan, *A Dictionary of Irish Biography*, Barnes and Noble, New York, 1978.
P. J. Drury, ed., *The Irish in America*, Cambridge Irish Studies, 1965.
D. Fitzpatrick, *Irish Emigration 1801–1921*, Dublin, 1985.
R. Hayes, *Old Irish Links with France*, Dublin, 1940.
R. Hayes, *Ireland and Irishmen in the French Revolution*, London, 1932.
M. Hennessey, *The Wild Geese*, Dublin, 1973.
R. Kearney, *Migrations: the Irish at Home and Abroad*, Wolfhound Press, 1990.
R. B. McDowell, *Ireland in the age of imperialism and revolution 1769–1801*, Oxford University Press, 1979.
M. G. McLaughlin & C. Warner, *The Wild Geese: the Irish Brigades of France and Spain*, London, 1980.
Abbé MacGeoghegan, *The History of Ireland: Ancient and Modern*, translated from the French by P. O'Kelly, James Duffy Publisher, Dublin 1844.
D. Hayton, ed., *Ireland after the Glorious Revolution, 1692–1715*, N.I. Public Record Office, Belfast, 1976.
T. W. Moody & W. E. Vaughan, eds., *Eighteenth-century Ireland 1691–1800*, vol. iv in *New History of Ireland*, Oxford University Press, 1986.
J. G. Simms, *The Williamite confiscation in Ireland, 1690–1703*, Faber and Faber, London, 1956.

Articles

C. Giblin, 'Irish exiles in Catholic Europe', in P. Corish, *Irish Catholicism*, vol. iv, chapter 3, Gill & Macmillan, Dublin, 1971.
R. Hayes, 'Irish associations with Nantes', *Studies*, xxxvii, 1948, 115–26.
L. M. Cullen, 'Catholic social classes under the penal laws' in T. P. Power & Kevin Whelan, *Endurance and Emergence*, Irish Academic Press, 1990.
V. Kiernan, 'Foreign mercenaries and absolute monarchy', *Past and Present*, no. 11, 1957, 66–86.
N. Canny, 'Migration and opportunity: Britain Ireland and the New World', *Irish Economic and Social History*, 12, 1985, 7–32.
H. McDonnell, 'Irishmen in the Stuart navy 1660–1690', *Irish Sword*, xvi, no. 63, 1985, 87–104.
P. Karsten, 'Irish soldiers in the British army 1792: suborned or subordinate', *Journal of Social History*, 17, Fall 1983, 31–64.
D. Mulloy, 'In search of wild geese', *Eire–Ireland*, v, 1970, 3–14. (Irish American Cultural Institute St Paul, Minnesota.)
J. McErlean, 'Ireland and world contact', *Studies*, viii, pt. i, 1919 (for legal privileges enjoyed by the Irish in Spanish territories).
R. Hayes, 'Irishmen in the naval services of continental Europe', *Irish Sword*, 1952–3, 304–15.
C. A. Petrie, 'Irishmen in the forty-five', *Irish Sword*, ii, 1954–6, 275–82.
The following O'Donnell lectures published by the National University of Ireland, Merrion Square, Dublin, contribute to the general theme of the wild geese, or the Irish as soldiers abroad in the more general sense.

M. Walsh, *The O'Neills in Spain*, N.U.I., 1957.

M. Walsh, *The MacDonnells of Antrim on the continent*, N.U.I., 1960.

G. A. Hayes-McCoy, *Captain Myles Walter Keogh: U.S.A. army 1840–1876*, N.U.I., 1965.

J. A. Murphy, *Justin MacCarthy, Lord Mountcashel*, Cork University Press, N.U.I., 1958.

3 Irish migration to Argentina

Patrick McKenna

Irish migration to Argentina is a subject that, to date, has attracted very little serious academic attention. Indeed, outside the immediate areas that contributed to the migration most people are completely unaware of its existence. For this reason I propose to examine the topic under five headings: (1) its early origins, (2) the formative period, (3) mass migration, (4) life on the Pampas and (5) assessment of the data.

Early origins

The first Irish to set foot on what was to become Argentina were probably the three Galwaymen who were part of the crew on Magellan's voyage to discover a route to the Pacific, through the straits which still bear his name, in 1520. One was named Guillen, who was a *grumete*, or ship's boy, on the *Concepción*. He died on 25 January that year. The other two were the brothers William and John ——. William was *grumete* on *La Trinidad*. John was *paje*, or cabin boy, on the same ship.[1] John and William are recorded as having served at the first Mass celebrated on Argentine soil, on 1 April 1520, at the mouth of the river Santa Cruz in Patagonia. While technically they were probably the first Irishmen to set foot on Argentine soil they did not settle there. They appear to have been ordinary seamen recruited in Galway by the Spanish navy. The first recorded Irish settlers were a small group who were members of the pioneering expedition led by Pedro Mendoza. Mendoza sailed from Cadiz in 1536. Among these first settlers were two brothers called John and Thomas Farel, natives of San Lucas de Barrameda, Spain. Other 'Irish' names listed in the expedition were Colman, Rea, Lucas, Galvan and Martin. The name 'Martin' is very common in both Ireland and Spain and it is therefore impossible to be certain which, if any, Martins were Irish. Other Irish names appear among sixteenth century settlers. A Juan Fays (probably Hays) and Isabel Farrel, the wife of a Captain Hernando de Sosa, a colonist in Corrientes.[2] Mendoza's expedition numbered about eight hundred, mostly German settlers. The expedition was financed by German banks, as Charles I of Spain was also Emperor Charles V of the Holy Roman Empire, which included a large part of Germany. The expedition, which consisted of about fourteen ships, brought with it cattle, sheep, horses and pigs, the first such animals ever to reach the American continent. Mendoza founded his settlement on the southern bank of the river Plate. He dedicated it in honour of the sailors who had brought the expedition safely from Cadiz; he included in the name of the settlement the patron saint of all sailors from that port, 'Our Lady of Fair Winds'. Thus the settlement of 'Santa Maria de Buenos Aires' began. Mendoza did not choose a good site for his new settlement, and it failed. This was due mainly to attacks from the native Indian population. The surviving settlers, the Farrels among them, went up river for about twelve hundred miles to another, more peaceful and successful settlement on the opposite bank called Asunción de paraguay. However, they were forced to abandon their horses in Buenos Aires. These horses flourished in the pampas and became the foundation stock of the 'native' Argentine horse. They spread rapidly across the pampas, as they had few natural enemies to restrict their growth in numbers.

About forty years later Buenos Aires was re-established from Asunción on a more defensible area, a few miles up river from its previous site, where it is now situated. The Farrels decided to stay in Asunción and exercise their right, as they were among the original settlers, to acquire lands there. The records show that a Rafeal Farel, son of one of the original settlers, acquired lands and Indians near Asunción in Corrientes Province in 1588.[3] The next Irishman recorded as having settled in Argentina was a Jesuit priest, Fr Thomas Field, from Limerick. He was sent down from Brazil to convert the native tribes of the La Plata provinces in 1586.[4] He died in Asunción in 1625.

Irish relationship with Spain

The reason the Irish reached the Americas so soon after its discovery was the combination of mythology, history and trading patterns then existing in Ireland, as well as the political changes taking place in the country.

The mythology was that the Gaels had originally settled Ireland from Galicia in Spain, led by their Queen Scotia, where they quickly became the governing elite. Some of Scotia's followers then invaded the northern part of the island to the east. For a time 'Scotia's Land', or Scotland, referred to both Ireland and present-day Scotland. Those of Scotia's followers who remained in Spain became the governing class there as well. This meant that the Spanish and Irish elites considered themselves cousins, and obligations of kin existed between them.

What is certain is that throughout the first millennium there was considerable contact between Ireland and the continent. The monastic settlements attracted not only wealth but also students from all over Europe. Ireland was one of the places Charlemagne turned to for priests and scholars to re-establish learning and religion in his empire. With the spread of the Reformation across northern Europe these old links became concentrated in Spain in particular.

Ireland, being a relatively short and safe journey by sea from France and

Spain, enjoyed a very considerable trade, especially in wine and leather. This inevitably led to population transfer as merchants in one country sought to expand their contacts with their trading partners. The trading ports became the focus of such transfers. This trade was generally between Galway and Cadiz. A similar trade existed between Youghal in the south and Bordeaux in France. Waterford, in the south-east, and Bristol also had a close trading relationship at that time.

A further reason for the Spanish desiring a strong relationship between Ireland and Catholic Europe was that Ireland's location blocked the Protestant north European gateway to the Atlantic. This alone made Ireland of great strategic importance to both Spain and England and was a major factor in England's invasion and subjugation of Ireland. After the defeat of the O'Neill at the battle of Kinsale in 1601, and because of continuous fighting due to the refusal of the Irish to conform to the New Religion or give up their tribal lands, the country was devastated. The population experienced probably worse privation than they were to experience 250 years later with the potato famine of 1845–9. The population of the island was reduced from about two million to under 750,000. Those who remained were, for the most part, left without land or livestock. To secure the land and pacify the countryside, the English moved most of the remaining population west across the river Shannon, further adding to the misery of the native Irish population. 'To Hell or to Connacht' is a phrase from that time still bitterly remembered in Ireland today.

Many of those who had the resources fled the country and settled in Catholic Europe. Spain, because of the strong trading connection between the two countries, and also because of the kinship which existed between them due to the Milesian legends, was host to the majority of these refugees. It is estimated that 50,000 men fled to Europe during that period. Women and children were not counted; say another 50,000,[5] if my assumption about the number of dependants migrating is correct, then about one in eight Irish-born were living in Europe by 1650, most of them in Spain. Another reason why Spain was such a willing host was that at that period in her history she was pushing the Moors back across the Mediterranean. This left her in control of extensive areas of her own country but without a population of sufficient education or skill to administer them. She needed Catholic administrators capable of filling the essential posts vacated by the retreating Moors. The Irish were not the only settlers in Spain at the time. There was also an influx of merchants from the city states of Italy. The preferred means of assimilation into the Spanish elite by these groups, the Irish included, was marrying the daughters of noble Spanish families. Not all these new settlers were completely trusted, and they tended to settle in the periphery of the country. The Cullens, for example, settled in the Canary Islands, and their family did not reach Argentina until 1812, when they settled in Santa Fe province.

The influx of merchants from northern Italy was what gave Spain her initial incentive for maritime adventure. The Irish, having shallow roots in their new country, were willing to try and restore their fortunes in the New World, then opening up to Spain owing to the endeavours of the Italian merchants, and were as a consequence to be found from the very beginning throughout Spanish America from the sierras of California to the southern Andes in Chile and Argentina.

Spanish and British settlement in America

Because the Spanish system of American settlement was fundamentally different from the English, mass Irish migration never occurred. Briefly, the Spanish were interested only in the extraction of valuable metals for shipment directly back, at the least possible cost, to Spain. This required the presence of a small number of a governing European elite and a large slave labour force. A peasant or artisan class was not needed. The slave labour was made up entirely of native Indians and later African populations. The English, in contrast, were interested in trade. Their initial contact with the New World was in search of new fishing grounds. Their allies the Dutch soon discovered that it was more efficient to sail out to the fishing grounds and purchase the fish from the fishing boats in the region. Coastal settlement soon followed. Some fishermen began to trap beaver when ashore. Beaver skins quickly became an expensive luxury in Europe which, in turn, attracted more settlers to the east coast of North America. In addition the English were anxious to remove all idle persons from their shores in order to prevent unrest in the home country. The Americas, and later Australia, provided the ideal sites for these resettlements. Furthermore Dissenting Protestants who were beginning to be persecuted in Protestant Europe saw America as a place of safety. Thus there were many incentives to English settlement of territories in America.

The role of the Irish in Spanish America

The function of the Spanish elites in Spanish America was to provide the military and civil administration necessary for the extraction of the gold and silver. As it was cheaper to produce the food locally than ship it from Spain, the large herds of wild cattle, sheep and horses which soon spread across the pampas were granted to those administrators who were willing to settle in the country. These settlers soon came to control personally not only the wild herds but also the lands over which the individual herds grazed. The 'estate' or *estancia* and its owner the *estanciero* had arrived. A large number of these *estancieros*, throughout Spanish America, bore Irish names.

These *estancieros* never made any effort to encourage migration from among the Irish peasant class. It was not until the ascent of the Bourbon kings to the throne of Spain that any Irish labourers were recruited for Argentina. By then the *estancieros* wanted to develop trade in hides and tallow to Europe and jerked beef to Brazil and Cuba to meet the ever increasing demand for food to feed their growing slave populations. One hundred Irish butchers and tanners were brought to Buenos Aires in 1785 to start the industry.[6] Others were recruited over the next twenty years. It was on the skill of these Irish migrants that the foundation of the Argentine meat industry was built.[7] Very little is known of these men or their origins at present. They appear to have been unmarried and, being Catholic, they assimilated immediately into the local community. Irish butchers would have been chosen because of the long established Spanish tradition of purchasing such goods in Ireland. Spain would be easily able to recruit the people with the required skills there.

Not all Irish migration to Argentina during this period was voluntary or indeed in the service of Spain. In 1762 a British warship commanded by a Captain MacNamara was captured in the river Plate estuary. MacNamara was killed in action but seventy-eight of his crew were taken prisoner and sent into the Argentine interior, chiefly to Córdoba and Mendoza.[8] Mulhall claims[9] the names 'Sarsfield, Carrol and Todd etc. are probably derived from these captives'. It is much more likely that Mulhall was unaware of the long connection between Ireland and Spain and that these names occurred as a direct result of Spanish-sponsored migration. Galvan also occurs frequently in Buenos Aires province and could very probably have Irish origins.[10] In 1770 more British troops were captured and sent to Córdoba and Mendoza following the battle of Egmont in the Falkland Islands. This pattern was continued following the invasion of the river Plate in 1806–7, when at least some of the troops who were taken prisoner were transported to Mendoza and Córdoba in line with the earlier custom.

None of these migrations was ever to form a nucleus of further Irish migration, despite the fact that the Mendoza region is the premier wine-growing district of Argentina, similar to Bordeaux in France. Bordeaux, however, attracted a number of very successful Irish migrants. The main difference between the migrants who settled in Mendoza and Bordeaux was essentially one of social class. Those who settled in France were the sons of the Catholic Irish elite, whereas those who were forced to settle in Mendoza came from the lower ranks of Irish society.

Córdoba city was to attract a reasonable number of Irish migrants at the beginning of the twentieth century. By then the railways were providing an important source of white-collar employment for more educated Irish migrants, and Córdoba city was the major interconnecting point on the railway system. There is no evidence, to date, to show any connection between the later 'railway migration' and the earlier 'military' ones.

Formative period

Under Spanish rule any foreign national found engaged in commerce in South America was subject to immediate execution by the authorities. Despite this, by the beginning of the nineteenth century a considerable smuggling trade in British manufactured goods had grown up between Liverpool and the river Plate. Irishmen such as the Catholic John Dillon from Dublin and the Protestant Thomas Armstrong from Athlone were among the principal 'merchants' involved in the smuggling of these goods along the river Plate. They traded between Buenos Aires and the Portuguese-held towns of Colônia del Sacramento and Montevideo across the river in what is now Uruguay.

These smugglers, or, from the British perspective, merchants and bankers, soon realized that the development of agricultural production was necessary to provide the economic base for expansion. Modern agricultural methods were needed to exploit the potential fully. The merchants concluded that a free white labour force, proficient in animal and crop husbandry, which was capable of owning and running its own enterprise, was the most efficient way to achieve their aim. The Irish, being Catholic, and with such a long association with Spain, were the preferred choice. This system of a free, land-based migrant work force was designed to leave the merchants in control of the transportation, processing and marketing of the produce. In addition the surplus earned by the producers was held in the form of cash balances in merchant-owned banks and was available to the merchants for further investment.

The growing trade between Britain and the river Plate basin at the end of the eighteenth century led to the British invasion in 1806–7. Though the invasion was a failure from a military point of view, it began a series of events on both sides of the Atlantic that were to combine to play a crucial role in directing mass Irish migration towards Argentina.

The independence movement was successful because it promised to open up the country's economy to a full trading relationship with all of Europe, especially England and the port of Liverpool. This movement was widely supported throughout the country by all the leading local governors. The euphoria was short-lived, Buenos Aires' 40,000 inhabitants tried to replace Madrid as the governor of territories equal in area to India. This attempt was greatly resented by the provinces and was directly responsible for a centralist–federalist split. This in turn led to a civil war and the breaking away of the states of Bolivia, Paraguay and ultimately Uruguay from Argentina. The loss of Bolivia, in particular, and with it the vast silver mines of Potosi, had the effect of turning Argentina into an east-coast, agriculture-based export economy which urgently needed an influx of settlers skilled in animal husbandry.

The invasion also caught the imagination of almost every adventurer in London. Rumours of undreamt-of riches, to be had for the taking, quickly swept the city. Consequently, Argentina experienced a huge increase in British investment and trade. That inevitably brought Argentina into conflict with Spain. Led by General San Martin, the Argentines rebelled on 25 May 1810. The general and others, such as his deputy, General Thomand O'Brien (from County Wicklow), expelled the Spanish from the land while the founder of the Argentine navy, Admiral William Brown (from Foxford, County Mayo), routed the Spanish at sea. The Spanish immediately retaliated by banning all emigration to Argentina from Spain, especially from the Basque country, adding to the growing shortage of free labour in Buenos Aires.

Another consequence of the invasion of the river Plate for Irish migration resulted from the fact that a large proportion of the troops involved were

Irish conscripts. These soldiers either deserted or were captured upon arrival in Buenos Aires. Many (possibly the deserters) were to live in the negro areas of San Telmo, along the docks in Buenos Aires, finding work deepening the river for shipping and using their knowledge of stone masonry to construct quays for the emerging port. A few moved inland some miles and began farming the fabulously rich grassland plains of the pampas. These soldiers, turned labourers and farmers, were exactly what the merchants needed and were to prove crucial in attracting other Irish migrants to the Argentine.

By 1822 the Argentine government was coming under increasing press-ure from the Buenos Aires merchants to take action on the growing shortage of manpower. In 1823 the Argentinian Prime Minister, Rivadavia, raised a loan in London of £1 million sterling to build a port and introduce Irish immigrants. The money was spent on a war with Brazil, however, and the project came to nothing.[11] Instead the merchants sent General O'Brien to Ireland to recruit 200 skilled labourers to be employed in public works. A new town named Belgrano, located a short distance outside the city, was founded to house them.[12] Belgrano is now one of the wealthier suburbs of Buenos Aires.

There is no record of exactly how many people returned with O'Brien or Armstrong who also paid a return visit to Ireland about 1826.[13] What is known is that two people from Streamstown, Patrick Bookey and his father-in-law, Thomas Mooney, did go out at that time. Mooney may well have been one of the soldiers involved in the invasion of 1806–7 and possibly returned to Ireland with O'Brien or Armstrong. What is certain is that, from that time, growing numbers of Irish began to emigrate to the Buenos Aires area from Westmeath and south Longford mainly, along with a few from northern Offaly and the western part of County Meath. The numbers from Westmeath and south Longford were to make up about two-thirds of the total number of Irish emigrants to Argentina.[14]

Another group who went to Argentina from Ireland during this period were from the Forth and Bargy area of Wexford. They were encouraged to migrate by a Patrick Browne who had been sent out to Buenos Aires to replace his brother as a manager of the Liverpool bank of Dickson & Montgomery in 1826.[15] Browne, quickly recognizing that a much larger fortune was to be made as a merchant than as a bank employee, started his own salt meat business (*saladero*). He sent home to Forth and Bargy for labour to work in his *saladeros* and to settle the land. Thus began the migration from Wexford. These migrants made up about 15 per cent of the total migration from Ireland.

Another tiny group, with no ostensible connections with any other group, emigrated from County Clare after the Famine in the 1850s. This appears to have been just one family, the Carmodys. They were Irish-speaking, unlike the rest of the emigrants, who spoke English. They remained bilingual Irish/Spanish speakers until around 1900. There is some evidence that Clare Irish was at least known, if not spoken, up to the 1930s, by which time this group had fully assimilated into the rest of the Irish community. Another interesting fact about the Carmody family is that they

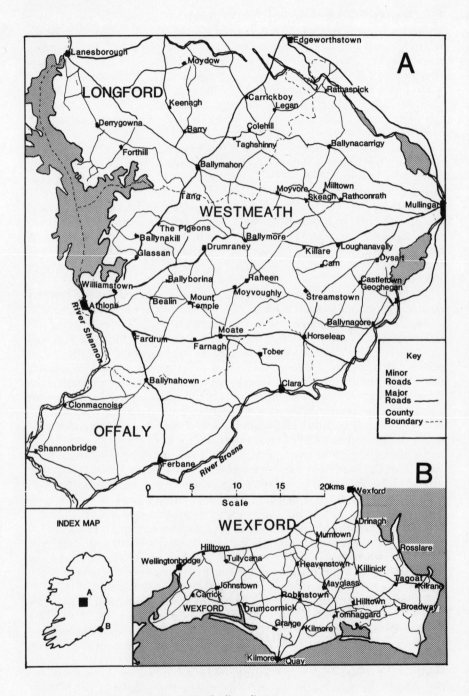

Figure 3.1   The 'Westmeath' and 'Wexford' sending areas

settled west of the Salado river and were initially completely cut off from the main Irish settlement areas in a *partido* (county) called 25 May.

Mass migration

The voyage out

There is circumstantial evidence of pre-selection of the early migrants. They came initially from the more commercial areas in Ireland, e.g. Forth and Bargy and the margins of commercial areas in Leinster. The great majority of the early migrants were the younger, non-inheriting sons, and later daughters, of the larger tenant farmers and leaseholders. Usually they were emigrating from farms which were in excess of twenty acres, and some were from farms considerably larger.

Regardless of where they originated in Ireland, the vast majority of migrants used Liverpool as the port of embarkation and most disembarked in or near the port of Buenos Aires. The journey lasted about three months.[16] Very few descriptions were ever written of the voyages out. They never captured the folk mind in the way the much shorter journey to the United Stated did. Yet in letters home many gave the long voyage as the reason for their never being able to return home.

The cost of a third-class ticket from Liverpool to Buenos Aires was £16.[17] A similar ticket from Ireland to North America cost £4 pre-Famine and as little as £0.75 after the Famine.[18] While there is general agreement among the sources that many of the migrants' fares were pre-paid in Buenos Aires by earlier migrants or potential employers, there is very little evidence of the mass privation that was experienced among the Famine migrants travelling to North America, with the exception of those migrants who actually arrived during the Famine years of 1845–9. The poor condition of these migrants led to the resident community establishing and financing what amounted to their own complete health, education and social services. Such was the organization of the Irish community in Buenos Aires by then, however, that the setting up of such a social system was inevitable.

Settlement areas

When the wave of migrants who began arriving in significant numbers in the mid-1820s landed they generally spent about a year in Buenos Aires, learning the language and saving some money. They found work in *saladeros* owned by the merchants such as Armstrong, Mooney, Bookey, Browne and many others. They could also find work as labourers in the building trade, as Buenos Aires city by then was experiencing rapid expansion.

Until 1833 the area under the control of the Buenos Aires government comprised the countryside north of a line which ran along the bank of the Rio Salado from the Atlantic inland through Lake Chascomus until it reached San Miguel del Monte (Monte). It then turned north-west to Junin

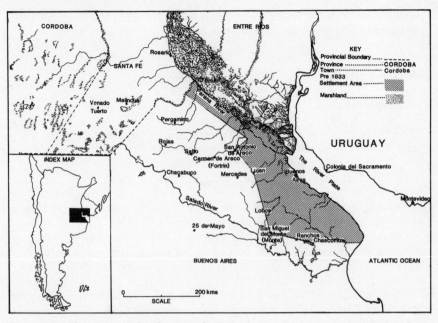

Figure 3.2   The region under the control of the Buenos Aires Government before 1833 (shaded) and before *c.* 1860 north of the Salado river

and on to San Antonio de Areco. From this point the line ran roughly north-east until it came to within a few kilometres of the Parana river, where it again turned north-west, following the river at this distance until it reached San Nicholas de Arroyos. The towns of Carmen de Areco (then known as Fortrin), Rojas, Pergamino and Melincue were at that time just military forts, deep in Indian country, protecting the road from Córdoba.[19]

In 1833 all the territory between the Salado and Parana rivers, which until then had been considered Indian territory, was annexed by Rosas, who was by then dictator of Argentina. The region is made up of loess and alluvium and is the most fertile land in Argentina. The fertility of the soil improves as it progresses northwards. The most fertile land is located in northern Buenos Aires and southern Santa Fe provinces, within the flood plain of the Parana river. The Irish, therefore, had every incentive to migrate north-wards as the land was cleared. Not only was the quality of the land improving, the distance from Buenos Aires was reducing as its hinterland was being cleared of Indians. Thus they had the double benefit of better land and closer access to markets. The Irish followed immediately behind the soldiers, renting the land from the government or from soldiers who were given it as grants and did not wish to farm it.

Here again the Irish had an advantage over the native Argentine. A native-born Argentine was subject to military service between the ages of seventeen and forty-five. Yet a condition of the land grant was that it had to be worked by the owner. Therefore even when the Creole owner wished to retain his land he was in practice obliged to use Irish migrants as shepherds, because a native Argentine could be conscripted literally at a moment's notice into the armed forces. A point to note here is that the Argentine-born children of Irish migrants who were legally Argentine citizens regularly avoided military service because very many could speak only English or at best very poor Spanish and were able to convince the authorities that they too were immigrants.

The first of these new lands to be settled were located around the military forts which served as the centres of communication for the surrounding countryside. These centres were to become important towns in the province of Buenos Aires. Later migrants settled the land in between the towns, so that a certain amount of 'leapfrogging' took place in the settling of these regions, though the progression was steadily north-west. These towns today are still settled by families bearing Irish names. San Antonio de Areco settlers have mostly Wexford names such as Casey and Devereaux, whereas near by, in Suipacha, Westmeath names – Lawlor, Kelly, Garahan and Geoghegan – still predominate.

Life on the pampas

Once they had mastered the language and customs of the country the first Irish migrants moved out of the city and began herding sheep in the Chascomus district, about seventy-five miles south of Buenos Aires city. The reason for choosing this region was that the greater the distance from Buenos Aires the cheaper and more freely available suitable land became, and prior to 1833 Chascomus was the most distant area under the control of the government of Buenos Aires close to a constant water supply.

The sheep were herded on a 'shares' basis, usually for the same merchant for whom the shepherds had worked in Buenos Aires. Some emigrants also worked for native Creole (or 'Criollo', as they are known in the Argentine) *estancieros*. This system, unknown in South America outside the province of Buenos Aires, was very similar to both the *métairie* system of France and to the system of tenure in Ireland under the native Brehon laws. The system operated as follows. The owner of a flock of about 2,000 sheep would go into partnership with the migrant. Under the contract the owner would agree to supply the flock for a specified number of years (usually four). The migrant was responsible for looking after the sheep and meeting all expenses out of his own pocket, including the provision of grazing. When the agreed number of years had expired the shepherd and the owner would divide the flock, the owner getting back his 2,000 sheep plus the agreed percentage of the increase (usually 50 per cent) as well as his share of the price for the wool clip for the contract period. By this time the flock, under good management, would have grown to 10,000 in number. The shepherd would then own up to 4,000 sheep. He would then divide his flock into, for example, two flocks of 2,000 and hire shepherds on a similar type of contract to that which he had worked. In this way one migrant brought out first his brothers and later his cousins and neighbours, and so a highly regionally specific chain migration began.

There is evidence in folk memory that the established Irish drove much harder bargains with the new migrants than did the Criollo *estanciero*. The Irish flock owner expected the migrant to purchase his half-share in the flock in addition to keeping the other conditions mentioned. If the new migrant did not have the cash for this he became a *tercero* (a one-third man) rather than a *medianero* (a halves man). The *tercero*, however, was provided with grazing, stock pens, etc., free of charge by the flock owner. At the end of the contract period the new migrant could become a *medianero* by using the share he was then due to buy his half-share in the flock.

Many of the later migrants were to move directly into the countryside to find employment as shepherds. As sheep became more valuable, and shepherds more plentiful, many of the established flock owners began to employ shepherds on a wage basis. Those shepherds who retained the old system saw their percentage share become steadily smaller and the number of years of the contract increase. The migrant who herded sheep for wages was called a *peón*. If in addition to herding he was also responsible for protecting a portion of the *estancia* he was a *puestero*, or (fence) 'post' man. Later migrants were also in great demand for digging ditches and wells on already settled land. They earned, on average, £30 a year for such work.[20]

The migrant's life style

Life was not easy for the migrant. It was not just a matter of riding off into the sunset with 2,000 of someone else's sheep and returning four years later a man of worth. Many never returned, or returned broken in body and spirit, sometimes insane from years of almost complete solitude. A broken leg or a fall from a horse frequently meant a lingering death from thirst or starvation. Life among the gauchos and Indians was cheap. Even if they did not want to steal his flock the migrant was just as likely to be killed for his horse or his clothes – a dead victim was less likely to seek to recover his possessions than a live one.

The land too had to be tamed. Over vast areas the vegetation consisted of tall, coarse grass which the sheep could not eat and thistles which were taller than a man on horseback. The thistle thorns not only blinded the sheep but also got entangled in their wool and left it worthless for shearing. The migrant had to search for a large area of land with sufficient suitable grass for his flock to graze. The land, around Chascomus at least, was generally more low-lying than other areas and was subject to flash-flooding in the spring months. Suitable land was also available farther into the interior; however, it was subject to prolonged drought in the summer. These were not annual occurrences but would take place usually once or twice in a decade. In a drought rivers and streams dried up altogether and the sea of lush pasture which had stretched to the horizon and beyond shrivelled and died, leaving the migrant to witness his flock, the culmination of his life's work, choke on the dust and blind themselves as they tried to eat the last of the surviving thistles. A migrant could lose the result of ten or fifteen years' hard work in a single night's thunderstorm and flood or, probably worse, watch the flock die of thirst over several weeks while he struggled vainly against the inevitable end.

The migrants soon discovered that it was possible to overcome the water shortage by digging wells. This meant that proximity to a constant flowing river was no longer essential for sheep grazing. It allowed the migrant to penetrate farther into the interior. In a dry period the water had to be raised from the well. A sheep drinks about two gallons of water per day, so 10,000 sheep require 20,000 gallons. The shepherd drew the water by lowering a container, made from horse hide, by means of a rope, the other end of which was attached to the saddle of his horse. He then walked his horse away from the well, filling the skin and raising it in the process. The water container was so designed that when it reached the top of the well it poured out the few gallons of water into a shallow channel from which the sheep were able to drink. The shepherd and his horse would walk back towards the well, lowering the empty skin back into it as they returned. He and his horse continued working in temperatures often approaching 40°C until all the sheep were satisfied.

In the evening when the sheep were safely penned for the night the shepherd cooked himself a meal of mutton – to kill a lamb would have been wasteful: the meat from an old ewe was valueless and therefore could be eaten, provided that the hide, along with the wool and fat, was kept for the partner or *estanciero*. After his meal the shepherd had to set about skinning all the sheep that had died that day; whilst the carcasses were worthless, the hide and wool could be sold. This done, he was free to rest.

The shepherd lived in a one-room mud cabin (*rancho*), roofed with rushes and the strong pampas grasses. His *rancho* was distinguished from that of the gaucho by the fact that the migrant's had a chimney and a ladder attached to the gable end to allow him to avail himself of the roof as a vantage point to keep in visual contact with his sheep. This roof, William Bulfin once remarked, kept the rain out on a fine night.[21] There was generally one opening into the *rancho* across which a horsehide was hung to serve as a door. The interior was sparsely furnished. The shepherd slept on wool or, if he could afford it, a horsehide which was stretched across a timber frame. His blanket was a sheepskin. In the centre of the room would be an upturned chest containing his tea, biscuit and some yerba leaf which was made into a drink, in the same way as tea, called *matte*.[22] This chest was always surrounded by a shallow channel which was kept filled with water, otherwise black ants would remove all the food in a matter of hours. The chest also served as a table. A chair consisted of an ox skull whose large curved horns served as the backrest.

As the shepherd began to prosper he could afford to marry and improve his home. The first sign of improving wealth was a wooden door. The timber had to be imported into this vast treeless plain. Windows were the next addition. When he could afford enough timber for flooring a second storey was added. The second storey faced in the same general direction as the lower one. The shepherd was not always an expert builder, nor was he noted for being houseproud.

Consolidation and change

The 1850s saw great changes in Argentina which were to have a profound effect on the Irish. The overthrow of the dictator Rosas and the formation of a democratic government ended the British and French blockade of Buenos Aires port. This opened up markets in continental Europe, especially Germany, as well as Great Britain and the United States.[23] The demand for wool and sheep soared, especially for the merino breeds which were owned mainly by the Irish. In addition the new government changed from a policy of renting the land it captured from the Indians to one of selling it outright. The timing, from an Irish point of view, was perfect. The shepherds were cash-rich after several years of high wool values and soaring sheep prices. Consequently they were able to outbid the Creole *estancieros* for the best land. The English merchants were also in competition with the Irish in purchasing large tracts of land to build lavish country estates on at the same time. However, they valued aspect and view as well as land quality, whereas the Irish valued land quality alone. This gave rise to the saying among the Irish that 'the Irish got the best land while the English got the best scenery'.[24]

Another consequence of Rosas's fall was that European migration to Argentina grew rapidly. The migrants came mostly from the Mediterranean basin, especially from southern Italy and Spain. Buenos Aires city grew, with a resulting demand for more land for building and for the production of food for domestic consumption. Land prices close to the city soared, and many Irish sold their recently purchased properties at a huge profit and could then afford to buy and develop much larger *estancias* farther out in the province. The railway network also expanded. It brought remote areas within a few hours' travelling time from the city. Land prices near the railways rose rapidly, benefiting, sometimes for the second time, some Irish landowners.

The 1850s brought unforeseen changes which were to fix the destiny of Irish migrants over the next forty years. The fencing of land, on a large scale, became possible with the introduction to Argentina of wire. It made the restriction of livestock feasible and allowed large areas to be ploughed and unsuitable grasses replaced by more productive European strains. There was widespread replacing of native grasses with alfalfa. Alfalfa has a deeper root system and was therefore more resistant to drought. Alfalfa cannot, however, sustain the close grazing due to the heavy stocking of sheep; it can nevertheless sustain heavy grazing by cattle. Combined with a growing demand for beef, this meant that it became more profitable, as the century progressed, for large landowners to devote more of their land to beef production. These changes greatly increased the productivity of the land, which in turn brought about great differences in wealth and social status between migrants. A migrant's standing in the community from the 1850s began to be judged more and more by how much land he owned rather than the number of sheep he possessed.

The change-over to alfalfa production took five years of intermediate tillage production. By the 1870s a system had developed whereby the landowner would rent a section of virgin, fenced, land to a migrant for five years. The migrant would clear the rough grass off his piece of land and sow wheat in its place for the period of the tenancy. When the soil was brought up to a condition where it was ready to grow alfalfa the tenant and his family had to move on and begin again elsewhere. Irish migrants were not prepared to accept such terms. The work was carried out mainly by southern Italians, who were willing to work for a relatively short period in the Argentine and then return to Italy with sufficient funds to retire. Incidentally this is how Argentina became a major wheat producer. Wheat was initially a by-hyproduct of the change-over from native grasses to alfalfa production.

Organization of Irish migrants

During the fifty-year period between 1825 and 1875, when the Irish migrated to Argentina in substantial numbers, a certain amount of social control was exercised. The first to organize the Irish were the merchants. They were joined by the middle of the century by the wealthy migrants. These groups exercised strict control over the poorer migrants to ensure an adequate supply of reliable labour. The Irish Catholic Church was to play the central role in the process. This came about as a result of one of those accidents of history whose consequences could not be foreseen at the time. In 1822 Rivadavia expelled all religious orders. Such was the standing of the Irish community in Buenos Aires at the time, because of the services rendered to Argentina by men like O'Brien, Brown, Dillon, etc., that the Irish were allowed to retain their own chaplain. When Rosas came to power a few years later he rescinded the ban, but the custom of the Irish having their own chaplain lived on.

   In the beginning the chaplain remained in the city and confined his work to spiritual duties. All this changed in 1843 when a Dominican priest, the son of a brewer from Loughrea in Galway, Fr Anthony Fahy, arrived in Argentina as chaplain to the Irish emigrants. Father Fahy immediately set about organizing the community in such a way that they were to remain a separate Irish colony, isolated socially and culturally from the rest of the population. He ensured that the Irish were met on the quay as soon as a ship from Liverpool arrived. From there they were sent to approved accommodation (i.e. an Irish boarding house in the city). If the emigrant was male, Fr Fahy found him employment immediately, either in a *saladero* or on an Irish *estancia*. If the emigrant was female she stayed in a boarding house for about three weeks or a month, during which time she was greatly encouraged to choose a husband from among the earlier emigrants.[25] The latter would be passing through town at the time, on their annual business of selling sheep and wool. Such was the organization of the community that each boarding house would hold 'dances' at prearranged times known to the men, who would time their visit to town to coincide with one of these events. All the newly arrived women would be shepherded off to whichever boarding house was holding the dance. There they could look the prospective grooms over and decide which one to marry. This is one reason why emigrants tended to marry others from their own areas. Their families at least, if not the individuals concerned, would be known to each other.

Every area of immigrant life was organized along Irish lines. Irish schools, hospitals and churches were built and maintained for the exclusive use of the Irish community. The churches also contained libraries, which, in addition to having suitable books to read, also subscribed to local Westmeath and Wexford newspapers. The majority of the migrants, by mid–century, learned little if any Spanish, and they certainly could not read it. The result was that they were kept far more aware of conditions in Ireland than they were of conditions around them in Argentina. The Irish community also raised enough money to pay for the education of twelve Irish priests for the Argentine mission in the Missionary College of All Hallows, Dublin. These priests were assistant chaplains and so remained under the sole control of Fr Fahy and did not have to report to the local Bishop of Buenos Aires. Irish Mercy nuns were also sent out to meet the nursing and educational needs of the growing community.

Father Fahy and Thomas Armstrong became lifelong friends. Father Fahy lived for the rest of his life in rooms in Armstrong's house in the centre of Buenos Aires. Between them they were to ensure the success of the Irish community. Armstrong was banker to the Irish community. With their money, which Fr Fahy collected when out on pastoral work among his community, Armstrong was able to found the stock exchange and a bank, making a fortune for himself in the process. Fahy – living very modestly, it must be said, in his rooms in Armstrong's house – was also well placed to know in advance how agricultural prices were likely to move. He passed word on to the Irish through the network of the church. Thus Fahy's flock sold when prices were high and bought when they were low. The profits were handed over to him when he next called, and were banked with Armstrong. This money became in turn available to the merchants for investment in the form of loans, and so the circle continued. Fahy and Armstrong were recognized as being among the most powerful business figures in Argentina. Father Fahy gained the complete confidence of his congregation in all matters. And the Irish could bank their money safely in one of the few properly run banks then in Argentina.

Fahy banked the Irish migrants' money in his own name at Armstrong's bank with the consent of the migrants, because they knew that if anything happened to them he would ensure that their heirs inherited. Very soon, on paper at least, Fahy had acquired huge assets against which he was able to borrow to fund hospitals, schools, orphanages, etc. He was also in a unique position to determine how much each of his congregation could contribute to the maintenance of these charities and so never defaulted on any of his loans, further reinforcing the myth of his personal wealth.

Fahy and Armstrong were the driving force behind the Irish community. Fahy spent half the year in Buenos Aires and the other half travelling through the countryside on horseback, visiting his parishioners. He gave his constant travelling as the reason why he was able to get legal exemption for himself and his assistant chaplains from wearing clerical garb. The effect was to draw a clear distinction between the clergy serving the Irish Catholic community and priests ministering to the rest of the population. Thus he was able to create a Church within a Church, the membership of which he controlled. Fahy's personality was such that he moved with complete ease whether he was mixing with the upper echelons of the Buenos Aires political and social classes or deep in the wilderness sitting on an ox skull, sharing boiled mutton with an illiterate shepherd who had not spoken to another human being for weeks. Nevertheless his views were very much those of the son of a wealthy Irish merchant. He saw his mission to the Irish in Argentina from that perspective. He saw it as God's will that a few were to lead and many were to follow. From his perspective the rich had a duty to subscribe to and maintain a welfare system for poorer Irish migrants. Equally the poorer migrants should be grateful for such charity and work hard and long for their employers in return.

It did not conflict with his Christianity that he was helping the isolation of the Irish from the rest of the community, preventing them from assimilating into what was their adopted home and, for an increasing number, the land of their birth. In fact Fahy saw his duty as 'protecting' his congregation from the influence of the 'natives', whose way of life life did not conform to the Irish Catholic ethos of the nineteenth century.[26] To maintain this isolation, and in order to prevent, as far as possible, any attempt to assimilate, the cultural and ethnic difference was emphasized to the point of racism. The maintenance of English, especially after the Famine, was a central element in preventing assimilation. Hurling was played exclusively among the Irish community and the hurling club was founded to promote the game solely among the various Irish communities, despite every effort the native Argentines made to become involved in the game. Hurling allowed the Irish from the various communities to socialize among themselves without having to come into contact with the rest of the population.

Education

The wealthy Irish funded education, which was always taught through the English language and followed an English curriculum. At the primary level it was the sole responsibility of the *estanciero* under the direction of the Irish Church. Further education was funded by the community in general, with the wealthy Irish contributing by far the largest share. Boys at this level were educated by the Pallotine and Passionist orders. The girls were educated by the Mercy nuns. The Mercy Sisters also ran orphanages for younger children of both sexes. All these religious orders were staffed exclusively either by Irish-born priests and nuns or in a few cases by the children of Irish migrants. Again the Irish ethos was rigidly maintained. Even the architecture reflected total commitment to Irishness. The schools were the Fahy Institute and Clonmacnoise for boys and St Brigid's for girls. The buildings always had a huge statue of St Patrick over the door, sometimes with the right hand, raised in blessing, holding a shamrock. The shamrock would be worked into every possible part of the decoration, from the ironwork around the buildings to the tiles on the floors and the decoration on the altar rails, to the beading around the altar and the carving on the pulpit and on the end of the pews – in fact anywhere the ingenuity of the architect could work them in. The stained glass windows often consisted of three panes of glass in a circle, one green, one white and one gold, with a centre circle of blue, the colour of St Patrick.

At these colleges the students acquired the skills necessary to run an *estancia* efficiently or to take up lower-grade clerical positions. The schools were nevertheless far superior to those available to the rest of the non-Irish community on a similar income. University education was the prerogative of the rich. The wealthy Irish sent their children back to Europe, some to Ireland, to be educated, usually to one of the more exclusive colleges such as Blackrock, Clongowes Wood or Castleknock.

This Irish system began to crumble when Perón came to power, about the time of the Second World War. The schools were forced to abandon ethnicity as a criterion of admission. By the 1960s the Irish no longer wished, nor could afford, to fund them on their own, and as a result, today these schools have either closed or have very few Irish students. The Irish still maintain a role in the management of the Fahy Institute and St Brigid's. They award a number of scholarships to these schools each year, as many of the Irish community can no longer afford to send their children to them to be educated.

These emigrants and their descendants were to remain a close-knit rural community until after the Second World War, when trade with Britain declined and the young people migrated into the city. There they obtained work, usually with American firms which needed bilingual staff to bridge the language barrier between Americans and the Argentines. Thus began the assimilation of the Irish into mainstream Argentine society, an assimilation which will be almost complete with the present generation.

Assessment of data

The precise number of Irish who emigrated to Argentina is disputed. The generally accepted figure is 30,000. Its source is a letter from Fr Fahy to the Archbishop of Dublin in 1864 in which he gives this estimate of the number under his care. The figure includes the Argentine-born children of the migrants and would exclude all out-migration, deaths and those (admittedly few) who were outside his congregation. Another estimate was derived statistically by Korol and Sabato in 1981[27] from the census periods 1855–69–96 for the province of Buenos Aires, where the great majority of Irish migrants settled. Korol and Sabato arrive at a figure of 10,672 for the city and province. My research is not yet able to resolve the difference with confidence[28].

Analysis of Coughlan's[29] work on the genealogy of the Irish in Argentina

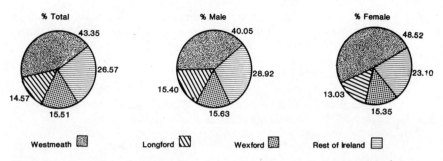

Figure 3.3 Proportion of migrants from the main sending areas in Ireland, calculated from Coughlan, *Los Irlandeses en la Argentina*

shows that 58·26 per cent of the migrants were male and 41·74 per cent female. Figure 3.3 represents the percentage breakdown by sex of those who migrated from the main sending areas in Ireland to Argentina, on the basis of Coughlin's work. Another feature that emerges from analysis of Coughlan's work is that female migration from the different areas began fifteen years after male migration started.

Taken together, these two facts indicate that unmarried women were willing to migrate to a given destination only when there was an established corps of successful male migrants from their local area settled at it. Female migration to Argentina did not outnumber male migration by a significant figure in any year as it was to do later for the United States. However, the proportion of females migrating over the fifty-year period between 1825 and 1875 steadily increased. By the end of the migration the sexes had almost reached parity.

Further analysis of Coughlin's data shows that the majority of migrants entered Argentina between the ages of fourteen and thirty-six, though there was a small number still migrating up to seventy years of age. The average age of all migrants arriving in Argentina was twenty-one. However, if voluntary migration is assumed to be between the ages of fourteen and fifty, and this group is looked at separately, the average age of the migrant rises to twenty-six years. This average age remained remarkably steady throughout the whole nineteenth century.

Conclusion

Though the numbers of Irish who emigrated to Argentina were tiny in comparison with the numbers who settled in English-speaking areas of the world, it is important not to overlook them in any broad study of Irish migration. While they improved their condition by migrating to Argentina, and some were to amass great wealth, they failed as a group to use their surplus to create the industrial base necessary to secure their own and their adopted country's future.

Closer study of the Irish settlements in the Argentine could do much not only to clarify the settlement history of that country but also to highlight other experiences of the Irish in more usual English–speaking destinations.

Notes

1. Peter Boyd-Bownan, *Indice geobiografico de 40,000 pobladores españoles de America en el siglo XVI*, Instituto Caro y Cuervo, Bogotà, 1964.
2. R. Lafuente Machain, *Conquistadores del Rio de la Plata*, Buenos Aires, 1937.
3. Thomas Murray, *The Story of The Irish in Argentina*, Kennedy, New York, 1919, p. 7.
4. Murray, *Irish in Argentina*, p. 1.
5. I know of no records which list the families and other dependants of those who migrated from Ireland at that time. It is certain that many of those fleeing the country brought dependants with them. The ratio of 1:1 is purely an assumption on my part, nothing more.
6. Andrew Graham-Yooll, *The Forgotten Colony*, Hutchinson, London, 1981, p. 32.
7. W. H. Koebel, *Argentina Past and Present*, Kegan Paul, London, 1910, p. 134.
8. Murray, *Irish in Argentina*, p. 8.
9. Michael Mulhall, *The English in South America*, Buenos Aires, 1878, p. 59.
10. Edward Maclysaght, *The Surnames of Ireland*, third edition, Irish Academic Press, Dublin, 1978, p. 118. He states that the name Galvan originated in Clare and spread to surrounding counties. This would place it in the area of Ireland in greatest contact with Spain.
11. M. and G. Mulhall *Handbook of the River Plate*, sixth edition, Standard Office, Buenos Aires, 1892, p. 61
12. Murray, *Irish in Argentina*, p. 53.
13. Murray, *Irish in Argentina*, p. 73.
14. Murray, *Irish in Argentina*, p. 56, estimates that about 2,000 Irish had emigrated to Buenos Aires between 1824 and 1832.
15. Murray, *Irish in Argentina*, p. 78
16. John Brabazon, writing in a diary, which he kept, about his life on the pampas between 1845 and 1855, a copy of which is in my possession.
17. Newspaper advertisement, *Westmeath Guardian*, 10 August 1865.
18. T. W. Freeman, *Pre-Famine Ireland*, Manchester University Press, Manchester, 1957, p. 38.
19. Murray, *Irish in Argentina*, p. 12.
20. M. and G. Mulhall, *Handbook of the River Plate*, first edition, Standard Office, Buenos Aires, 1869, section C, chapter 1.
21. William Bulfin was a journalist in Argentina who wrote from the 1870s to the 1890s about the lives of the early Irish migrants under the name of 'Che Bono'. Most of his work appeared in the Irish migrants' newspaper *The Southern Cross* around that period.
22. *Matte* is the South American equivalent of tea or coffee in Europe and the United State.
23. John Brabazon's diary.
24. The evidence for this is anecdotal but generally accepted among the Irish-Argentine community.
25. Kathleen Nevin, *You'll Never Go Back*, Boston: Bruce Humphries, Boston, Mass., 1946. While Nevin's work is a novel, it is regarded as an accurate account of female migration to Argentina.

26. When examining baptismal records in the parish churches of San Patricio parish Mercedes, San Antonio de Areco, Suipacha, Arrecifes and Las Heras, in October–November 1990 I found illegitimate births among the gaucho population were around 80 per cent compared with a total of two illegitimate births for about 5,000 Irish migrants in the records I examined. In the case of the gaucho the figure should be seen in the context of a lack of concern about a formal marriage certificate rather than promiscuity. In the Irish case, however, the figure should be seen as a result of the total social control of the population – as was also the case in Ireland at the same time – by the Catholic Church, or by the landowners working through the Church, depending on your point of view.

27. Juan C. Korol and Hilda Sabato, *Como fue la inmigración irlandesa en Argentina*, Editorial Plus Ultra, Buenos Aires, 1981, pp. 189–95

28. Immigration figures for the 1860s given by the Mulhalls in their *Handbook of the River Plate* series would suggest that Korol and Sabato greatly underestimate the number of Irish migrants

29. Eduardo Coughlan, *Los Irlandeses en la Argentina*, published privately in Buenos Aires in a limited edition, 1987. A number of copies were given to the Irish Department of Foreign Affairs, St Stephen's Green, Dublin. A number of other copies are in private libraries (including mine) in Ireland and Argentina. This work represents over thirty years' work by Coughlan tracing the genealogy of almost every member of the Irish community still living in Argentina, which he traces back to 3,667 original migrants.

4 The Murphys and Breens of the overland parties to California, 1844 and 1846

Joseph A. King

On 18 July 1881 what has been called 'California's Grandest Party' began on the Murphy ranch, north of San Jose. It was the occasion of the golden wedding anniversary of pioneers Martin Murphy Jr and Mary Bolger. For three days and nights the Murphys welcomed thousands of partygoers, including the cream of California's business, political and professional elite.

California historian Hubert H. Bancroft in *Chronicles of the Builders of the Commonwealth* wrote that 'far into the night the multitude lingered among the illuminated groves, for the scene was of surpassing loveliness that has never before or since been witnessed in California'. The *San Francisco Examiner* reported that it was 'a feast that has never been equaled in point of stupendous liberality and profusion on this Coast'. The businesses and the courts of San Jose closed; a marching band escorted guests from the train depot, Murphy's Station, on the site of the present city of Sunnyvale.[1]

A famous Los Angeles chef, skilled in the tradition of the *fiesta*, was hired for the occasion. A barbecue pit was dug, 114 ft long, fuelled by seven wagonloads of wood. Into it went seven steers, fourteen sheep, ten hogs. There were 500 chickens, 150 turkeys, fifty barrels of beer, 500 gallons of coffee, many hogsheads of punch and lemonade, and an ample supply of California and imported wines. Eight hundred people were served at a time, and 10,000 the first day. An elaborate pavilion was constructed in an oak grove under the supervision of John Gash, a leading California architect. The pavilion and dance hall, measuring 8,000 sq. ft, accommodated one thousand dancers and an eighteen-piece band. Prominent Californians, including Senator William Gwin, industrialist Colonel Peter Donahue and Judge Ryland of San Jose, toasted Martin and Mary. Greetings arrived from Archbishop Joseph S. Alemany. The material for the pavilion and platform was afterward donated to the Church for the construction of the first Catholic chapel in Mountain View.

This was quite a celebration for two natives of Ireland who could neither read nor write.[2] They were, however, members of a large extended family that, in 1844, had organized the first company of overland migrants to bring wagons across the High Sierras into the Sacramento valley of California, opening up a route that was soon to be followed by thousands of others. By 1860 Martin Murphy Jr, his brothers and their father had become the largest landowners, farmers and cattlemen on the central coast of California.

Their story needs telling, reflecting as it does a dimension of the Irish diaspora in America that has been slighted by historians, at least until recent years. The tendency of historians has been to focus mainly on the Irish who settled in the cities of the eastern seaboard, or who worked in the mines or dug the canals or laid railroad tracks. They have thus told a story largely about the urban and the poor. Another story, however, can be told, about the Irish who shunned the cities.[3] Among them were two families from south-east Ireland, the Murphys and the Breens.

The Murphys

Ireland

Patriarch Martin Murphy was born in 1785, probably east of Enniscorthy, in the old barony of Ballaghkeen, County Wexford.[4] He married Mary Foley about 1805, and the oldest of nine children, Martin Murphy Jr, was born on 9 November 1807, according to family records. Five more children were born to them in Ireland: James (1809), Margaret (1811), Johanna (1813), Bernard, also known as Brian (1815), and Mary (1816).[5]

It is not known exactly why the Murphy family emigrated, but some good guesses can be made. One has to do with enormous population growth. Between 1780 and 1821 the population of Ireland grew by 75 per cent.[6] During the same period most Irish tenant farmers were practising partible inheritance, subdividing their leases to provide for all their sons. This, together with dramatic population growth, was a certain recipe for poverty. In Wexford and neighbouring counties of south Leinster, how-ever, from the late eighteenth century onward farmers seem to have favoured impartible inheritance, the oldest son inheriting the land.[7] As a consequence, tenants of south Leinster, where holdings of ten to sixty acres were common, were better-off than those of the west and south-west. At the same time, this led to a great increase in landless labourers. Fewer victims were Protestants, because they were more likely to keep their lands intact.[8]

It should be noted, for initiates to Irish history, that all land in County Wexford as elsewhere in Ireland was held by a relatively small group of head landlords. Few of them were of Irish stock, even fewer were Roman Catholic (only 5 per cent by the end of the eighteenth century), and many were absentee landlords, with residence perhaps in Dublin or England. Typically, small farms would be leased through a layer or two (or more) of middlemen. A quite usual lease might be for a period of thirty-one years, or the 'lives' of the tenant and his immediate family.[9] There is considerable evidence that, especially in Wexford and neighbouring counties, Catholic and Protestant tenants were not treated equally by some landlords when leases fell in. A bitter Catholic farmer of County Carlow complained of 'the exclusive, orange system of letting now practised in this Country', and a Wexford shopkeeper reported that 'the people are so divided . . . [that] Landlords are driving their unfortunate Tennants out Especially Roman Catholick'.[10] The prejudice against Catholics had been exacerbated by the events of 1798, when County Wexford was the major centre of the bloody rebellion. The battles, indeed massacres, at Vinegar Hill and Oulart Hill, close by the farms of the Murphys of this study, were still fresh in the minds of a fearful Protestant class at the time the Murphys chose to leave Ireland in 1820.

In the late eighteenth and early nineteenth centuries County Wexford exceeded all counties in Ireland in the production of barley for the malt industry. Additionally, one-eighth of Ireland's entire export of oats was shipped from the ports of New Ross and Wexford town.[11] Ireland had experienced a period of relative prosperity during the Napoleonic wars at the turn of the nineteenth century when European ports were closed to British trade. Irish grain, beef, pork and bacon brought premium prices on the British market. With the end of hostilities in 1814, however, the price of Irish grain crops dropped dramatically. The average day labourer wage of 10*d* a day paid during the wars dropped to 8*d* in the summer and 5*d* in the winter.[12] Grazing became more profitable than farming. Head landlords consolidated their holdings to increase pasture land, and small farmers were evicted or threatened with eviction all over Ireland. This was an immense spur to emigration for those who could afford it.[13]

After 1815 emigration from County Wexford began in earnest, mainly to British North America.[14] A Quaker merchant in New Ross, seeking government or other aid for potential emigrants, drew up two lists – one Protestant, the other Catholic – of Wexford and Carlow families who were anxious to emigrate in the spring of 1817.[15] The Protestant list included 714 families, 4,027 people; the Catholics numbered 281 families, 1,475 people.[16] 'Most of the Catholic families are quite unable to bear the expenses of a passage to Quebec and providing for their subsistence on arriving,' noted the Quaker merchant Joseph Elly. The cost of passage on a sailing ship was £5 (or even more) for an adult and hence affordable only to strong tenant farmers and artisans, mainly Protestant.[17] The research of Bruce Elliott reveals that a majority of the emigrants sailing from the ports of Wexford, New Ross, Waterford and Dublin in the early days (after 1814) disembarked at Quebec.[18]

Martin Murphy must have been among the relatively small class of strong Catholic tenant farmers with the means to emigrate. In 1820, for whatever reasons, Martin and Mary Murphy sailed to Quebec with four of their children, leaving behind their oldest son, Martin Jr, aged thirteen, and eldest daughter, Margaret, aged nine.[19]

Why were Martin Jr and his sister left behind? It was increasingly the policy of many head landlords and middlemen, determined to expand pasture lands, to prohibit sub-letting. Further, as late as the 1820s many farmers were prevented from selling their lease without the consent of their eldest son after he had reached the age of twenty-one.[20] It seems likely that Martin Jr was left behind until he reached maturity. He and his sister perhaps were left with their grandparents.

Canada

When Martin Sr arrived in Canada he purchased land in Frampton, south-east of Quebec, where his family was among the first in a growing Irish community served by St Edward's Catholic Church. Three more children were born: Ellen (1822), John M. (1824) and Daniel (1826). It was not until 1828 that Martin Jr, now aged twenty-one, and his sister Margaret, seven-teen, arrived in Canada, sailing on 9 April 1828, from Wexford city on the *Thomas Farrell.*[21] Three days out, in rough seas, the ship was damaged and had to make port in Waterford for repairs, after which it had a safe twenty-eight day journey across the Atlantic. Margaret joined her parents in Frampton, while Martin remained in Quebec city, selling merchandise. By 1830 Quebec city had a substantial Irish population, 7,000 in a population of about 32,000.[22] Among them were the Bolgers of Oylgate township, Edermine parish,[23] barony of Ballaghkeen, who were friends of the Murphys from the Old Country. On 18 July 1831 Martin married Mary Bolger in the French cathedral in Quebec, Father McMahon officiating.

Life was not easy for the junior Martin and Mary in Quebec city. After an epidemic of cholera had taken the lives of two of their children (Mary and Nellie), Martin purchased 200 acres near Frampton, where his father had settled a decade before. There he and his spouse felled the trees, cleared the land and built a home for their family, which included four sons: James T. (1832), Martin J. (1836), Patrick W. (1838) and Bernard D. (1841).

Meanwhile the other children of Martin Murphy Sr and Mary Foley had grown up. James Murphy married Ann Martin, daughter of Irish-born Patrick Martin. Mary Murphy married Wexford-born James Miller in 1834.[24] In time, however, the marginal soil, harsh climate and other factors led the Murphys, the Millers and some of their neighbours to seek brighter prospects in life on the western frontier of the United States.[25]

Missouri

In 1840 Martin Sr and most of his children left Frampton for Missouri. The route followed by the Murphys was not an easy one, mainly by river and lake boats to Montreal, Kingston, Buffalo, Cleveland, Portsmouth on the Ohio river, Cincinnati, Louisville, Cairo, then on the Mississippi to St Louis.[26] From St Louis the Murphys sailed up the Missouri river and purchased land in Holt County, south of the town of St Joseph, which at the time contained only a few farms and one grist mill. They were soon followed by a number of their friends and relatives from Canada, and their settlement became known as Irish Grove. In September 1842 Martin Jr arrived with his family and purchased 320 acres, on which he cultivated maize and wheat. The land was productive, but the Murphys had reason to be dissatisfied. Malaria epidemics regularly swept the river ports. Educational opportunities for the children were lacking. Catholic church facilities and priests, except for occasional visits from missionaries, were also lacking. Stories reached the Missouri settlers of a better life in far-off Oregon and California, where huge tracts of desirable land, so they heard, were available practically for the asking.

A tragedy occurred in 1843 when Martin Sr's wife Mary, aged fifty-five, and Martin Jr's infant daughter Ann Elizabeth, aged six months, died of malaria. Consoled by missionary priest Fr Christian Hoecken, the Murphys listened to tales the priest had heard of California. The climate was more favourable and they would be better able to practise Catholicism in a country under Mexican rule, where Catholicism was the established religion.

The overland trail to California

In 1844 very little was known of the overland route to California. West of the Missouri river were only a few small trading posts, such as Fort Laramie and Fort Hall, maintained by fur companies. Two attempts had been made, in 1841 and 1843, to bring wagons into California and both had failed, the wagons being abandoned in the deserts of Nevada. Nevertheless the Murphys and several other families gathered at Council Bluffs, Iowa, in May 1844 for the 2,000 mile journey by covered wagon over the plains, deserts and mountains. One historian of the journey, George R. Stewart, in *The California Trail*, wrote that 'one of the remarkable features of the remarkable expedition of '44 is its isolation from everything that had happened before. It seemed to spring from some fresh impulse.'[27]

This party of migrants is given various names in the history books, including the 'Murphy–Stevens' and the 'Stevens–Murphy–Townsend Party', but there is little question that the chief organizers were members of the Murphy clan. They included Martin Murphy Sr, his four adult but unmarried children, two married sons with their wives, one married daughter with her husband, and eight grandchildren. Additionally, travelling with the train were Patrick Martin and his two sons (Patrick's daughter Ann was the wife of James Murphy, son of Martin Murphy Sr). The Murphy family and its 'connections' therefore consisted of at least twenty-two people, to be increased with the birth of Ellen Independence Miller and Elizabeth Yuba Murphy on the trail. Together with John Sullivan, his sister Mary and younger brothers, Michael and Robert, the Irish (and Catholic) contingent numbered more than half the company.

Elisha Stevens, an experienced mountain man, was elected captain of the company. Caleb Greenwood, an old trapper, and his two half Indian sons were hired as guides. The party of about fifty people with eleven wagons left Council Bluffs on 6 May 1844. They had to travel through Indian country at the pace of the oxen, two miles an hour, about fifteen miles a day. They followed the Platte river across Nebraska, stopping at the small fur-trading post at Fort Laramie in present-day Wyoming, then up the Sweetwater to its origin in the Rocky mountains at the continental divide, where the waters for the first time flowed westward; then they went north-west by the Greenwood cut-off to Fort Hall, a British fur-trading post in present-day Idaho; then south-west to the lazy Humboldt river and across Nevada to the river's sink. There a Piute Indian, whom they named Chief Truckee and with whom Caleb Greenwood conversed in sign language, told them of a river to the west that flowed down from a lake and a high pass. They followed the river, which they named the Truckee, through today's Reno and up its difficult canyon to where it flowed south, with a fork to the west. It was already mid-November, the peaks were snow-covered, food was getting scarce, the high pass had yet to be crossed, and Sutter's Fort in the Sacramento valley was a very long 120 miles away, although the company had no notion of the distance.

At the fork the company made a wise decision, splitting into three groups. One contingent of four men and two women on horseback proceeded south on horseback, being the first white people to set foot on the shores of Lake Tahoe. They then went west across a pass and followed the American river, arriving at Sutter's Fort in the second week of December. The main body went west a few miles and camped at Truckee (Donner) Lake, below a difficult 7,200 ft pass. At the lake they constructed a rude cabin for three young men who had volunteered to stay behind to guard six of the wagons from Indian depredations. (One of these men, Moses Schallenberger, aged seventeen, spent the entire winter there alone, living on coyotes and foxes which he was able to trap.) The main group, with five wagons, crossed the pass, floundering in deep snow, driving their remaining oxen, and were forced to camp at Big Bend on the Yuba river, where Mary Bolger Murphy gave birth to Elizabeth Yuba Murphy on 28 November 1844. They could go no farther with the wagons in the snow. So another wise decision was made. They butchered most of the cattle for food, built a cabin, and left James Miller, old Patrick Martin, the women and children, and the five wagons, at Big Bend for the winter. About 6 December the others proceeded westward, driving a few cattle ahead of them, down the Bear River valley, and reached Sutter's Fort about a week later, a few days after the horseback party of six had arrived there.

The contingent at Big Bend, after being reduced to eating the hides of the animals, were rescued in March by a group that included Martin Murphy Jr. Young Moses Schallenberger was rescued by Denis Martin, who arrived at the lake camp alone and on snowshoes, a feat of heroism hard to match in the history of the American west. Eventually ox teams were driven up from the valley and all the wagons were brought down.

It was an amazing performance. Historian Bancroft wrote, 'The Murphy–Stevens party were the first to open up a wagon trail to California, their route being mainly traversed by the Union Pacific Railroad in later years.

They were the first to cross the Sierra by way of the Truckee and Bear Rivers.'[28]

The Murphys in California

What was just as amazing, however, was the success of the Murphys in California. They and other Irish members of the migrant company established fiefdoms that would have been the envy of the chiefs of ancient Ireland. In the Santa Clara and Salinas valleys alone, a stretch of land about forty miles long and seven miles wide was owned by one or other member of the Murphy clan. Today it is almost impossible to drive on Interstate Highway 101 from Sunnyvale to Gilroy without passing through, or being within sight of, land that was once part of the Murphy fiefdoms. Travelling farther south, one will pass through or come close to the Santa Margarita, Atascadero and Asuncion *ranchos*, also once Murphy territory, in San Luis Obispo County; and still farther south, a *rancho* at Point Concepcion in Santa Barbara County.[29]

Martin Murphy Sr. The senior Martin Murphy settled in Santa Clara County below San Jose. He and his sons acquired thousands of acres of land around present-day Coyote, Gilroy and San Martin, including the Rancho Ojo de Agua de la Coche of almost 9,000 acres. The town of San Martin was named after his patron saint, as was the chapel he built, dedicated by Archbishop Alemany, who had often visited and said Mass at the Murphy home. The Murphy adobe house became a famous stopping-off place in a sparsely populated valley without inns. One guest, a surveyor and former Protestant missionary in Hawaii named Chester L. Lyman, made this entry in his diary 10 August 1847, after stopping at the senior Murphy's home: 'Our principal entertainer was Miss Ellen Murphy, a girl of much good sense. . . . They had been 2 years in the country & possess a fine farm.' Another visitor, General William T. Sherman, wrote that Ellen Murphy was 'a sweet and attractive girl, bright and witty and like a sunbeam, especially in a country where members of the gentler sex were so rare'.[30] Martin Murphy Sr died in 1865 at the age of eighty at the home of his daughter Margaret and her husband, Thomas Kell.

Martin Murphy Jr. In 1845 the junior Martin Murphy purchased two square leagues of land (one league is about nine square miles) for $250 from a German settler, Ernest Rufus, on the Cosumnes river, eighteen miles below the present city of Sacramento. The first overt act of Americans against the Mexican government of California – the Bear Flag revolt – occurred at the Murphy ranch on 10 June 1846, when a party of Americans surprised a Mexican company under Lieutenant Francisco Arce that had stopped at the ranch for the night, and made off with 125 horses that the Mexican company had stabled in the Murphy corral. Murphy, who (like his father) had become a Mexican citizen, then provided each of Arce's men with a horse, maintaining the cordial relations that had been established with the Mexican authorities.

In his 'Memorias' Arce recalled that the American raiders intended to kill him but that he was saved by the intercession of Martin and Mary Murphy. In 1959 a plaque was placed on the west side of Highway 99, designated California Registered Landmark No. 680, with this inscription:

MURPHY RANCH

This is the site of the beginning of the Conquest of California by the United States. On June 10, 1846, American settlers led by Ezekiel Merritt overpowered the soldiers under Lieutenant Francisco Arce and took their Mexican Army horses from the corral of the Murphy Ranch on the north side of the Cosumnes River. The 'Bear Flag' action in Sonoma followed on June 14, 1846.

According to the research of Patrick Dowling in *California: the Irish Dream*, Murphy's wheat crop was harvested in the old-fashioned manner with scythes and reaping hooks, using Indian labour. At a threshing bee Murphy 'improvised a method of extracting the grain from the straw by having his horses stomp the sheaves'. Captain John Sutter's journal at the fort indicated that Murphy delivered eleven wagonloads of wheat in 1847. Other entries reveal that Murphy made almost forty visits to the fort with horses and cattle as well as wheat for sale. Murphy's cattle and wheat ranch was well situated after gold was discovered in 1848 and the Gold Rush began. Bayard Taylor gave an account of a visit to the ranch in 1849:

About two hours after dark, however, a faint light glimmered in the distance, and I finally reached the place of my destination – Murphy's Ranch on the Cosumnes River. An Indian boy tied my horse to a haystack, and Mrs. Murphy set about making some biscuit in a pan, and roasting a piece of beef for me on a wooden spit. A company of gold-diggers, on their way from the Yuba to winter on the Mariposa, had possession of one end of the house, where they lay rolled in their blankets, their forms barely discernible through the smoke sent out by the rainsoaked wood of which their fire was made. I talked an hour with them about the prospects of mining on the different rivers, and then lay down to sleep on the clay floor. . . . Mr. Murphy, I found, was the son of the old gentleman whose hospitality I had shared in the valley of San Jose. He had been living three years on the river, and his three sturdy sons could ride and throw a lariat equal to any Californian.[31]

The first school in the Sacramento valley was established at the Murphy ranch when Murphy hired a roving Irish schoolmaster named Patrick O'Brien to tutor his children. When O'Brien, an army deserter, was apprehended upon the arrival of General William T. Sherman, Murphy's influence on the general prevailed when Murphy explained that O'Brien was the only teacher in the valley. O'Brien was released and continued to teach.

In 1850 Martin Jr sold about half the ranch and 3,000 head of cattle for $50,000, and departed for the Santa Clara valley. His son Bernard D. gave an account of his father's first purchase of land in that valley, the scene-to-be of California's Grandest Party:

> In 1849 my father was trading with the miners, supplying them with cattle and horses, and he came down here intending to purchase a band of cattle to take up to the mines. The owner here [Santa Clara County] would not sell at the agreed price. Father had the money with him, as it was at that time customary to carry large sums of money about the person, and accordingly he bought the rancho Pastoria De Las Voregus [Borregas]. . . . My father went to Judge Wallace to get him to draw up the deed for him, he paying five dollars per acre for the land, and Wallace said to him, 'Old man, you have the h—l of a lot of nerve to settle in that wild country.' We all moved down bag and baggage.[32]

Land records indicate that the first purchase was consummated in January 1851, Mariano Castro deeding 3,207 acres of the Rancho Pastoria de las Borregas ('sheep pasture') to Martin Murphy for $12,500. In a second indenture, in May that year, Castro deeded 1,688 acres to Murphy for $5,000. Murphy soon became the first rancher to grow wheat crops of significance in the valley.

Martin built a thirty-room house at his 'Bay View Ranch', where priests from Mission Santa Clara often came to say Mass in a room set aside for an altar with a consecrated altar stone. Another room was kept ready for the comfort of Archbishop Alemany during tours of his churches. Church records include this 15 December 1863 note by Alemany: 'Visited Murphy home where I blessed the Church under title Saint Patrick.' The Murphy home became a social and political, as well as religious, centre for the Santa Clara valley.

Devoted to the Catholic Church, Martin Murphy Jr was the principal benefactor in the establishment in 1851 of the schools that came to be the University of Santa Clara and the College of Notre Dame for Women. His daughters and sons received their education at these institutions.

At the time of Martin's death at the age of seventy-seven in October 1884 the value of his estate was estimated variously at $3 million to $5 million, which meant he was a billionaire by today's standards. The estate included over 70,000 acres in San Luis Obispo County, 12,000 acres in Santa Clara County, 10,000 in Santa Barbara County and considerable real estate in the cities of San Jose and San Francisco.

Martin Murphy Jr's funeral was a major event. Archbishop Alemany, Martin's old friend, who was appointed first Bishop of California in 1850, the same year that Martin settled in Santa Clara County, celebrated a Requiem Mass at St Joseph's Church in San Jose. Flags were lowered at government buildings to half-mast, state and city government offices and business houses were closed for the day. Martin's widow, Mary Bolger, outlived him by eight years. She died in San Jose in 1892. Their children were active in business and politics, three of them serving as state senators from Santa Clara and San Luis Obispo counties.

James Murphy. James and his wife, Ann Martin, first settled at Corte Madera ('wood-cutting place') in Marin County. From there James supplied timbers for Liedesdorf's Wharf at Yerba Buena, now San Francisco. After spending some time in the goldfields at Coloma and Placerville, he joined his father in 1849 in Santa Clara County, when he purchased the Rancho de las Llagas near Gilroy. This became the showplace Ringwood Farm, where James and Ann raised seven children. James died in 1888, Ann in 1900.

Bernard Murphy. Bernard, known as Brian, married Catherine O'Toole, and they lived with Bernard's father at San Martin. In 1853 Bernard acquired Rancho Uvas, adjoining the ranches of his father and brothers, and during that same year was killed in the explosion of the steamer *Jenny Lind* in San Francisco Bay on a voyage from Monterey to San Francisco. His only son, Martin J. C., inherited the estate. Catherine O'Toole Murphy's second husband was James Dunne. She died in 1925.

John W. Murphy. John served in Captain Fremont's California Battalion during the hostilities between Mexico and the United States. On 2 January 1847 he was one of the leaders in the skirmish known as the battle of Santa Clara. John and his brother Daniel ventured to the Mother Lode in July 1848, among the first prospectors after the discovery of gold by John Marshall, an employee of Captain Sutter, earlier in the year. They struck rich deposits in Calaveras County at a spot known as 'Murphys Diggins' near today's village of Murphys. William Redmond Ryan, a travelling journalist, reported that 'the camp of Mr. Murphy [presumably John] is in the midst of a small tribe of wild Indians, who gather gold for him, and receive in return provisions and blankets'.[33] Ryan further reported that Murphy was 'married' to the sister of the Indian chief, an item of genealogical information that has never been acknowledged in Murphy family records. Reports vary as to the amount of gold John and Daniel took out of the mines, but it had to be enormous, considering their later huge purchases of land in the Santa Clara valley and elsewhere. Henry Walsh, SJ, in *Hallowed were the Gold Dust Trails*, estimated that John Murphy 'took $2,000,000 in gold from the Murphys Diggings in about a year's time'. Earl Schmidt estimated that the weight of that gold would have been over 8,000 lb at $20 per troy ounce and (quoting an unnamed source) that 'when John Murphy left the mines in December 1848, he took out 17 hides [pouches] of gold dust, all that six mules could haul from the camp [and] he had more gold than any other man in California'.[34] This was the result of less than one year of work.

In 1850 John married Virginia Backenstoe Reed, a survivor of the tragic Donner party of 1846–7, against the wishes of her stepfather, James Frazier Reed, a staunch Mason and Ulster-born Protestant. Reed threatened to kill Murphy whom Virginia announced her intention to wed.[35] His objections were based perhaps as much on stories of John's liaison with the Indian woman as on John's Catholicism. Since Reed had a reputation for violence (he had been expelled from the Donner overland party in 1846 after killing a member of the company in Nevada), the threat was not to be taken lightly. Nevertheless, Virginia and John were wed, Virginia accepting the Catholic faith of her husband and therefore keeping a promise she had made during her ordeal in the mountains when she said prayers by firelight nightly with the Catholic Breen family as storms raged and wolves howled about them.[36] Her father grudgingly became reconciled to his son-in-law after the birth of his first grandchild. John Murphy became eminently respectable, serving on the San Jose City Council and as sheriff, recorder and treasurer of Santa Clara County, often working closely with his father-in-law, who was also active in local politics. He and Virginia raised nine children before John's death in 1892. Virginia died in 1921.

Daniel Murphy. Daniel, who also served with the California Battalion in the Mexican war, became fabulously rich after the short stint with his brother John in the gold country. In 1849 he joined his father at San Martin, assisted in the operation of the family ranches, and acquired immense tracts of land elsewhere in California and in Nevada, Arizona and Mexico (where one ranch, in Durango, covered a million and a half acres). He served as a director of what became the mammoth utility company Pacific Gas & Electric, the only investor listed as 'capitalist' by occupation in early records of that company. At the time of his death at Halleck, Nevada, in 1882, he may have been the greatest stock-raiser in the world. Daniel married Mary Fisher by whom he had five children. One of them, Diane, married Hiram Morgan Hill, for whom the town of Morgan Hill, near San Martin, was named. After Hill's death in 1913, Diane married Sir George Rhodes. She died in 1937.

Margaret Murphy. She married Thomas Kell, an Englishman, and they settled in San Jose. The house that Kell built in 1848 was still standing in recent years, reportedly the oldest frame house in Santa Clara County. Thomas died in 1878, Margaret in 1881.

Johanna Murphy. She married John (a.k.a. Patrick) Fitzgerald, owner of a ranch near Gilroy. Johanna, who died in 1899, was the mother of Sister Anna Raphael of the Notre Dame Convent, San Jose.

Mary Murphy. In 1845 Mary and her husband, James Miller, took up land in Marin County, which Miller acquired from Timothy ('Don Timoteo') Murphy, an early settler from Coolaknick, parish of Edermine, County Wexford, and perhaps a distant cousin of the Murphys of this study.[37] A copy of the deed to 680 acres was recorded on 8 November 1850, the first such deed recorded in English in the Marin County records. Miller conducted extensive real estate and dairy operations, marketing butter and milk to San Francisco, and by 1880 owned much real estate in the town of San Rafael and was the proprietor of 8,000 acres of land in Marin County. A large contributor to Catholic and other charities, James Miller died on 25 November 1890. His funeral services were conducted at St Vincent's Orphanage, which had been a beneficiary of his many charities. Mary Murphy Miller preceded him in death in 1880. They raised ten children.

Ellen [a.k.a. Helen] Murphy. In 1850 she married German-born Charles M. Weber (1814–81), founder of the city of Stockton, who had laid out that river port in 1847.[38] The ceremony was performed by Father John Nobili, SJ. Charles, a Protestant, accepted the Catholic faith of his wife, a requirement for joining the closely knit and very Catholic Murphy clan. Their first child, Charles M. Weber II, was born 22 September 1851. Charles Sr died in 1881, Ellen in 1895.

Historians of the Irish diaspora

In recent years the notion has been advanced that Irish Catholics, because of their forced exile and the religious and Gaelic cultural baggage which they brought with them from across the ocean, were peculiarly handicapped in adjusting to the New World. Ancient values of kinship, group equality, dependence on others and adherence to an authoritarian religion and family-based work patterns, so this notion goes, were markedly at variance with the rugged individualism of Irish Protestants and the prevailing Anglo-Protestant culture.[39] Ironically, however, it was these same allegedly crippling values of Irish Catholics that contributed mightily to the fact that the Murphy party, more than 50 per cent of whose members were Irish Catholics, suffered no casualties and, indeed, arrived in the Sacramento valley with two more members than when they began their long and historic journey. It is interesting to compare this record with that of the members of the unfortunate Donner party of 1846–7, who, like the Murphy party, were caught in the snows of the High Sierras. Thirty-nine perished either on the trail or in the mountain camps of entrapment. Of eighty-seven men, women and children, Carlow-born Patrick Breen and Margaret Bulger and their seven children were the only Irish Catholic family in the company, and they all survived.

The Breens of the Donner party

At four in the afternoon on 12 March 1847 seven brave men on a rescue mission from Sutter's Fort reached the head of the Yuba river in the Summit valley, 7,000 ft elevation, in the High Sierras of California. There they found a pit in the snow, 24 ft deep, created by a camp fire that had been kept burning for nine days and nights, gradually descending as it melted the snow. At the bottom of the pit around the camp fire were huddled eleven miserable human beings, barely alive. At the surface were the mutilated bodies of three other human beings, a woman and two children, their flesh stripped from their arms and legs, their hearts and livers and brains removed. A pot was boiling on the fire. It was one of the most pitiful sights in the history of the American west.[40]

The eleven survivors numbered two adults and nine children, aged one to fifteen. The adults were two immigrants from County Carlow, Patrick Breen, fifty-one, and his spouse Margaret, whom he called Peggy, forty-one. They were members of the tragic Donner party, of which Patrick Breen was the main chronicler. He kept a diary of the four months of entrapment near what has come to be known as Donner Lake. The original document is today a prized possession of the Bancroft Library in Berkeley, California.

Patrick was baptized on 11 June 1795, the son of Edward (Ned) Breen and Mary Wilson of Barnahasken townland, near the tiny village of Killedmund.[41] Patrick's paternal grandfather and grandmother were Patrick Breen and Bridget Ryan. They and their son Edward, and a daughter Mary,

are buried in the old Kiltennel cemetery under a headstone with the following inscription, still readable today:[42]

> Erected by Patrick Breen in memory of his wife Bridget Breen, also Ryan
> [maiden name], who Departed this life December 29th 1799 aged 73 years also
> lieth the body of Patrick Breen who Departed this life January the 1st 1802 aged
> 77 years. Also his son Edwd. Breen who depd August the 9th 1816 aged 50 years.
> Also Edwd Breens daughter Mary who dept January 2, 1819 aged 23 years. *Reqt
> in Pace. Amen.*

Edward Breen and Mary Wilson had at least nine children, of whom
Patrick Breen was the eldest son. After the death of Edward in 1816 the land
was divided among his widow and her three eldest children, the family
thereby reduced by partible inheritance from 'strong' to 'middle' tenant
status. In 1826 in Ballinvally and Barnahasken (adjoining townlands), six
lots totalling 161 Irish acres (257 English acres) were occupied by the widow
Breen and her sons Patrick, Samuel and William.[43] Patrick Breen's portion
was twenty-one Irish acres. In addition to the rents paid to the head landlord
(the fourth Earl of Courtown), the widow Breen and her children were
forced to pay £4 14s 11d in annual tithes to the Established Protestant
Church of Ireland, a substantial sum equalling what a labourer might earn
for six months of work at the rate of 5d–10d per day.

The rents paid to the earl and the tithes paid to a Church not of their
choosing were festering sores which contributed to the rising of 1798, when
the village of Killedmund was burned by insurrectionists; to the bursting
forth of the O'Connellite movement of the 1820s; and to the Tithe Wars of
the 1830s.

We do not know precisely the reasons for the entire family of Breens
emigrating to Canada in the late 1820s, but some good guesses can be made
and they have to do with partible inheritance, religion and tithes, leases, and
general economic conditions affecting both Protestant and Catholic. Some
of these reasons have already been discussed in connection with the emigration of the Murphy family of neighbouring County Wexford. In County
Carlow during the 1820s especially strong support was given to the movement headed by Daniel O'Connell which led to the Catholic Emancipation
Act of 1829, granting Catholic freeholders such as the Breens the right to
vote. One of the counter-reactions to Catholic political agitation was the so-
called 'Protestant crusade'. This was a vigorous, last-ditch movement by
Protestant evangelicals to finally impose the Reformation on a people who,
in the great majority, stubbornly clung to the creed of the 'Whore of
Babylon'. Counties Wexford and Carlow had only 13 per cent and 9 per
cent Protestant populations respectively (1831 census figures) and were
promising soil for the evangelists.

Among the zealous missionaries toiling in the south of Leinster was the
Rev. Robert Daly, described by one Protestant historian as the 'most
narrow-minded, bigoted and intolerant man in the Irish [Anglican]
Church', with an 'invincible dislike of any man, especially any clergyman,
who dissented from his opinion'.[44] In November 1824 the Rev. Daly,

Richard Pope and Edward Wingfield debated four prominent priests at a meeting of the Carlow Bible Society. The meeting ended in a riot, with the three evangelicals being helped over an 8 ft wall to escape from an angry mob.

In 1827 the situation was exacerbated with the arrival in the Carlow area of the Rev. Robert Fishbourne of the British Society for Promoting the Religious Principles of the Reformation. Fishbourne's genius for controversy contributed greatly to keeping County Carlow in a more or less continuous uproar over religious divisions in the pre-Famine years.

The decision of the Breens to emigrate in 1828 came one year after the arrival of the Rev. Fishbourne, one year before the Emancipation Act, and a few years before the bloody Tithe Wars provoked by the continued evictions of Catholic tenants for non-payment of the hated and burdensome tithes.

To Canada

Patrick Breen, aged thirty-three, sailed for Canada in 1828, perhaps from the port of New Ross in County Wexford. Margaret Bulger, Patrick's wife-to-be, emigrated about the same time. The register at Borris notes that she was baptized on 2 March 1806, the daughter of Simon Bulger and Margaret Bulger, no doubt distant cousins, of Rathgeran townland. Both the Breen and Bulger families attended the Catholic chapel at Ballymurphy. Margaret carried with her to the New World a letter from the priest who served that chapel:

> I, John Walsh, Parish Priest of Borris do certify that I know Margret Bulger the bearer of this letter and of my Parish since she was a child I never heard or knew any thing of her prejudicial to her character. [I] always esteemed her an honest and well conducted girl. Given at Borris this 5th day of March 1826 [last digit hard to decipher, perhaps 1828].

It was a six-week journey across the ocean. Patrick and his brother William purchased lots in Southwold township near the village of St Thomas in southern Ontario. On 7 September 1830 Patrick Breen was among ten signatories of a petition to Bishop Alexander Macdonnell of Kingston, requesting a resident priest for 200 Catholic settlers in sixty-seven families. About that time Patrick Breen married Margaret Bulger, and sons John and Edward were born in 1832 and 1833.

In 1834 or 1835 Patrick and Margaret with their two infant sons headed for the American west. They stopped at Springfield, Illinois, briefly, and then in 1835 moved 200 miles south, across the Mississippi, to Keokuk, Iowa, where Patrick worked for a time on a riverboat. In 1841 he purchased 320 acres a few miles north of Keokuk from Richard F. Barrett for $100, to be paid in five equal instalments at 12 per cent interest. On 15 October 1844 Patrick's final papers for United States citizenship were accepted by the district court at West Point, Lee County, Iowa. His Irish-born neighbour, bachelor Patrick Dolan, testified that Patrick had been in the United States at least five years.

California Bound

Precisely why Patrick Breen decided to uproot his family in the spring of 1846 and head for California is, like the matter of his emigration from Ireland and from Canada, another matter of guesswork. First, the year 1846 has been called the 'year of decision' when about 2,000 people in 500 covered wagons crossed the plains and the mountains and deserts from Missouri to both Oregon and California. The precedent was the Murphy party of 1844, who had proved it could be done with wagons.

Secondly, epidemic diseases such as malaria were a constant plague of the port towns in the Mississippi and Missouri river valleys. California was a healthier place, emigrants were told. Thirdly, there was the lure of cheap land. Fourth, at least for the fiercely Catholic Breens, was residence in a Catholic country where clergy, so they thought, would be more accessible and where nativist prejudice against Catholics did not exist. This was the age of Know Nothingism, a movement of native American Protestant zealots directed mainly against Irish Catholic migrants. Catholic convents and churches were being attacked and some burned in the east and, although the movement was not as virulent on the western frontier, it was nevertheless a fact of life.

The Breens set out from Keokuk for Independence, Missouri, with their friend Dolan and seven children (five had been born in Keokuk) on 5 April 1846. The Breens had three wagons drawn by fourteen oxen (seven yoke) and Dolan had one wagon. Before they left, missionary priest Father Lucien Galtier gave Patrick Breen a prayer book, which would serve the family well during the months of their ordeal in the Sierra snows.

The Breens and Dolan travelled alone for the first part of the journey across the plains, following roughly the same route along the Platte river traversed by the Murphys two years previously. Wagons were strung out across the plains in various companies, individual families joining one group, then another. By the time the Breens and Dolan reached Fort Bridger in western Wyoming they had joined a group headed by the Donner brothers, Jacob and George, and James Frazier Reed, prosperous farmers and merchants of Springfield, Illinois. Reed, a vigorous and head-strong man, had convinced the company that they should spurn the tried California trail through Fort Hall in Idaho and save themselves a few hundred miles by taking a new and untried route due west, called the Hastings cut-off, across the Wasatch mountains, then south of the Great Salt Lake and across the Salt Desert of present-day Utah. Lansford Hastings, a lawyer from Ohio, had promoted the route in a popular book, *The Emigrants' Guide to Oregon and California* (1845), but he had travelled the route only on horseback and he vastly underestimated the distance and obstacles.

It is beyond the scope of this chapter to tell the whole story of what came to be known as the Donner party, and the facts will be only briefly sketched here. The company consisted of eighty-seven people with about twenty-three wagons as it crossed the Wasatch mountains into the valley of the Great Salt Lake. Huge problems ignored by Hastings in his *Guide* were encountered. It took almost three weeks to cut a new trail through the Wasatch. It took three to five days (it was more or less every desperate family for itself) to cross a stretch of seventy-five miles of desert in Utah (Hastings had described it as a forty-eight-hour march). Indians in Nevada, with primitive bows and arrows, maimed their cattle, horses and mules, or stole off with them in the night. Some livestock just lay down and died of starvation and thirst. Provisions were running low and time was running out if they were to cross the mountains before the first snows. It was already late in October before the company reached Truckee Meadows, now Reno, Nevada. Before they had arrived at Truckee Lake (soon to be called Donner Lake), below the final pass in the High Sierras, five men were dead, three by disease, weakness and starvation, one (perhaps two) killed by other members of the party, and another accidentally shot by his brother-in-law in the act of carelessly handling a loaded pistol. Meanwhile, four men had gone ahead on horseback (one being banished from the party for killing another in a brawl in Nevada) to California, and it was hoped they would obtain supplies at Sutter's Fort in the Sacramento valley and return. One of these men, Charles Stanton, had returned with two Sutter's Fort Indians and six mules loaded with provisions, meeting the party as they were ascending the canyon leading to the lake and the high pass. Stanton and the two Indians would soon meet a sad end.

The Entrapment

On 31 October 1846 Breen and Dolan, with their wagons, were the first to try the pass, but were bogged down in heavy snow and had to return to the eastern end of the lake, six miles away. They took occupancy of a rude log shelter, about 16 ft x 24 ft, constructed two years previously by members of the Murphy party. Several other families constructed shelters at camp sites near by. The Donner brothers and their large families, along with several teamsters, trailing behind, were caught in a snowstorm and had to make camp about six miles away at Alder Creek. Another try for the pass was made but was again unsuccessful. The Breens and others returned to the lake in five feet of snow. They were seventy miles from the nearest settlement, Johnson's Ranch, at the edge of the Sacramento valley, and over 100 miles from Sutter's Fort. At the beginning of the entrapment there were fifty-six persons at the lake camps and twenty-five at Alder Creek, a total of eighty-one. Only forty-six of them would live to see the California settlements.

The Breens and Dolan settled in for the winter, and they seem to have been more prudent, patient and even luckier than other families. They quickly accepted their fate, killed their cattle, horses and mules, and dried the meat before the animals were lost beneath ten and even twenty feet of snow. Other families later probed the deep snow, usually unsuccessfully, for livestock which had wandered off in search of grass and had been buried by new snowfalls. The Breens were also careful to hoard what meat they had in favour of eating, first, the hides of the animals. The hairs had to be removed by scorching, after which the hides were boiled for many hours into a gluey mass which some stomachs could not take. The Breens also exercised a daily discipline at variance with the behaviour of other trapped families. Patrick Breen led his family in the recitation of the long Thirty Days' Prayer every evening by firelight; he made almost daily entries in his diary; and he played the violin.

In the Breen cabin were ten souls. Besides Patrick and Margaret Breen and their friend Dolan were the seven Breen children: John (fourteen), Edward (thirteen), Patrick Jr (eleven), Simon (nine), Peter (seven), James (five), and Margaret Isabella (one). In January and February the Breens took into their cabin Margaret Reed (wife of James Frazier Reed, who had been expelled from the party in Nevada for killing young John Snyder, a teamster for the Graves family) and her four children, ages three to thirteen. (Interestingly, the Breens and the Protestant Reeds were the only two families to survive intact, and both had Irish-born household heads.) In addition to the Reeds, the Breens took in Augustus Spitzer, a German immigrant, shortly before he died beside their fireplace in early February 1847. Although the survival of their own children always came first with Patrick and Margaret Breen, the record shows that they were more generous than others in sharing their food and shelter.

The diary of Patrick Breen

Patrick Breen made the first entry in his famous diary on 20 November in a little book which he fashioned from eight small sheets of letter paper, trimmed and folded to make a book of thirty-two pages, each 3³/₄ in. by 6 in. He filled twenty-nine of these pages with over a hundred entries by the efforts of his numbed fingers.

> Friday Nov. 20th 1846 came to this place on the 31st of last month' that it snowed we went on to the pass the snow so deep we were unable to find the road, when within 3 miles of the summit then turned back to this shanty on the Lake, Stanton came one day after we arrived here we again took our teams & waggons & made another unsuccessful attempt to cross in company with Stanton we returned to the shanty it continueing to snow all the time we were here we now have killed most part of our cattle having to stay here until next spring & live on poor beef without bread or salt it snowed during the space of eight days with little intermission, after our arrival here, the remainder of time up to this day was clear & pleasant frezeing at night the snow nearly gone from the valleys.

Other entries such as the following, always very brief, tell the story of the long ordeal:

Sunday 13th [Dec.] Snows faster than any previous day   wind N:W   Stanton & Graves with several others makeing preparations to cross the mountains on snow shoes, snow 8 feet deep on the level   dull [*sic*].

Thursd. 17th [Dec.]. Pleasant sunshine today   wind about S. E. Bill Murp[hy] returned from the mountain party last evening. Bealis [Baylis Williams, employee of the Reeds] died night before last. . . .

Sundd. 20 [Dec.]. Night clear   froze a little   now clear & pleasant   wind N W thawing a little   Mrs. Reid here, no account of Milt [Milford Elliot, a Reed teamster]   Dutch Charley [Burger, a Donner teamster] started for Donnghs [Donners]   turned back   not able to proceed   tough times, but not discouraged   our hopes are in God. *Amen.*

Mond. 21 [Dec.] Milt got back last night from Donos camp   sad news. Jake Donno   Sam Shoemaker   Rinechard & Smith are dead   the rest of them in a low situation   snowed all night with a strong S-W wind. . . .

Tuesd. 22nd [Dec.] Snowd. all last night   Continued to snow all day with some few intermissions   had a severe fit of the gravel [kidney stones] yesterday   I am well to day, Praise be to the God of Heaven

Wend. 23rd [Dec.] Snowd. a little last night   clear to day & thawing a little . . . began this day to read the Thirty days prayer, may Almighty God grant the request of an unworthy sinner that I am. *Amen.*

The entries continue almost daily through January and February, with reports of sickness and death and burials in the snow, difficulties in obtaining kindling wood and food for some families, and always the weather. On 26 February Breen noted talk of cannibalism for the first time:

Frid 26th [Feb.] . . . Marthas [Martha, known as 'Patty', Reed] jaw swelled with the toothache; hungry times in camp, plenty hides but the folks will not eat them   we eat them with a tolerable good apetite. Thanks be to Almighty God. *Amen.* Mrs Murphy [Lavinia Murphy, a widow with seven children] said here yesterday that [she] thought she would commence on Milt [Elliott] and eat him. I don't [think] that she has done so yet, it is distressing The Donnos told the California folks [members of first relief party] that they [would] commence to eat the dead people 4 days ago, if they did not succeed that day or next in finding their cattle then under ten or twelve feet of snow & did not know the spot or near it, I suppose they have done so ere this time.

On 27 February Breen noted a 'beautiful morning sun shineing brillantly' and, as a first sign of spring, 'heard some geese fly over last night . . .' On 3 March, Breen's last diary entry reads:

. . . there has 10 men arrived this morning from Bear Valley with provisions   we are to start in two of three days & cash [cache] our goods here   there
is amongst them some old [mountaineers?]   they say the snow will be here until
June.

The ten men were members of the third of four relief parties that brought
out surviving migrants in February, March and early April. The first of the
migrants to reach the valley did, however, bring themselves out, as survivors of what came to be known as the Snowshoe party. They numbered
fifteen, ten men and five women. Equipped with snowshoes and six days'
rations, they left the high camp on 15 December, got lost on the trail and
took thirty days to reach the first settlement. All five women survived, but
only two of the men, William Eddy and William Foster. To do so they had
consumed the bodies of seven of the eight dead. One of them was Patrick
Dolan, who received the unwanted distinction of being the first person
cannibalized by Donner company members. Two others were the Sutter's
Fort Indians, whose deaths were hastened when Foster or Eddy shot them
through the head as they were gathering acorns.

The first relief party led out eighteen migrants in late February, two of
them being Edward and Simon Breen. Eighteen survived the seventy-mile
journey, two children and one adult dying *en route*.

Starved Camp

The second relief party of seven men left the high camps in early March
with another seventeen survivors, including Patrick and Margaret Breen
and five of their children. Three reliefers were sent ahead to bring back food
at a cache. Things went well the first two nights on the trail. Patrick Breen
even entertained the party with his fiddle-playing around the camp fire. But
on the third night a terrible storm began. It raged for three days. Before it
was over, Isaac Donner, aged five, was dead.

The four relief party members – James Frazier Reed, Hiram O. Miller,
William McCutchen and Brit Greenwood – took with them from Starved
Camp only three children, and two of them were Reed's own. The rescuers
in their weakened condition could offer no help to the others. The Breens
figured it was better to take their chances that another rescue party would
arrive soon with food. Besides, they could not leave the weak behind.
Margaret Breen was the strongest of the thirteen and would have had to
carry her year-old infant, leaving her other children to their own devices.
Her husband was very weak, as was her eldest son, John. She was not about
to leave her husband and family to certain death, not to mention the
Graveses and the Donner child. So the rescuers left behind the seven Breens,
Mrs Graves and her four small children, and little Mary Donner, aged
seven. They left some firewood but no food.

Mrs Graves and her five-year-old son died the first night after the rescuers
had abandoned them. The migrants were to spend another six nights in the

pit created by the fire, which gradually descended to earth level, over 20 ft below the surface of the snow. Margaret Breen held her own infant to her breast, which had long since ceased to produce milk, and gave what comfort she could to the one-year-old Graves infant and the other children. Without food, save for a few seeds, some tea and coffee, and a one-pound ball of sugar that Margaret Breen had stashed on her person, the Breens ate human flesh for the first time, after the Donner girl, who had eaten of her uncle's and her father's bodies at Alder Creek, had innocently suggested doing so. The starved bodies of Mrs Graves, her dead child and Isaac Donner were quickly consumed, giving the survivors the strength to be led out by a member of the third rescue party, a giant of a man named John Stark who took responsibility for nine of the eleven survivors.

Of eighty-one persons (of the original eighty-seven members of the company) – twenty-five men, fifteen women and forty-one children – who were entrapped at the high camps, over two-thirds of the men perished, and most of them died during the first two months of the ordeal. The adult men travelling without family tended to perish first, only two of nineteen surviving. About one-third of the children died, mostly in the beginning and middle of the entrapment, and boys in the highest ratio. About one-fourth of the women died, mostly toward the end of the tragedy.

The Breens in California

The Breens recuperated at Sutter's Fort, where they met Martin Murphy Jr. He extended them hospitality at his ranch on the Consumnes river, south of the fort, and in the summer of 1847 helped Patrick Breen and his older sons retrieve their wagons and personal possessions at the lake camp.

The Breens soon thereafter settled in San Juan Bautista with the encouragement of Fr Jose Anzar, who gave the Breens the use of the mission orchard, in run-down condition. The priest also introduced the Breens to General José Maria Castro, once head of the Mexican military district. (California had been conquered by United States forces during the time the Donner party had crossed from Missouri.) Castro kindly gave the Breens the use of a two-storey adobe house he owned but used only occasionally. All the Breens quickly became fluent in Spanish, the language of all of the residents of San Juan before they arrived. In 1849 Patrick Breen purchased the adobe from Castro with money his eldest son, John, had made in the goldfields, and also 401 acres adjoining the mission. The house unofficially became 'The Inn', as it was opened to wayfarers needing lodging for the night on their way to the Mother Lode. Another son, William Breen, was born in 1849.

By 1850, according to the assessment rolls for Monterey County (San Juan was later to become part of newly formed San Benito County), Patrick Breen had twenty milk cows, six saddle horses, thirty 'wild cattle', thirty sheep, and four hogs on his 401 acres. By 1854, his livestock had increased to sixteen horses, thirty mares, 460 head of cattle, 359 sheep, seventy-five hogs, and one mule. A mare at the time was worth $20, a mule $220. During this period Breen increased his agricultural holdings in the county to almost 1000 acres of good land and had fenced in 100 acres of it. He died at the age of seventy-three on 21 December 1868, his family at his bedside as he received the sacraments of Penance, Communion and Extreme Unction from Fr Cipriano Rubio of the mission. In 1880 an historian of the Donner party, C. F. McGlashan, wrote that Breen was 'a man of more than ordinary intelligence . . . his life furnishes a rare type of the pioneer Californian.'

During his last years Patrick Breen enjoyed playing his fiddle and watching his sons, all of whom became expert horsemen, assume more and more of the work of managing his property. Breen's estate was appraised at $100,000, the equivalent of many millions today. Besides the San Juan ranch, his property included a 24,000 acre cattle ranch near King City, several smaller parcels elsewhere, 1,500 head of cattle and forty Spanish horses and mares.

Widow Margaret Breen received an interesting letter from Father P. Carey, parish priest of Borris, County Carlow, dated 30 December 1869, in which the priest thanked her for a gift of £9 towards the erection of a belfry and bell and also a cross for her native chapel at Ballymurphy. After giving some details of the present chapel, and the total cost of the new additions (£200, including £60 for the bell of 7 cwt to be constructed in Dublin, and mentioning that the congregation had already raised £60), the priest wrote:

> I announced from the pulpit in Ballymurphy where you have so many relatives, your generous donation, that came 3,500 miles across the Continent of America and 3,500 miles across the Atlantic and asked the Congregation's fervent prayers for your family and also for your deceased husband. . . . I have said the number of Masses I promised and everyday I make a memento for you at the altar.

Margaret Bulger Breen died six years after her husband. Both are buried on a hill in the district cemetery, a short distance from the old mission at San Juan. The Breen children fared well. James attended the institution that became the University of Santa Clara, obtained a law degree and became a superior court judge for Monterey and later San Benito County. Edward was part owner and manager of the 24,000 acre 'Topo Ranch' near King City for many years. Patrick Jr acquired thousands of acres of farming and grazing land, which in 1991 were still in the possession of a consortium of Patrick Jr's descendants. In 1991, among the hundreds of direct living descendants of Patrick Sr and Margaret Breen were Harvey Nyland, sheriff of San Benito County since 1987; Thomas P. Breen, judge of the superior court in the same county; Philip Hudner of Kentfield, California, partner in the law firm of Pillsbury Madison & Sutro in San Francisco, and former head of the Society of California Pioneers; and Dr Philip Raven, Director of the Missouri Botanical Garden, Secretary to the American Academy of Science, author of twenty books and over 400 articles on botany and biology, and holder of a number of honorary degrees awarded by institutions in Europe and America. They are all great-great-grandchildren of Patrick and Margaret Breen.

The Irish in Rural California

The Murphys and the Breens, although more successful than most pioneers, were not isolated examples of Irish settlers who made a significant mark in California. In the Far West there was no entrenched Protestant class holding tenaciously to its property, power and perquisites against the tide of newly arrived foreigners from the east. Everybody, more or less, could begin at the same starting line.[45]

By 1860 a large number of Irish Catholics had become part of the San Francisco and rural California political, business and professional elite. By 1881 four Irish Catholics had been elected to the United States Senate, and another, John Downey, from southern California, had served as governor of the state. In 1870 California's Irish-born numbered 54,000 of a total population of 537,000. Of 187,000 foreign-born, 29 per cent were Irish-born, and they were the dominant foreign-born presence in thirty-eight of California's fifty counties. Not counted as 'Irish' in these figures are the first-generation sons and daughters of Irish born in 'British America' or in Maine, Massachusetts, California or elsewhere. A cursory check of surnames on the 1870 census reveals that the Irish were represented significantly in the 10,690 enumerations of California residents born in 'Canada East' and 'New Brunswick', and among the 350,416 native-born, including 119,904 California-born. By 1870 the typical Irish immigrant was married with a family, the children California-born.[46]

Interestingly, in 1870 in California the Irish were as much a rural as an urban people. In San Francisco, California's only fully urbanized county, the Irish-born numbered 25,864 of a total population of 149,473. That was less than half California's total Irish-born population. Even in partly urbanized Los Angeles County 19 per cent of the Irish-born were listed in the 1870 census as farmers.

Although no family, Irish or otherwise, matched the Murphys, and few matched the Breens, in the acquisition of property, many achieved material success on the farms and grazing lands of California's rich valleys. Many of these Irish pioneers spent at least some time in the goldfields, where they quickly made their poke and invested it in fertile valley land. (The migration of the Irish from the gold country to the farms has been little studied.[47])

California today is not thought of as a particularly Irish state. It may even be true, as one scholar has suggested, that the Irish-born, by 1900, had ceased to be an important contributing factor to the state.[48] By the end of the century, however, families such as the Murphys had laid an enormous foundation in churches, schools, universities, charitable organizations, local and state governance, labour unions and business enterprises. Occasionally the Irish pioneers are remembered. In 1981 the city of Sunnyvale commemorated the hundredth anniversary of California's Grandest Party by sponsoring another party in the grand manner to honour the city's founding father and mother, Martin Murphy Jr and Mary Bolger of County Wexford.

Notes

1. A description of the party, from various contemporary newspaper and other sources, can be found in Sister Gabrielle Sullivan, *Martin Murphy Jr.: California Pioneer, 1844–1884*, Pacific Center for Historical Studies, University of the Pacific, Stockton, Cal., 1974, appendix 7, pp. 62–5; also Patrick J. Dowling, *California: the Irish Dream*, Golden Gate Publishers, San Francisco, 1988, pp. 120–4.
2. Martin Murphy Jr signed with an 'X' mark, according to the research of Sullivan, p. ii. Sullivan had access to a trunkful of Murphy family papers.
3. See Margaret E. Fitzgerald and Joseph A. King, *The Uncounted Irish in Canada and the United States*, Meany, Toronto, 1990; focus on the Irish who settled in rural Canada and America, especially before the Great Famine.
4. Various secondary sources, often repeating one another, give 'Balnamough' and 'near the towers of Oulecree' as the residence of the Murphys. These place names, which nobody has been able to locate, may be corruptions of Ballynamuddagh and Outlartleigh, neighbouring townlands about four miles south-east of Enniscorthy in the civil parish of Ballyhuskard; another possibility: Ballynamona in the parish of Castle Ellis, just east of Ballyhuskard. The name Murphy is almost ubiquitous in County Wexford, but the only Foleys in Ballyhuskard in 1834 were in 'Ballinamudda [*sic*] Townland'. There a Martin Murphy and a James Foley are listed as occupiers of five and four-acre parcels. Given the custom of naming children after the grandparents (usually the paternal grandparents first), these could be the parents of Martin Murphy and Mary Foley, who named their first boys Martin and James. See Tithe Applotment Books, Parish of Ballyhuskard, Diocese of Ferns, year 1834, film 256,571, LDS (Mormon) Library, Salt Lake City; and *General Index to the Townlands and Towns, Parishes, and Baronies of Ireland*, Dublin, 1851 (Genealogical Publishing, Baltimore, Md, 1984).
5. For biographical material, chief sources are Bernard D. Murphy (1841–1911), Dictation to Alfred Bates for Hubert H. Bancroft's *Chronicles of the Builders of the Commonwealth* (1891), Bancroft Library, Berkeley, Cal., MS C–D 792, file folder 46·1 (hand), 28·1 (typed transcript), 17·1 (typed transcript); and Sullivan, *Martin Murphy Jr.*, a well researched study with extensive notes and appendices, including records of land transactions and other documents from the Murphy family papers. I have generally drawn from these two sources (citing them only occasionally), except where otherwise noted.
6. Kerby Miller, *Emigrants and Exiles*, Oxford University Press, New York and Oxford, 1985, p. 78. Estimates vary, as the first systematic population count was not taken until the census of 1821. Cecil Woodham-Smith gives a figure of 172 per cent increase between 1779 and 1841, when the population count was 8,200,000. See *The Great Hunger*, Hamish Hamilton, London, 1961, p. 29, citing G. Talbot Griffith, *Population Problems of the Age of Malthus*, 1926, p. 50.
7. Partible inheritance was virtually abandoned in Ireland after the Great Famine of 1845–8, when the older male children tended to emigrate first. See Miller, *Emigrants and Exiles*, p. 403.

8. Miller, *Emigrants and Exiles*, pp. 37–8, 57–9, 217–20.
9. Patrick J. Corish, 'Two centuries of Catholicism in County Wexford', pp. 222–47; T. Jones Hughes, 'Continuity and change in rural County Wexford in the nineteenth century', pp. 342–72; both in *Wexford: History and Society*, ed. Kevin Whelan, Geography Publications, Templeogue, Dublin, 1987.
10. Quotations are from Miller, *Emigrants and Exiles*, who cites several sources, pp. 245, 612.
11. Abstracts of Irish Exports and Imports, 1764–1823, National Library of Ireland MSS 357–76, cited by Mary Gwinnell, 'Some aspects of the economic life of County Wexford in the nineteenth century', *Journal of the Wexford Historical Society*, 10, 1984–5, p. 5.
12. Gwinnell, 'Some aspects', p. 18. A few benign Wexford landlords, even during the period of declining prices, paid wages of 1s 1d per day, well above average.
13. Miller, *Emigrants and Exiles*, p. 59.
14. The Wexford emigration has been studied by the Canadian historian Bruce Elliott, 'Emigration from south Leinster to Eastern Upper Canada', in Whelan, *Wexford History and Society*, pp. 422–45. See also William Forbes Adams, *Ireland and Irish Emigration to the New World from 1815 to the Famine*, Genealogical Publishing, Baltimore, Md, 1980; and J. A. King, 'The Tyrrells of County Wexford', *Journal of the Old Wexford Society*, 7, 1978–9.
15. File P.R.O., C.O. 384/1, Public Archives of Canada, Ottawa, reel B-876, reproduced by Elliott, 'Emigration', pp. 442–5.
16. According to the 1831 census, 60,000 of 400,000 residents of the three counties of south Leinster (Wicklow, Wexford, Carlow) were Protestant, nearly 15 per cent. For Wicklow, 20 per cent, Wexford 13 per cent, Carlow 9 per cent.
17. In 1817 the *Duchess of Richmond* carried nineteen adult passengers from Dublin to Miramichi, New Brunswick, for £5 apiece, and a child for £2 10s. See the passenger list in William Sweetman, 'A Wexford shipbuilder', *Journal of the Old Wexford Society*, 7, 1978; Joseph A. King, *The Irish Lumberman–Farmer*, K&K Publications, Lafayette, Cal., 1982, p. 55.
18. Elliott, 'Emigration', p. 428.
19. Hubert H. Bancroft, *Chronicles of the Builders of the Commonwealth*, History Company, San Francisco, Cal., 1891, p. 16.
20. Adams, *Ireland and Irish Emigration*, p. 9, citing report of Devon Commission.
21. Bancroft, *Chronicles*, pp. 16–17.
22. Sister Marianna O'Gallagher, *St. Patrick's, Quebec*, Carraig, Quebec, 1981, p. 31.
23. Sullivan, *Martin Murphy Jr.*, p. 9: 'In a visit to Wexford in June of 1967, the writer located the Bolger homestead in Oylegate, north of the city of Wexford'. Sullivan provides no confirming evidence. The surname Bolger (Bulger) is very common in County Wexford.
24. Dowling, *California*, had access to Miller family records and gives James Miller's birth date as 1 May 1814, in the 'townland of Upton, Parish of Livermore', his parents being William Miller and Catherine Duff. 'Livermore' should doubtless be *Litter Mor*, a townland in the civil parish of Kilmuckridge, barony of Ballaghkeen, on the coast about twelve miles east of Enniscorthy. Upton House is close by.
25. Sullivan, *Martin Murphy Jr.*, p. 4. She cites a number of sources on conditions in Canada spurring the emigration, including Edgar McInnis, *Canada: Political and Social History*, Rinehart, New York, 1959.
26. Sullivan, *Martin Murphy Jr.*, p. 5, citing Bancroft, *Chronicles*, p. 18.
27. George F. Stewart, *The California Trail*, University of Nebraska Press, Lincoln

and London, 1983, pp. 53–82. For the events that follow I have drawn mainly from this source.

28. Cited by Dowling, *California*, p. 132.

29. A reliable source of information on Murphy family acquisition of land is Mildred B. Hoover *et al.*, *Historic Spots in California*, third edition, ed. William N. Abeloe, Stanford University Press, Stanford, Cal., 1966. For the biographies of family members I have used this source as well as Bernard D. Murphy's dictation, Sullivan's *Martin Murphy Jr.* and Henry L. Walsh, SJ, *Hallowed were the Gold Dust Trails*, University of Santa Clara Press, Santa Clara, Cal. 1946, pp. 473–4.

30. Thomas F. Prendergast, *Forgotten Pioneers: Irish Leaders in early California*, Trade Pressroom, San Francisco, Cal., 1942, p. 103.

31. Bayard Taylor, *Eldorado, or, Adventures in the Path of Empire*, Putnam, New York, 1892, pp. 229–30, quoted by Sullivan, *Martin Murphy Jr.*, p. 13.

32. Bernard D. Murphy dictation, p. 5.

33. William Redmond Ryan, *Personal Adventures in Upper and Lower California*, London, 1852.

34. Earl F. Schmidt, *Who were the Murphys? California's first Irish family*, Mooney Flat Ventures, Box 239, Murphys, California, 1989, p. 24

35. The account of Reed's wrath is told in an obscure pamphlet, the information obviously furnished by descendants of Reed: *Hazeldell Charavari: Christmas at Zayanta, 1856, being the story of the wedding of Patty Reed to Frank Lewis*, published by the editor of the *Frontier Gazette*, Santa Cruz, 1959, copy in the library of the Society of California Pioneers, San Francisco, file 'Donner Papers'.

36. Virginia Reed Murphy, *Across the Plains in the Donner Party*, Outbooks, Golden, Colo., 1980, p. 40.

37. Timothy Murphy's birth year is given as 1800 and the place 'Coolaneck, County Wexford' by Jack Mason in *Early Marin*, second edition revised, Marin County Historical Society, San Rafael, Ca, 1976, p. 34. This is doubtless Coolaknick in the civil parish of Edermine, several miles south of Enniscorthy on the river Slaney. The birthplace of his nephew, John Lucas, who sailed from Ireland to California in 1852, is given, with allowances for corruptions in spelling ('Barney of Ballaghkune'!), as the townland of Coolnaboy, civil parish of Edermine, barony of Ballaghkeen, on 12 March 1826. See *Index to Townlands*, 1851.

38. The Weber connection with the Murphy family is thoroughly explored by George P. Hammond in *The Weber Era in Stockton History*, Friends of the Bancroft Library, University of California, Berkeley, Cal., 1982.

39. The major advocate of the Catholic Irishman-as-misfit in the New World is Miller in *Emigrants and Exiles*. For a critique of Miller see Fitzgerald and King, *The Uncounted Irish*, IX, pp. 188, 251, 318–22.

40. The events concerning the Breens and the Donner party are drawn largely from manuscript sources consulted for the book *Winter of Entrapment: a new look at the Donner Party*, scheduled for publication by Meany, Toronto, 1992, which contains extensive notes and bibliography. Major collections are the Breen and McGlashan papers at Bancroft Library, Berkeley, Cal., and the Reed papers, Sutter's Fort Historical Museum, Sacramento, Cal.. Private collections include those of Breen descendants Philip Hudner of Kentfield, Cal., and Dr Peter Raven, St Louis, Mo. Secondary sources include C. F. McGlashan, *History of the Donner Party: a Tragedy of the Sierra*, Stanford, Cal., 1947 (first published 1880), and George R. Stewart, *Ordeal by Hunger*, University of Nebraska Press, Lincoln and London, 1986 (first published 1936, revised 1960).

41. Baptismal register of the Roman Catholic parish of Borris, County Carlow.
42. *County Carlow Tombstone Inscriptions: Ballicopagan Cemetery, New Cemetery Borris, Clonagoose Cemetery, Kiltennel Cemetery*, published by St Mullins Muintir na Tire, County Carlow, 1985.
43. Tithe Applotment Books, year 1826, townlands of Ballonvally [*sic*] and Barnahasken, parish of Kiltennel, barony of Idrone East, County Carlow, National Library of Ireland.
44. For the account of the evangelism in County Carlow, I have drawn mainly from Desmond Bowen, *The Protestant Crusade in Ireland, 1800–70*, Gill & Macmillan, Dublin, 1978.
45. See especially R. A. Burchell, *The San Francisco Irish, 1848–1880*, Manchester Univesity Press, Manchester, and University of California Press, Berkeley, Cal., 1980; David M. Emmons, *The Butte Irish*, University of Illinois Press, Urbana and Chicago, 1990; King, *The Irish Lumberman–Farmer*; Fitzgerald and King, *The Uncounted Irish*; Denis Clark, *Hibernia America*, Greenwood Press, N. Y., 1986.
46. For statistics cited see Fitzgerald and King, *The Uncounted Irish*, especially pp. 213–54.
47. A number of Irishmen who turned to farming and grazing after a stint in the goldfields are cited in Fitzgerald and King, *The Uncounted Irish*, pp. 213–54.
48. Patrick Blessing, 'West among Strangers Irish migration to California, 1850–1880', unpublished Doctoral dissertation, U.C.L.A., 1977, p. 426.

5 Irish hooligans Ned Kelly (Australia) and William Donnelly (Canada) in comparative perspective

James Sturgis

Ned Kelly and William Donnelly never set eyes on each other. Moreover, they lived thousands of miles apart in separate continents. Yet their lives shared so many striking similarities as to be compelling subjects of study. To start with, they were both second-generation immigrants whose fathers had left Tipperary in the same year of 1841, and both were to meet their fate a few months apart in 1880. By mere chance William Donnelly was to escape his attackers, only to live out his remaining years in a kind of melancholy daze. This chapter is a deliberate exercise in the comparative method – the use of which, it is hoped, will aid in the understanding of two sets of events which both had their genesis in Ireland in the pre-Famine days but which culminated on the widely separated stages provided by Canada and Australia.

In part the desirability of seeking out the commonalities and differences arises from the obvious puzzlement which has set in concerning the motivation of Ned Kelly's actions. Was he still fighting the battles of his ancestors? Or do we see him acting in response to the iniquities of the social divides which existed in north-eastern Victoria? Or was his the kind of thuggish behaviour one would expect from a family already bearing certain caste marks of notoriety? And, in the case of William Donnelly, to what extent was he programmed by his Irish past to act in certain ways? And how much did family deprivation in one form or another explain aspects of Ned's and William's behaviour? The questions abound, as do the difficulties. Naturally, hard facts, as opposed to folk memories, are at a premium. Popular historians have been drawn irresistibly to these episodes. Their sparring with the evidence has not always been subtle, resulting in many telegraphed ideological punches and much dime-store psychology. What we want to see is whether understanding of one circumstance can be advanced by reference to the other and whether any general conclusions regarding the Irish experience overseas can be drawn.

The Tipperary inheritance

One half of our story concerns the family and background of the Australian bushranger Ned Kelly, and the other half the less well known (except in his home locale of south-western Ontario) William Donnelly. In many ways it is inappropriate to introduce them as individuals, because so much of their significance derives from the meshing of their lives with that of their wider families. And tracing the ramifications of this clannishness, or what one prominent historian has called the proclivity to 'aggregation',[1] leads us back to Ireland. Both families emerged from the tortured body and distracted soul of a country sapped in strength, as it was, by the bitterness and recrimination flowing from its long contested inheritance. As Catholics the Kellys and the Donnellys were automatically assumed to be imbued with certain cultural loyalties as surely as if they were to wear military uniform. Even more, as poor peasants they had to find the means of living upon a landscape the social dimensions of which were controlled – by day – by the forces of Church and state enjoining conformity with the law and – by night – the unofficial apparatuses of a beleaguered, but ever stubborn, opposition which demanded unity in resisting encroachments upon the means of a niggardly survival. The penalties for defying either were uncompromising.

Overseas, to come from Ireland might speak volumes about identity and background, but to come from Tipperary was to be even more exact about the familial exposure to an environment of social conflict and violence. The Home Secretary in 1829, Robert Peel, wrote irritably that Tipperary was 'by far the most troublesome county in Ireland'.[2] It was entirely fitting that the Whiteboys, the prototype of later secret societies, should have had their beginnings there in 1761. Made up mainly of labourers and cottiers, their clandestine operations were in the beginning designed to counter enclosure of common land and the imposition of excessive tithes.[3] In addition, Tipperary shared to the full the ills of Ireland, such as the fact that over half the county's landowners were absentees and few of them bore a Gaelic family name. It was not as if Tipperary was uniquely poor. Indeed, its soil and fertility were above average. But perhaps it was this very fact that led to an alarming increase in the densities of rural poor after the late eighteenth century.[4] On the eve of the departure of the Kelly and Donnelly families, so ingrained were certain modes of action that:

> to some extent the Whiteboys fed on their own tradition of activity as well as an earlier one of social banditry. By 1840, a Whiteboy in Tipperary could look back on some eighty years of peasant protest, with some idea of what had been done and could be achieved in various situations.[5]

In view of the identification later of Ned Kelly and Will Donnelly with Irishness, should it not be expected that their families would stand in some kind of apostolic connection with this Hibernian tradition of protest? For a long time, in the case of Ned Kelly, did it appear to be so. His father, John 'Red' Kelly, was popularly supposed to have been sentenced to transportation to Australia in 1840 for having stolen two pigs. The implication of injustice was obvious. But recent research by Bob Reece paints another picture – one in which 'Red' Kelly is an accomplice of other, and sometimes more serious, robberies and in which he lessened his own sentence by offering evidence to the police.[6] James Donnelly also left Ireland under a cloud. He came from Borrisokane in north Tipperary, where the proportion of Protestants was nearly 25 per cent, compared with the more usual number of about 4 per cent, as in Cashel, the main urban centre of Kelly's neighbourhood.[7] Legend has it that Donnelly eloped with a Protestant girl, Johannah McGee, and paid for it by being installed behind bars by an outraged father. It meant that his escape precipitated a hurried exit to Canada, followed shortly by Johannah, with infant in tow.[8]

Embattled families

James Donnelly settled in Biddulph township, near the village of Lucan and some fifteen miles from London. He was able to establish himself on a 100 acre plot of the fertile, gently rolling land of the Canada Company along the so-called Roman Line, a road adjoining a settlement of Tipperary Protestants on concessions 2–5 to the west and Tipperary Catholics on concessions 6–11 to the east. By 1858 the Donnellys had a family of seven boys and one girl. Their second child was William, who was born, to their consternation, with a deformed foot in January 1845. It might seem, even overlooking the demands of a pioneering existence, that the family's successes were such as to put any alternative which Ireland might have offered in the shade. Yet, during those formative years in the life of the Donnellys and the Irish community, there were tensions and conflict which pockmarked what might have been an Arcadian paradise. Feuds and faction fights erupted, one of which involved James Donnelly as a fringe character and another which caused his brother, John, to leave the area and Canada altogether.[9] But all this was a mere preamble for what was to come. James Donnelly's title to his land arose more from occupation than from legal documents. In 1855 the Donnellys were ejected from the southern half of their homestead by Patrick Farrell. Whether the roots of the enmity which existed between them went back to Ireland or not, there could be no denying the intent with which Donnelly tried to warn off Farrell and any other potential occupier of his land. Then came the climactic moment in June 1857 when at a logging bee Donnelly became embroiled, when drunk, in a fight with Farrell and with what was undoubtedly preternatural accuracy threw a wooden handspike at Farrell which caused his death. For nearly the whole of a year Donnelly, by various stratagems, escaped apprehension, to some extent because the community had generally disliked Farrell and partly because it was felt that Donnelly had not wilfully committed murder. Eventually he handed himself in and was saved from the gallows only by the energetic intervention of Johannah, who petitioned for mercy. Nevertheless the father was to be in Kingston penitentiary between August 1858 and 1865.

As for Kelly, he was sent to Tasmania and served out his sentence by

1848, at which point he crossed to the mainland and took up residence near Melbourne. In 1850 he married Ellen Quinn, but only after elopement, as James Quinn presumably disliked the idea of his young daughter marrying an ex-convict. This was a brave act, because the Quinns, a Catholic family from County Antrim in Ulster, were ruled firmly by the father. Ned Kelly was by 1854 the third-born but first boy in a family of seven which included younger brothers Jim and Dan. John Kelly, despite the reputation he had acquired in Ireland, seems to have made a determined effort to avoid entanglements with the law. This might explain his gradual edging away from the environs of Melbourne towards wilder and less agricultural territory to the north. If so, it failed as a plan, since he was arrested in 1865 and charged with cattle stealing. His constitution, again under the siege of penal conditions, gave way and he died in late 1866.[10]

Strong mothers and family honour

Johannah Donnelly had shown her mettle long before she faced the world alone with a young brood. She brooked no insult to the family name. If there was one thing the Donnellys were known for, other than their pugnacity, it was cohesiveness. A quarrel with one was a quarrel with all. And what she taught did not prohibit the incidents which led the Donnelly boys to have their first brushes with the law shortly after the incarceration of their father. Indeed, in 1864, when Will was charged with stealing wood, the mother faced the accusation of accepting stolen goods. Local folklore still tends to blame her for the family's difficulties: the family memory of one Lucan resident in the 1970s led to the description of Johannah as 'a large vengeful ill-educated Irishwoman'.[11]

Ellen Kelly, whose personality had always overshadowed that of her husband, was an equally formidable character. She decided to move north, closer to the Quinns, but not before being fined for threatening language against the family which had brought charges against her husband. She took up land of her own near Glenrowan but fought a losing battle against the terms imposed upon the selectors (smallholders) to gain title to it. According to Manning Clark she and her husband, when alive, had 'both taught their children that no Irishman could expect justice in an English law-court; both taught their children that the police were the paid hirelings of English landlords who had robbed Irishmen of their rightful inheritance on the land'.[12] To help make ends meet she sold grog on the side; she also took a man named Frost to court for maintenance to help pay for the upkeep of a child, the result of a two-year relationship. Ellen's remarriage in 1874 at the age of forty-two to a Californian almost half her age by the name of King, who was also an expert horse thief, could not have but speeded the family's progress towards new danger zones.

Boys become men

Thus at a critical stage of their lives both Will Donnelly and Ned Kelly faced up to responsibilities within a one-parent family. True, Will was not the eldest, but he was widely recognized, both within and outside the family, as the most intelligent and resourceful of all the siblings. Among the more dubious visitors to both sets of homes were men whom the fathers had known in convict days. In Ned's case, authorities agree that for a time in 1870 he was in the company of one of the most notable bushrangers, Harry Power, whose bravado could easily have turned the head of an impressionable young lad. As for Will Donnelly, more and more of his time and that of his brothers was spent in the numerous drinking establishments of Lucan, of which there were eight in 1870 – and this for a hamlet striving to reach a population of 1,000 people. Moreover, some of the Donnelly's closest friends were more often than not either in the public gaze or in the public jail. This was certainly true of Andrew Keefe and his numerous boys, who managed a drinking establishment at Elginfield, between London and Lucan. A close perusal of local newspapers at any time in the 1870s will uncover items such as the notice that a warrant for the arrest of the wife of a man named Keefe had been issued because she had hit him with a plank while he was repairing a fence.[13]

What is most uncanny is the number of character traits which Kelly and Donnelly can be seen to have shared. One way of describing it is to say that they both had 'style' or, perhaps better, a sense of self that others believed in. For those on the right side of them, they had an undoubted charisma which weakened any wavering as to a proposed course of action among the doubtful. Charm and menace were alternative social tools for effecting their purpose. Both also liked to be the centre of attention. Will had sartorial pretensions that matched his ability to master whatever line of endeavour he turned to. Adept with the fiddle, his playing enlivened more than a few evenings with brothers and friends – as did his propensity for playing practical jokes. His mental sharpness was such that he earned the nickname of 'the Lawyer', while others thought that different circumstances might have seen him become a priest.[14] That he was neither he blamed on the fact that his mother had often lacked the means to clothe him properly for school. He also self-consciously possessed a facility of verbal and written expression that added to his persona of confidence and audacity, qualities that over the years he carefully cultivated. He also knew how to threaten. When frustrated in an elopement attempt in 1874, the letter to the father catches the essence of the menace which Donnelly could conjure up:

> And now, Dear Sir, I want you to understand that I will have my revenge if it cost the lives of both families, which I am sure it will not, for I can get crowd enough in almost any town to carry out my design without any trouble, except a little law from you, but I do [not?] care for that, as I have plenty of money to pay my way through all.[15]

Will guarded the citadel of individual and family pride by gathering around him a gang of uncritical admirers and by deploying an expedient morality.

The personal description in the previous sentence could equally apply to Ned Kelly. He had that same swagger which infuriated the respectable bourgeoisie and caused one police superintendent, early on, to recommend that Kelly and his friends should be arrested on any sort of paltry charge, since it would be 'a very good way of taking the flashness out of them'. At an early court appearance Ned was described in one newspaper as adopting a 'jaunty air'.[16] There is also the same acuity that owed less to any family pedigree or formal learning than to an intuitive grasp of the meaning of things and led him to acquire a reputation as a 'bush lawyer'.[17] And he too had a naive verbal dash that enabled him to stand tall among his more tongue-tied mates. We can see this in the two long epistles in which Kelly represented to the world the justification of his lifetime's actions – the Cameron letter and especially the Jerilderie letter of 1879. The latter also displayed an impish, yet pointed, humour which was directed at his favourite target, the police.

> The Queen must surely be proud of such heroic men as the Police and Irish soldiers, as It takes eight or eleven of the biggest mud crushers in Melbourne to take one poor half starved larrakin to the watchhouse. I have seen as many as eleven, big and ugly enough to lift Mount Macedon out of a crab hole, more like a species of baboon or Guerilla than a man, actually come into a court house and swear they could not arrest one eight stone larrakin . . .[18]

But there were, too, all the time germinating within him dangerous delusions regarding the degree to which his *fiat* was to hold sway, even in the neutral realm of the bush. On the one hand there was his own stated vulnerability as 'a widow's son' combined, on the other, with the determination that 'my orders *must be obeyed*'.[19]

The troubled 1870s

The Australian dream in the 1870s seemed more certain of realization than did the Canadian, where the onset of hard times soured ambitions. Yet things were not much different in north-eastern Victoria, where the land was so marginal that a desperate man's hope that somehow a decent living might be squeezed from it were more often than not dashed. In neither place was it a reasonable expectation to find much generosity of spirit. Besides the economy, some attention needs to be paid to the political and legal framework of both Ontario and Victoria. The grip of Canadian political parties upon the loyalties of the individual voter, newspaper editors and elite groups was substantial. Political conflict was played out with gusto and often marked by outright intimidation. This was because there were differences in ideas and ethnic flavour between the parties but even more because there were real favours to be won in patronage terms. Executive power was maintained by a police force that was so decentralized that it was difficult to ensure impartiality in its running. Although extra reinforcements might be provided by the county in exceptional circumstances, Lucan, which was formally incorporated as a village in 1872, appointed its own constables. The advantages flowing from having law enforcers with local knowledge were considerable but at the same time the clear danger was that the system was always likely to be skewed by political or factional considerations.

Victorian politics bore many similarities to Ontario's. Nevertheless, there was the difference that political alliances tended to be of a more shifting and transient kind, owing to the part-time nature of political life and the assumption of the mantle of independence by members of the Assembly. This lifted the yoke of party politics somewhat but it also helped develop a political climate within which there was widespread suspicion that individual ideals meant less than offers of office. In a colony where the opening up of the land was such a big issue there was a visceral certainty among the less well-off that pledges to fight the battles of the little man were forgotten once the temptations of Melbourne hove into view. As for the police, the situation could hardly have been more different from Ontario. Here they were directed from the capital. Their greater immunity from local pressures was often small recompense for their lack of knowledge of local conditions and people.

In trouble with the law

In the 1870s it is observable that a pattern emerges which holds true for both Ned Kelly and Will Donnelly. First, there were youthful brushes with the law. This stage was followed by attempts to take up legitimate occupations and to distance themselves from the epicentre of conflict. Such efforts were to prove unavailing, from which point the aroma of historical inevitability wafts over the remaining records. Slowly, but not always very surely, the forces pursuing Kelly and Donnelly closed in on their respective prey. Part of the explanation was that neither individual could break free from the suspicion which was attached to the family name. Ned was part of the Quinn clan, whose reputation for quarrelsomeness, 'getting even', brawling and thieving increased with each passing year. His father's brother, Jim Kelly, was sent to prison in 1868 as the result of a drunken rampage at the home of one of the married Quinn's daughters, whose own husband was in jail.[20] Similarly, the constant injunction from Johannah Donnelly to her boys never to forgive or to forget was no recipe for social peace.[21]

Ned Kelly served his first sentence in early 1871 on a charge of violent assault. He was charged, within a month of release, for stealing a horse. Now it has to be said that in north-eastern Victoria to be found guilty of this charge was in many ways as arbitrary and unlucky as acquiring a parking ticket today. Ned had been led to believe by a family friend, Wild Wright, that he (Wright) owned the horse. For this misinformation, which led to Kelly suffering a pistol whipping and a three-year sentence, he exacted his revenge upon Wright, after release, in a primitive twenty-round bare-knuckle fight. Soon it seemed that almost every member of the Quinn–Kelly clan was behind bars. Ned's brother, Jim, was sentenced to five years for cattle stealing in 1873. When Ned got out in 1874 he made a determined effort to change his ways. He took a job lumbering and did well. But a drunken spree in 1877 led to his arrest. Even worse, the policeman who escorted him to court, balked by Kelly's refusal to be handcuffed, humiliated and hurt the prisoner by grabbing his genitals in order to move him towards the doors of justice.

Will Donnelly faced his first suspicion of theft in 1871 and actually spent two weeks in the London jail before successfully proving that it was a case of mistaken identity. Shortly thereafter both Will and his brother, Jim, were again arrested on suspicion of theft but positive identification was not possible. However, when new evidence was brought forward, Jim quickly departed for Michigan, despite recently having taken up a farm of his own in Biddulph. The vacant farm proved too much of a temptation for a man by the name of Caswell, who tried to gain possession of it from the Canada Company. Having moved in, he began to suffer various depredations. When Jim did eventually return in 1874–5, he put pressure on Caswell to allow him to reclaim his land. There was haggling over the amount of compensation for improvements which Caswell should be allowed. Caswell's demands were turned down, only for the barn and sheds to be destroyed in a fire shortly afterwards. Slightly later, two of his horses were discovered with their throats slit. Eventually Caswell felt it more prudent to leave the area.

Such was their reputation that it led to great trouble when the Donnelly boys pursued romantic interests, a line of endeavour at which Will and his brothers proved to be adept. The object of Will's attentions was Margaret Thompson, but the difficulty was that her father would not abide the match. The result was the failure of an attempted elopement, engineered by Will and his friends. The bitter disappointment was partly assuaged by Will and Dan Keefe retiring to Lucan for liquid replenishment, only to be goaded into fisticuffs by the boasting of Margaret's brother William and his friend, James Toohey, of how they had foiled Donnelly's plans. The next year, 1875, Will did succeed in taking a wife, but only with the exertion of another elopement and the alienation of his wife's brothers, Joseph and Rhody Kennedy.

It was the opinion of one astute observer of the Lucan scene, the post-master, William Porte, that Will's influence over his brothers and friends was the main impetus behind the operations of what people called the Donnelly gang. Will's financial backing for a new venture, which began in May 1873, did little to change the Donnelly reputation. This was a stagecoach franchise which ran the thirty miles between London and Exeter. The difficulty was that there was stiff competition with a rival line. Soon incidents such as the breaking of axles began to happen to these competitors which bore every appearance of being the result of sabotage. Transcending this in importance, however, was an incident which occurred in Lucan in early 1876 on the occasion of the jollifications attendant upon an Irish wedding. Police-constable Coursey chose this completely inappropriate time to arrest Jim Donnelly on a charge of assault. Donnelly was being led peacefully away when Will scornfully rebuked him for deferring to such an unworthy fellow. Coursey retreated, but later that evening, as the celebrations were in full swing at Fitzhenry's Hotel, all hell broke loose when the police weighed in again. Will, besides wielding the shillelagh, brandished pistols and fired at least one inaccurate shot. His companion, William Farrell, did actually seriously wound one constable by gunfire. For his part in the affray Will got nine months, but (some said), by feigning sickness, he managed to breathe free air again within a month. All of this does seem to have had its effect on Will. Perhaps also he could see the writing on the wall so far as the stagecoach business was concerned, as the London Huron and Bruce railway was nearing completion. Will dropped his connection with the business and advised his brothers to do the same. Shortly he was to move to a farm in an adjoining township and begin a horse-breeding business. Thus it was, as Ray Fazakas says, that 'peace broke out in Lucan'.[22]

Final showdown in Kelly country, 1877–80

Ned Kelly always blamed the start of his troubles on the machinations of James Whitty, a powerful squatter, who when his stock began to disappear during 1877 fastened upon Kelly as the explanation. Through the Benalla Stock Preservation Association he was able to arrange for the advertisement of rewards for apprehension of the guilty parties. Early in 1878 warrants were issued for the arrest of both Ned and Dan Kelly on charges of horse stealing. There followed a confusing incident in which an incompetent police officer by the name of Fitzpatrick attempted to arrest the Kelly boys but succeeded only in getting himself shot in the wrist. In October Ellen Kelly was arrested as an accomplice of what was termed an attempted murder of Fitzpatrick. In the very same month that she had finally to give up her land, something which a neighbouring squatter had been angling to bring about over a long period, she also faced the court, along with a recently arrived infant, and was sentenced to three years in prison. This treatment of his mother marks a turning point in Kelly's life. Thus Ned and Dan, in company with companions of similar ethnic background, Steve Hart and Joe Byrne, took to the protection of the Wombat Hills. Only a few weeks later, with indignation undiminished, occurred at Stringybark Creek the fateful clash with a police patrol that ended in the death of three of the policemen. Naturally accounts of what happened differ as to who shot first and whether one of the policemen had been tortured and had his ear severed. John McQuilton thinks that the murders can be categorized as neither purely self-defence nor premeditated[23] but located presumably somewhere in the murky middle of these extremes.

Obviously, there was no question of going back now. If he had been arrested at this point there would have been no historical undertow from the life of Ned Kelly. Instead the police proceeded to alienate public opinion by holding numerous people on remand for excessively long periods on suspicion of aiding the Kelly gang. In addition, they also, by their bumbling inefficiency and cowardice, lost the sympathy of the public. Instead it was Kelly and his mates who gained growing admiration from the small selectors, the same class from which they themselves all came. One senior police officer wrote that 'the outlaws are considered heroes by a large portion of the population of the North Eastern District who, inured to the crime of horse and cattle stealing from an early age, look upon the police as their natural enemies.'[24] News of the movement of the police was quickly made known to Kelly by bush telegraph. The gang pulled off two daring bank robberies, one at Eoroa and another at Jerilderie, in both of which Kelly eschewed shows of violence and instead indulged in ostentatious acts of courtesy. It was also apparent that funds from these raids were filtering back to members of the family. Meanwhile the price on the gang's heads was being constantly upped by an increasingly jittery government.

In order to gain information regarding the gang's whereabouts the police hired informers. One of these, Aaron Sherritt, became a victim of the conflict when he was shot by his former friend, Joe Byrne, on Saturday 27 June 1880. This action was in concert with a much larger plan to take over the village of Glenrowan the following day and derail the train so as to prevent the arrival of police reinforcements. By Monday, partying and lack of sleep had somewhat blunted their readiness. But the biggest error was Ned's decision to allow a local schoolmaster to leave the siege on compassionate grounds. He was thus able to warn the train, enabling the police to surround the gang. Ned eluded them for a time but returned to fight it out with the police when it was obvious that other members of the gang were doomed. Ned appeared out of the morning mist, seemingly larger than life, encased in home-made iron armour. Bullets aimed at his exposed knees eventually brought him down. The rest of the gang lost their lives in the shoot-out or in the burning down of the hotel. Ned faced trial before Sir Redmond Barry, and when condemned to death by the Corkonian-born judge retorted 'I will see you there where I go.' This has become only slightly less famous than his comment 'Such is life' before being hanged on 11 November 1880 in Melbourne jail.

The Biddulph tragedy, 1877–80

However much Will Donnelly wished to change his ways or suffered a sense of foreboding, he neither could nor would do anything other than defend family honour when it was necessary to do so. And the fact was that several of his brothers, especially Tom and Bob, were arousing as much hostility as ever among an increasingly resentful community. When they managed to release their friend, Tommy Ryan, from the local lock-up the boasting of the Donnellys, Keefes and Feeheleys was intolerable to many. The family also stoutly, but somewhat improbably, maintained that young Jim Donnelly died of natural causes in 1877, the very day after a constable in Lucan had succeeded in wounding someone who was apparently attempting to set fire to a building. Adding to the enmity were those who felt that the Donnellys, especially Will, were doing better than others mainly because they were not averse to robbery and theft. Of course, as time went on, the possibility that any kind of misdemeanour would be blamed on a member of gang was all too likely.

That events in the township careered out of control can be attributed to a number of fundamental causes. One was when Bishop John Walsh made the mistake of appointing John Connolly as priest of St Patrick's in Biddulph.[25] Connolly seems to have been in no doubt that the primary cause of the violence and arson was the evil influence of the Donnellys. In no uncertain terms he let his congregation know of his judgement, going so far on several occasions as to refer to Will as a devil. When the priest tried to run Tommy Ryan out of the area, because he was suspected of having broken down a horse owned by a man called Kelly by running it up and down the township roads, Ryan came to Will for help. As a result Will penned a letter objecting to the priest's part in the affair. Superimposed upon this incident was the tension arising from the refusal of the Donnellys, as was true of many of their Catholic neighbours, to change their original political allegiance from the Liberal to the Conservative party. This exceptionalism only added to Connolly's determination to break the back of the Donnelly faction, who, upon Will's urging, now ceased to maintain their former sporadic attendance at church. Thus in June 1879 Connolly announced in church that he was inviting his congregation to join a 'property protection society'.

This attack on the Donnellys had been preceded by the growth of a permanent and organized secular opposition. The man who engineered it was James Carroll, who was also a second-generation immigrant from north Tipperary. He, like many of his co-adjutors, lamented the area's reputation and especially the slur it cast upon the Catholic Church and community. For a time in the late 1870s nearly every other court case in Lucan or London appeared to feature some variant of the Donnelly–Carroll dispute. Taking their cue in part from Connolly's well known opinions, Carroll's allies also began to meet regularly as a consequence of Tom Donnelly's ban on anyone threshing the grain of a particular individual whose testimony he believed had wrongly sent him to prison. This marked the conversion of the priest's open society into a secret one, bound together by oaths and by numerous blood ties. This development was also inspired by knowledge of such vigilante groups in the United States. It was even more ominous for the Donnellys when their opponents succeeded in getting James Carroll appointed as constable. As more and more properties went up in flames both in Lucan and in the township, the Donnellys suffered increased harassment at the hands of Carroll. By late 1879 the attempt of the Carroll faction to ostracize them was increasingly effective; the Donnellys felt keenly the cold-shouldering of many former friends. The slender thread by which the more reasonable heads within the vigilantes restrained the calls for action snapped when the barn of Grouchy Ryder, near neighbour of the Donnellys and member of the so-called 'Peace Society', was burned down in January 1880. Ryder laid a charge against the Donnellys but owing to the difficulty of getting witnesses the initial hearing was postponed until 4 February. Much greater retribution, however, was near at hand.

As the Donnellys lay in bed on the night of 3 February, attackers numbering thirty or so broke in and brutally murdered James, Johannah and Tom as well as their recently arrived niece from Tipperary. The attackers then moved on the few miles to Will's place to continue their grim business. It was only the next day that they discovered that the person who had been shot upon opening the door was John Donnelly, and not Will. The subsequent trial failed to establish the guilt of the parties, who were, nevertheless, well known and identified by a witness. Will Donnelly eventually moved away, his only consolation being perhaps the diary he kept until his death in 1897, in which he recorded the untimely end of so many of those individuals who had murdered his family.

Conclusion

This comparative study of two individuals and families in such disparate economic and geographical areas highlights the importance of certain common ethnic and cultural elements. This does not mean that one is forced to accept the idea that cultural forces are uppermost in the determining of Irish history or that some stereotypical 'wild' Irishman is being brought back to life.[26] Nevertheless, such a study does lead one to re-examine the notions of Kerby Miller regarding the tradition-bound *mentalité* of the Catholic peasantry, trying to cling to whatever it had by any possible means.[27] Qualifications, it is true, do come rushing to mind. One can hardly but be struck, for instance, by the entire lack of fatalism which characterized the Donnellys. Part of their present-day attraction derives from the way they shook their fist in the face of implacable odds.[28] Nor were the Kelly or Donnelly women at all downtrodden. Nor was either family afraid of the market economy. Yet it is in reading descriptions of the life style and attitudes of the southern Italian peasantry, especially the high regard for family and personal honour,[29] that one recognizes common modes of action and ways of thinking. And Celtic folkways were not ephemeral. Even in the urban setting of Chicago, for example, religious and ethnic self-sufficiency, in combination with nativism, ensured by the 1890s a retention of Irishness well into the third generation.[30]

It is difficult, however, to follow those biographers of the Donnellys, such as Miller and to a lesser extent Fazakas, who see the passions and violence of Biddulph as re-creations of feuds and rivalries inherited from Ireland. Both authors give credence to the view that violence was much more likely to break out on key Irish dates such as the anniversary of the hanging of the martyr Father Sheehy in Tipperary on 15 March 1766. Yet, even in Tipperary itself, this date had no relevance during the period 1837–47 compared with those which coincided with 'the cycle of the peasant economy, and rural custom'.[31] Another reason for discounting this view is that after nearly forty years in Canada the battle lines which were drawn up reflected mainly the tensions of the new society. However much their reputation for fraternization with Protestants may have tainted their reputation in Ireland, it is difficult to see that it counted for much in the enclosed world of Biddulph. It is equally difficult to accept those interpretations of Ned Kelly, most notably that of McQuilton, which rely mainly for their authenticity on the interaction between the conditions imposed by a marginal, scrub landscape and a struggle between selectors and squatters for possession of the land. The validity of this geographical interpretation is diminished by the fact that it can hardly accommodate the situation in Ontario at this time, where most land was owner-occupied and only 17 per cent was rented in 1881.[32]

Both the Kelly and the Donnelly families were involved in struggles over the possession of land. No issue could strike a more elemental Irish chord.[33] John Kelly passed on to his son the idea that 'land was life itself'.[34] The manner in which James Donnelly tried to preserve his 100 acres bore the imprint of his own upbringing. Previous studies by Mannion and others have shown a relationship between the density of the Irish population and the retention of cultural traits.[35] Biddulph was unusual in Canada in that the settlement was so ethnically and religiously homogeneous. In nearby Westminster township, on the other hand, there was an admixture of Irish Catholics and Protestants who coexisted in harmony.[36] Kelly did not emanate from such a 'pure' background. Yet the Irish were the second largest ethnic group in Australia and numerically in the majority in the rural areas of Victoria.[37] Similarly, Doug Morrissey has shown that the most active supporters of Ned Kelly were second-generation Irish immigrants.[38]

The instincts of the families were those which had been ingrained in them over generations by the necessity of finding a means of survival. Both Johannah and Will Donnelly were known to swear vengeance against those who disputed the family's cultural right of way, as did Ned when he heard that his mother had been sentenced to prison.[39] Any offence, however slight, demanded punishment. One walked warily near the Donnellys and Kellys. If one was on friendly terms, then all was well, but if their opinion changed, for whatever reason, then violence was always likely.[40] Sometimes there would be a warning shot first, perhaps by some injury inflicted upon an animal. Or a threatening letter might be despatched. It was a Manichaean world which they inhabited. Also, as at home, protest could collude with acts of criminality. An obvious corollary to this was the feeling that self-policing was the natural way to solve disputes and much preferable to having to submit to outside interference. No more than Ned Kelly did the Biddulph Irish expect to get justice from English law or courts.[41] An added factor in the creation of social conflict was the fondness for strong drink exhibited by both families and individuals under study. Those who were taking up the new fad of temperance were not those, on the whole, who remained the most stubbornly Irish.

The Donnellys were the victim of new colonial attitudes regarding the Church and respectability. As pre-Famine immigrants the Kellys and Donnellys did not come from a particularly religious society. Ellen Kelly left the Church, choosing to get married in 1874 via a Primitive Methodist ceremony.[42] In remote Victoria, where the reach of the Church was feeble, that did not matter very much, but in Ontario, surrounded by a resurgent Church, Will Donnelly could not adjust to its new pretensions. The arson and violence associated with the family lowered the reputation of the

Church and the community. Similarly, Ned Kelly's horse stealing and defiance of authority offended the moral sensibilities of the Victorian elite and promised to set an example of disrespect for property and authority of frightening dimensions. It was the moral anarchy which was set loose in both societies that constituted the demand for its own extinction.

The boys' upbringing had imposed few, if any, restraints upon the exercise of their will. Yet this should not condone an interpretation which dispenses with Ned by calling him a paranoid and William by labelling his family as the Black Donnellys.[43] Their lives, of course, cannot be explained entirely by the inheritance of family and social conflict. Yet if the substance of what Ned and Will fought for was that for which their parents had prepared them, the style with which they went about it was the result of an intricate weave of Irish and colonial materials. Ned Kelly's flash dress, talk and behaviour were meant to impress his friends and intimidate his enemies. As a pose it appealed mightily to the larrikin elements' liking of anti-social behaviour. The hat, the sash, the pipe – all in place with a jaunty self-confidence – partook of an Australian leveller–larrikin sense of distinctiveness in dress and speech as well as of the very similar concerns of an Irish tradition of flamboyant bandit leaders.[44] Similarly, Will Donnelly's attire and general demeanour were meant to impress his peers with his superiority and invincibility. As Hobsbawm reminds us, it was part of the peasant outlook to feel that oppression could only be countered by 'being tough or the friends of toughs'.[45]

All this added to the theatricality that was so essential a part of each man. Ned was especially conscious of himself fitting into a tradition and playing a role. One of his toasts at the last at Glenrowan was to the memory of Harry Power and the other bushrangers who had gone before. Will too seemed to seek the spotlight of public attention. As one astute commentator put it:

A Donnelly [display of] magnetic exuberance rouses and impresses those watchers around them. Donnellys seem to *need* that added intensity of living which the consciousness of an influenced circle of persons around them provides. The historical William Donnelly who gathers a gang about him ('me and my adventurers') is understandable in this light – a Donnelly deliberately generating an audience, a sphere of influence, which enlarges his own experience of life.[46]

What comes to mind is Will seeing off a menacing crowd in search of a stolen heifer in 1879 by pulling out his fiddle and playing to such effect that it must have made the members of the 'Peace Society' feel like criminals at a child's birthday party. Or could anything theatrically match Kelly's iron-clad finale at Glenrowan? Some have seen this armour as the beginnings of an army whose destiny it was to proclaim a republic of Victoria.[47] That Ned showed a disposition to harangue his captured audience is undeniable but the main theme was always the iniquities of police persecution suffered by his family at the hands of traitorous Irish personnel (those who had 'deserted the shamrock'). Therefore the armour was just one more prop – as extraordinarily 'unique and impracticable as it was true to Kelly's spirit; a grand, misguided gesture.'[48]

Such playing to the crowd fitted in well with Ned's assumption of the traditional Australian role of the social bandit.[49] In many ways the caprice which this allows is flattering to the actor. Ned could then also articulate the grievances of the small man. That it had later resonance was due to the fact that the values of egalitarianism and mateship were taken up and propagated by a set of urban writers mainly associated with the *Bulletin*.[50] In addition, until well into the 1930s Irish particularalism provided a ready-made audience. Social banditry was an ideal vehicle for Ned in that it allowed of a marriage between the smouldering sense of wrong suffered both in the before and in the now. The materials with which to portray the Donnellys as social bandits are probably there. They had a habit of collecting and helping the oddities and strays in the community. The William Farrell who was present at the showdown at Fitzhenry's Hotel was the son of the man killed by James Donnelly. Nothing in the way of factual incongruity, however, should have stood in the way, as the evolution of the original Robin Hood story makes clear, or the even more astonishing inclusion of Jessie James among the canon.[51] But the majority of Canadians have been uncomfortable with the legacy of William Donnelly. For a province guarded over by Orange Toronto, the Belfast of the North, it was always unlikely that any kind of exceptionalism would operate in the favour of a Catholic.[52] Also, Will was a victim of his own people and stood for the fear, as had the assassination of D'Arcy McGee in 1868, that the ills of old Ireland would be visited upon the new land. As well, geography imposed conditions inimical to survival, as James Donnelly discovered. In the end the mythical social bandit was not demanded by the Canadian experience. Perversely, Canadians took as their cultural icon the Mountie, who stood not for the gallant individual but for social cohesion and the maintenance of law and order.[53] Little wonder that the impact of Ned Kelly and Will Donnelly has been so different in their respective societies.[54]

Yet, if categorized differently by their national histories, Ned and Will can quite legitimately, for the sake of one last comparison, be joined together and placed alongside a plentiful company of American adventurers such as Jessie James, Billie the Kid and the feuding families of West Virginia and Kentucky. The dates on the tombstones have an eerie conspiratorial sameness about them. But always nemesis took identical form. The obtrusive agent of modernity was the railway. All these actors had invested the meaning of their lives within the confines of a culture now under threat. Will Donnelly's stagecoach company is emblematic of the rest. What we have seen played out in these dramas is the forlorn retreat of a band of anachronistic battlers in the face of the advancing tide of a new stage of economic development

Notes

1. Patrick J. O'Farrell, 'The Irish in Australia and New Zealand, 1791–1870', in *A New History of Ireland*, V, *Ireland under the Union, 1801–70*, Clarendon Press, Oxford, 1989, p. 673.
2. As quoted in Thomas G. McGrath, 'Interdenominational relations in pre-Famine Tipperary', in Wm. William Nolan, ed., and Thomas G. McGrath, associate ed., *Tipperary: History and Society. Interdisciplinary Essays on the History of an Irish County*, Geography Publications, Dublin, 1985, p. 276.
3. J. S. Donnelly, Jr, 'The Whiteboy movement, 1761–5', *Irish Historical Studies*, XXI, 1978, pp. 20, 21, 37.
4. T. Jones Hughes, 'Landholding and settlement in County Tipperary in the nineteenth century', in Nolan and McGrath, *Tipperary*, pp. 340–53.
5. Michael Beames, *Peasants and Power: the Whiteboy Movements and their Control in pre-Famine Ireland*, Harvester Press, Brighton, 1983, p. 97.
6. Bob Reece, 'Ned Kelly and the Irish connection', in Carl Bridge, ed., *New Perspectives in Australian History*, Sir Robert Menzies Centre for Australian Studies, London, 1990, pp. 77–9.
7. McGrath 'Interdenominational relations', pp. 283–4.
8. W. D. Butt, 'The Donnellys: History, Legend, Literature', Ph.D. thesis, University of Western Ontario, 1977, II, p. 369. Dr Tom Power has pointed out to me that elopement was a relatively common social happening in pre-Famine Ireland, often spurred on by hopes of economic improvement.
9. Ray Fazakas, *The Donnelly Album*, Macmillan, Toronto, 1977, chapter 3. Information concerning the Donnellys comes from this book, unless otherwise noted.
10. John McQuilton, *The Kelly Outbreak, 1878–1880: the Geographical Dimensions of Social Banditry*, Melbourne University Press, Melbourne, 1979, pp. 74–5. Information concerning the Kellys comes from this book unless otherwise noted.
11. Butt, 'The Donnellys', II, p. 371.
12. C. M. H. Clark, *A History of Australia*, IV, Melbourne University Press, Melbourne, 1978, p. 325.
13. *The Daily Advertiser* (London, Ontario), 17 April 1872.
14. Orlo Miller, *The Donnellys must Die*, Macmillan, Toronto, 1987, p. 65.
15. Miller, *The Donnellys must Die*, p. 80.
16. Charles Osborne, *Ned Kelly*, Blond, London, 1970, pp. 17–19.
17. F. Clune, *The Kelly Hunters*, Angus & Robertson, Sydney, 1955, pp. 125–6.
18. McQuilton, *The Kelly Outbreak*, pp. 208–9.
19. Clark, *History of Australia*, pp. 328–9.
20. Clune, *The Kelly Hunters*, pp. 32–3, 48, 62–4
21. T. P. Kelley *The Black Donnellys*, Signet, New York, 1955, p. 12.
22. Fazakas, *The Donnelly Album*, p. 114.
23. McQuilton, *The Kelly Outbreak*, pp. 100, 147.
24. McQuilton, *The Kelly Outbreak*, p. 139.
25. M. Power, 'John Walsh', in *Dictionary of Canadian Biography*, XII, University of Toronto Press, Toronto, 1990, p. 1086.
26. Patrick J. O'Farrell, *Ireland's English Question*, Batsford, London, 1971; David A. Wilson, *The Irish in Canada*, Canadian Historical Association, Ottawa, 1989, p. 12.
27. Kerby A. Miller, *Emigrants and Exiles*, Oxford University Press, Oxford, 1985, p. 556.

28. This is true for James Reaney both in his creative writing and in his entry on James Donnelly in the *Dictionary of Canadian Biography*, X, University of Toronto Press, Toronto, 1972, pp. 234–5.

29. Francis A. J. Ianni, 'The Mafia and the web of kinship', in Francis A. J. Ianni and Elizabeth Reuss Ianni, eds., *The Crime Society*, New American Library, New York, 1976, pp. 41–5.

30. Ellen, Skerett, 'The Catholic dimension', in Lawrence J. McCaffrey, Ellen Skerett, M. F. Funchion and Charles Fanning, eds., *The Irish in Chicago*, University of Illinois Press, Urbana, Ill., 1987, pp. 40–1.

31. M. R. Beames, 'Rural conflict in pre-Famine Ireland: peasant assassinations in Tipperary, 1837–1847', in C. H. E. Philpin, ed., *Nationalism and Popular Protest in Ireland*, Cambridge University Press, Cambridge, 1987, p. 276.

32. W. L. Marr, 'Nineteenth-century tenancy rates in Ontario's counties, 1881 to 1891', *Journal of Social History*, 21, 1987–8, p. 753.

33. It is worth while to keep in mind Michael Katz's surprise at finding such a high rate of house ownership in Hamilton, Ontario, among Irish Catholic labourers, as compared with British immigrants, in the mid-nineteenth century. See M. Katz, *The People of Hamilton, Canada West*, Harvard University Press, Cambridge, Mass., 1975, p. 83.

34. K. McMenomy, *Ned Kelly: the Authentic Illustrated Story*, Curry O'Neil Ross, South Yarra, 1984, p. 20.

35. John J. Mannion, *Irish Settlements in Eastern Canada*, University of Toronto Press, Toronto, 1974.

36. Cecil J. Houston and William J. Smyth, *Irish Emigration and Canadian Settlement: Patterns, Links, and Letters*, University of Toronto Press, Toronto, 1990, pp. 178–80.

37. Donald H. Akenson, *Small Differences: Irish Catholics and Irish Protestants, 1815–1922*, McGill–Queen's University Press, Kingston, Ont., 1988, p. 66.

38. Doug Morrissey, 'Ned Kelly's sympathisers', *Historical Studies*, 18, 1978, p. 296.

39. Fazakas, *The Donnelly Album*, pp. 104–5, 154.

40. Max Brown, *Australian Son: the Story of Ned Kelly*, Georgian House, Melbourne, 1956, pp. 30, 54.

41. Miller, *Emigrants and Exiles*, p. 107. In the end this tendency, of course, worked against the Donnellys. It seems to me that traditional peasant views about justice fitted in well with the localism, instrumentalism and, indeed, legalism of vigilantism. For the latter see R. M. Brown, *Strain of Violence: Historical Studies of American Violence and Vigilantism*, Oxford University Press, New York, 1975, p. 153.

42. Clune, *The Kelly Hunters*, pp. 106–7.

43. K. Dunstan, *Saint Ned*, Methuen, Sydney, 1980, p. 12.

44. Most informative on this subject is Patrick O'Sullivan, 'A literary difficulty in explaining Ireland: Tom Moore and Captain Rock, 1824', in Roger Swift and Sheridan Gilley, eds., *The Irish in Britain, 1815–1939*, Pinter, London, 1989, especially pp. 248–9. For the Australian tradition see Noel McLachlan, *Waiting for the Revolution: a History of Australian Nationalism*, Penguin, Harmondsworth, 1989, p. 120.

45. E. Hobsbawm, *Primitive Rebels*, Manchester University Press, Manchester, 1959, p. 39.

46. Butt, 'The Donnellys', II, p. 380.

47. Ian Jones, 'A new view of Ned Kelly', in Wangaratta Adult Education Centre, *Ned Kelly: Man and Myth*, Cassell, Wangaratta, Australia, 1968, pp. 169–73.

48. McMenomy, *Ned Kelly*, p. 143.

49. Russel Ward, *The Australian Legend*, Oxford University Press, Melbourne, Press, Melbourne, 1958, pp. 25–31.

50. Richard White, *Inventing Australia*, Allen & Unwin, Sydney, 1981, pp. 106–9, 153–4.

51. R. B. Dobson and J. Taylor, *Rymes of Robyn Hood*, Sutton, Gloucester, 1989, pp. 278–9.

52. See J. R. Miller, 'Anti-Catholic thought in Victorian Canada', *Canadian Historical Review*, IXVI, 1985; Canada's greatest sporting hero at this time, Ned Hanlon, the rower, was always held somewhat at arm's length by his home town, Toronto, because of his working-class Irish background. See Don Morrow, Mary Keyes, W. Simpson, F. Cosentino and R. Lappage, eds., *A Concise History of Sport in Canada*, Oxford University Press, Don Mills, 1989, p. 32.

53. R. Thacker, 'Mountie versus outlaw: inventing the western hero', *Journal of Canadian Studies*, 20, 1985, pp. 161–8.

54. Perhaps I should not assume too easily Ned Kelly's status in present-day Australia. Upon informing one academic from Victoria of the object of my study, her instant retort was 'Why, he was nothing but a horse thief.' For the view that if 'you ask a schoolchild to name a national hero he might just come up with Kelly' see Linda Christmas, *The Ribbon and the Ragged Square: an Australian Journey*, Penguin, Harmondsworth, 1987, p. 62.

Acknowledgements

I should like to thank Professor Roy Foster, Dr Tom Power and Dr Ged Martin for their kind willingness to read and comment upon a draft of this chapter.

6 A 'Bigger, better and busier Boston' The pursuit of political legitimacy in America: the Boston Irish, 1890–1920

Alun Munslow

This chapter examines the search for Irish Catholic political acceptance beyond the homeland, specifically in Boston, Massachusetts, during the period of the rise of the American corporate state.[1] Because the search for Irish legitimacy necessitates understanding the context of Irish emigrationism to post-Civil War America,[2] the narrative encompasses the complex relationship of ethnocultural dominance and subordination, the Irish Catholic politico as cultural mediator, and, finally, a judgement on the part played by the Irish leadership in helping shape and cohere the wider corporate industrial state. The key figure explored in this context is John F. Fitzgerald, the first American-born Irish Catholic mayor of Boston.

Placed in its global framework, Irish emigrationism was mainly directed to the United States from the mid-1870s through to the early 1920s and the advent of immigration restriction legislation.[3] By the mid-nineteenth century Irish Catholics were entering the United States in their millions. By 1890 virtually half the total American Catholics had parents born in Ireland.[4] While the celebrated historian of the Irish, Roy Foster, seems content not to question the Irish preference for city life in America, even echoing David Fitzpatrick's view that they constituted a model industrial proletariat, Donald Akenson reminds us we would do well to view the urban predilection of the Irish in its fullest perspective, by which he means noting their rural inclinations right up to the 1870s.[5] The cultural preference of the Irish for life in the American city may, however, be readily grasped from the statistics.[6] Of the forty-three most populous cities in America in 1870 the Irish were the largest first-generation immigrant group in twenty-seven, and second in the rest.[7] In Jersey City in 1870, for example, 55·2 per cent of the foreign-born were first-generation Irish, and they were not displaced until 1920, by the Italians.[8] While, as Akenson says, the pattern of Irish settlement remains highly complex, it is clear that the Irish Catholic inflows during the period of America's *postbellum* industrial revolution were metropolitan in destination.[9]

As Kerby Miller points out, Irish emigrationism was one response to the advent of the modern industrialization process. Irish nationalism was another, and Irish–American nationalism linked both.[10] Like Akenson Miller emphasizes the diversity of the American experience, but also insists that the Irish 'remained in figurative if not in literal "exile", increasingly divided from Ireland in time and circumstance . . .'.[11] This estrangement from the homeland grew out of the experience of living in the new environment of the industrial city and business enterprise culture, and it had several effects. While there was a continued if increasingly irrelevant Irish–American nationalism for the majority, of even more significance was a great if often thwarted desire to overcome what Miller describes as the 'scars of poverty and proscription'.[12]

It was as 'the pioneers of the American urban ghetto' with their poverty, alcohol abuse, crime and psychological trauma that the Irish still managed to become 'the masters of urban America'.[13] While becoming the masters they continued to experience the feelings of marginality acknowledged by Miller and recognized at the time by commentators like Viscount Bryce, who in his monumental *American Commonwealth* claimed that the urban Irish 'retained their national spirit and disposition to act together', thus becoming 'potent in city politics'.[14] In 1894 nativist John Paul Bocock judged the influence of the Irish to be the result of 'an hereditary aptitude for securing such offices as those of alderman, councilman, policeman, municipal clerk, bureau chief and mayor', concluding they had 'entered the race with unflagging effort and unfailing success'.[15]

For the Irish Catholics urban politics was the primary means of negotiating the contours of cultural dominance and subordinance in the New World. Municipal politics became the key discourse that in Boston mediated the dominant Yankee Protestant and subordinate Irish Catholic relationship. The intercessionist role between the two cultures was acted out by the Catholic Church and the Irish political leadership. But while Catholicism constituted an alternative, even oppositional institutional and cultural framework that served to defend the essence of Irishness, separate cultural development was never destined to be a viable proposition. The great irony of the Irish experience in urban America is that pride in a national Catholic culture was nurtured by a politics of separatism, which in its turn demanded civic and, ultimately, a kind of social assimilation. The history of Irish Catholics in the American city is thus the negotiation of the terms of exile by their political leaders.

The emergence of the industrialized corporate state was accompanied by the urban reform movement called Progressivism, a response to industrialism that challenged the new age of the trust, the slum, the political boss, the culture of inequality, Social Darwinism and the Gospel of Wealth.[16] The search for Irish political accommodation led by Fitzgerald among others is thus to be found within the constitution of a cultural hegemony rooted in the decline of entrepreneurial and individualistic values and their replacement by the progressive discourse and practices of a new age of welfare-oriented corporate capitalism.[17]

The political history of Boston during the industrial and Progressive era, though usually described by historians as an ethnocultural confrontation between the dominant Protestant native elite and the emergent immigrant Catholic masses, was never simply a transfer of political power institutionalized within the confines of the Democratic Party.[18] There were clashes within the ranks of the Catholic leadership itself, as one might expect during an era of cultural transformation. Not only were the Irish succeeded by the 'new' immigrant influx in the 1890s and 1900s, but there was also an intra-Irish conflict in the Democratic Party as a result of the emergence of a new generation of Irish politicos like Fitzgerald, who turned out to be the most significant figure in the most Irish of cities outside the homeland. He stood for the emergent Irish bourgeoisie, a case of poacher turned gamekeeper as an ex-ward boss driven to seek political office by personal ambition and the desire to unify all the Irish in the city, and show the Yankees they were just as good Americans. Fitzgerald's importance is further established through his recognition that as the process of post-industrial modernization advanced ethnicity ceased to follow strict class boundaries. Because the ideology of class cut across ethnicity, his leadership increasingly served a burgeoning industrial and business bourgeoisie decoupled from its ethnic origins – a new social formation rooted in economic power rather than ethnic cleavage.[19]

Behind the electoral fights for control of Boston's city hall, as in many other American cities there was, therefore, a more significant development – the creation of values that would incorporate immigrants, allow the indigenous elites not only to come to terms with a transformed political culture, but which also rapidly destroyed the ethnic bloc vote and the Irish boss system. While it is clear the Irish and Anglo bourgeoisie came into conflict,[20] what is obscured is the process whereby a class-based political culture was created as the central feature of a new corporate neo-liberalism.[21] The appeal of neo-liberal ideas to the foreign-born was a central element in the metropolitian Progressive movement. That the politico could be central to this highly complex process is shown in the history of Progressive politics in Boston, and specifically the clash of Irish Catholic and native Yankee.[22]

Along with many other so-called bosses Fitzgerald acted as an agent of political incorporation, mediating the dominant reform values of Progressive bourgeois neo-liberalism for the foreign-born.[23] He recast these values to allow both the Yankee cultural elite and the subordinate immigrant groups jointly to create America's post-industrial corporate state.[24] In cultural terms the function of neo-liberal reformism was to accommodate and assimilate subordinate ethnic cultures. As a functionary of Progressive ideology the problem that faced Fitzgerald was not could this be done, but how?

From the 1880s, the decade before Fitzgerald rose to prominence, Boston's Irish Catholics began to acquire political power in order to smooth the accommodation process, constitute an American-Irish consciousness, and contribute to the creation of modern America.[25] For historian Daniel

Moynihan this made them essentially conservative and antagonistic to social change.[26] The history of the Irish in Boston's politics, however, shows it not to have been so. The Irish took their political tone from the radicalism of American urban liberalism as personified by the first Irish mayor of the city, Hugh O'Brien. Mayor O'Brien's career attests to the accuracy of the interpretation of the historian of Irish politics Thomas N. Brown, that the Irish may have been rebels in Ireland, but they were politicians in America.[27]

Primarily O'Brien attempted to facilitate a relationship between government and citizen hallmarked by co-operation rather than conflict. This was witnessed in the alliance of Yankee Democrat and Irish Catholic Democrat in the 1880s and 1890s, and then again in the 1900s and 1910s when a mature and responsible Irish Catholic leadership experienced political power and office. The mayoralty of Hugh O'Brien (1885–8) can be seen as firmly establishing the template for the search for Irish political legitimacy followed by John Fitzgerald. O'Brien's platform was built on by expedient coalition politics, with Yankee Democrats as well as the ward bosses led by Irish Democratic ward boss Patrick J. 'Pea Jacket' Maguire. O'Brien's policy of co-operation, mediation and facilitation centred not only only on issues of common interest which crossed the Yankee–Irish divide like 'home rule' (the demand for the separation of certain city government functions from control by the state) and control of the city's police, but also on others like female suffrage, prohibition, controlling the physical growth of the city (the annexation movement), and defusing the parochial–public school debate. His policy of *rapprochement* appealed both to the burgeoning bureaucratic-reformer elements and the Yankee business bourgeoisie, prompting 100 prominent citizens to renominate him in 1885. Nevertheless, the established anti-Catholic nativists were successful in defeating him in the 1888 election.[28]

The worst economic depression of the nineteenth century began in 1893 and, as retrenchment replaced growth, an unofficial municipal welfarism emerged to cope with the unemployment.[29] The Irish ward bosses increasingly took it upon themselves also to lend comfort to their expanding 'new' immigrant as well as poor native clientele. The sharpening class cleavages within the city produced by the depression presented new challenges to the Irish leaders as they also faced up to the increasingly varied character of their immigrant constituencies, and the collapse of traditional solid Irish support and ethnic bloc voting.[30]

It is with John Fitzgerald, then, that the search for Irish political legitimacy reaches its apogee. As the first American-born son of Irish immigrants to be elected mayor of Boston he was ideally placed to mediate between the two cultures. He possessed all the classic trappings of the political boss, not least a mellifluous voice given to bursting into song, plus an affable and avuncular personality.[31] Born in 1863 in a tenement in Boston's North End, his father died in 1885, and he became responsible for his large family. Unable to get a job in a bank 'or a white collar job with a railroad',[32] he turned to the boss of Ward 6, Matthew Keany, for help. He was soon working for Keany with the Irish and the growing numbers of 'new' immigrants from central and south-eastern Europe. In 1890 he was elected to represent the North End's Ward 6 on Boston's common council. His political career thus coincided with the reform movement as well as the influx of 'new' immigrants. After a brief but successful council career during which he helped shape the built environment in which immigrants lived by having several hundred thousand dollars voted to construct a public park in the North End, Fitzgerald succeeded as boss of Ward 6 in 1892 upon the demise of Keany.[33]

The role of the corrupt ward boss was too limiting for Fitzgerald, however, and he soon set his eyes on establishing a reformist reputation, preferably at the level of state and national politics, but only as a means toward his ultimate goal, that of becoming mayor of Boston. Recognizing the factional nature of the city's Democratic Party politics, with as many bosses as wards, Fitzgerald determined on a more circuitous route to the mayoral office by standing for the thirty-five-member state senate.[34] He quickly built a personal machine, the Jefferson Club, to facilitate his 1892 fight for office,[35] and the two terms he served as state senator were to be crucial to his later development as a mediator between the two cultures. In the State House he established his Progressive credentials by supporting legislation to outlaw sweat-shops, Bills to limit the hours of work of women and children, and attempts to establish minimum wage levels in Massachusetts factories.[36] Throughout the 1890s, while moving in bourgeois Progressive circles, he continued to pursue Irish political legitimacy. Rather than being simply the corrupt politico he was depicted as by the Yankee press, he was in effect proving to be the restrained, even polite face of political accommodation. Meanwhile his ultimate ambition to be mayor of Boston remained. His political advance was to be achieved in the interim by running for the Ninth Congressional District in the House of Representatives.[37]

As always Fitzgerald was in need of allies, and he found himself seeking the goodwill of the independent-minded local boss Martin Lomasney to obtain the Democratic nomination. In 1894, as at so many other times in Boston's Democratic Party history, the collapse of one coalition spawned another.[38] At this time Lomasney happened to be in conflict with the Irish leadership.[39] Lomasney saw Fitzgerald's run for office as an opportunity to dish his opponents within the party. Calling upon all his political reserves, Lomasney boosted Fitzgerald's career by not only getting him the nomination but ultimately assuring his electoral success.[40] Fitzgerald's election to the House indicated more than Lomasney's influence, however. More significantly, it revealed the force of Fitzgerald's defence of his immigrant constituency amid the growth of virulent anti-Catholic hysteria, particularly at a time of industrial disputes, lock-outs and strikes.[41]

Fitzgerald spent the rest of the 1890s in Washington, serving three terms. One of only three Catholics in the House, he defended his religion and the immigrant against the attacks of the radical right. This policy met with the substantial approval of the voice of the Archdiocese of Boston, the Irish nationalist newspaper the Boston *Pilot*. Reporting on Fitzgerald's 4 July 1896 speech at the civic celebration, the *Pilot* claimed that it was 'a masterly oration, defending the right of asylum for foreigners in the land of free-dom'.[42] This speech was the confirmation of Fitzgerald's *rapprochement* with the Yankee elite. He spoke of the recently built monument to the Irish poet and patriot John Boyle O'Reilly, saying:

> . . . it not only commemorates the virtue of a great soul, but also emphasises the fact that our so-called foreign citizens are equally interested in adorning our city with the most beautiful creations of art and sculpture. It serves as another instance of the broad Americanism of all classes.[43]

Although such comments were more likely to influence the Irish and other 'so-called foreign citizens' in 1896, he was nevertheless establishing himself as the voice of a new cultural unity.[44]

By the late 1890s the city looked to be tightly controlled by the Democratic Party. Fitzgerald judged that his time had come to bid for the mayoralty. Prepared though he was, there was one politician even he could not successfully challenge, and that was the ex-US consul-general in London and Irish nationalist Patrick Andrew Collins. When Collins returned from his London appointment he found the Boston Democratic Party in disarray after the death of Maguire in 1896, and he sought to inject a degree of coherence through a bid for its leadership. Like Fitzgerald, Collins felt that a Democrat would undoubtedly win the 1899 mayoral election. Certainly the pro-Collins Boston *Herald* saw no reason to expect anything different:

> The mayoralty election does not seem likely to be productive of any degree of excitement . . . General Collins possesses the qualities of popularity . . . that when the votes are counted . . . it will be found that he has been elected by a majority [because] his popularity is not confined to members of his own party.[45]

Unfortunately the *Herald*, the Democratic Party, the Democratic bosses' informal club called the Board of Strategy and Collins had all misjudged the state of ethnocultural politics in the city. They had not realized it was in terminal decline.[46] Collins's opponent was Thomas N. Hart, a conservative Republican first elected to the mayoralty a decade earlier. Running on an anti-extravagance and anti-boss platform that also included promises to introduce the eight-hour day, lower taxes, home rule for the city and sound business practice, Hart was elected by a solid majority.[47] The electoral upset confirmed in Fitzgerald's mind the correctness of his policies. As he realized, the breadth of Hart's appeal was the most crucial factor in the victory, although it was undoubtedly helped by the Democratic boss John R. Murphy bolting the regular Democratic machine.[48] Rather than simple intra-Irish squabbling throwing an election to the Republicans, Collins's defeat was, as Fitzgerald knew, the result of the growing desertion of the Democratic Party by their traditional ethnic constituents. A more basic cultural transformation was under way in Boston's political structure, a shift not only recognized by Fitzgerald but one he could exploit.

With mixed feelings Fitzgerald witnessed Collins's stand and two substantial electoral victories in 1901 and 1903, but he knew they were not the
result of massive Irish or 'new' immigrant votes. In fact there was actually a
reduction in immigrant support for the Democratic nominee within the
context of an overall fall in the political participation rate.[49] The boss
factionalism of 1899 and Republican electoral success were in effect the
product of structural changes in the electorate and the consequent uncertainty of traditional Irish partisanship rather than a cause. Collins's victories
were the successes of possessing a national name and reputation and an
appeal for many sections of Boston's electorate. As the Boston *Pilot* interpreted his 1901 victory, 'General Collins won his election by the votes of
citizens of all races and classes.'[50]

The hegemonic process is evidenced by Fitzgerald's continuance of
O'Brien's and Collins's policy to appeal to a broad constituency. The
significance lay in his strategy to create a new working alliance between the
increasingly unbossed immigrant groups, the ward politicos themselves and
the growing power of the reform impulse represented by the founding of
the Good Government Association in 1903.[51] This was his task if he wanted
to become mayor and forge a new political culture out of an amalgam of
middle-class reformism and the practical traditions of active boss politics.
The contingent then intervened in Fitzgerald's career with the unexpected
death of Patrick Collins in September 1905. The gap that was left in the
Democratic ranks precipitated a seismic contest for his successor.[52] The
other bosses on the Board of Strategy sensed Fitzgerald waiting ready, with
his machine, his populist-Progressive politics and his driving personality.
The Strategy Board made the primaries, as the Boston *Herald* said, 'the fight
of their lives', realizing that in Fitzgerald they had an opponent who had an
organization 'in nearly every ward in the city'.[53]

Using the latest technology – the automobile – to campaign in all wards
was insufficient for Fitzgerald to ensure victory. He had to respond in kind
to the attack of the other bosses. He called a secret meeting at the Somerset
Hotel of the regulars as well as the other, less powerful, younger, ambitious
and out-of-favour bosses. At this meeting Fitzgerald promised them that
any administration of his would assure their interests.[54] The anti-Fitzgerald
coalition soon collapsed.[55] To further ensure the success of his bid,
Fitzgerald invoked the discourse of Progressivism whenever possible to
appeal to liberals and was even seen associating with starchy reformers like
John B. Moran, who since the mid-1890s had been among the most
outspoken critics of the Democratic machine. Fitzgerald's desire to win
even prompted him to claim that Moran's victory in the district attorney
election encouraged him to believe that the policy which he, Fitzgerald,
advocated 'to banish graft and jail the grafters' was a policy which 'the
people will endorse on primary day'.[56]

Through this appropriation of Progressive discourse as well as secret
pledges of patronage to the party regulars Fitzgerald succeeded at the
primaries by nearly 4,000 votes, inflicting the greatest defeat on the
Democratic Party machine in its history.[57] With Fitzgerald's name on the
ticket, regulars fell in behind the rising star and his Somerset House clique –

all except Lomasney, who had supported another Democratic candidate in the primaries.[58] Lomasney's response was to try to teach Fitzgerald and the regulars a lesson on the day of the poll. Until the eve of the 1905 election he refused to say which candidate he would support, although the rumours were proved correct when he came out for the Republican candidate, Louis Frothingham.[59]

Fitzgerald's victory was assisted substantially because there were two Republican candidates, the official party candidate and Republican Speaker of the Massachusetts House of Representatives, Louis Frothingham, and a former judge of the municipal court of Boston, Henry Dewey, running as an independent Republican. Dewey had been determined for several months before the death of Collins to head the Republican ticket. After Collins's death and the split in the Democratic ranks Republican managers saw a greater chance of victory with a better-known candidate than Dewey, hence the nomination of Frothingham. An angry Dewey stayed in the race and effectively split the Republican vote.[60]

Fitzgerald's 1905 campaign proved to be the most important in the history of Irish accommodation, given his neo-liberal policies and cross-cultural electoral coalition. His campaign successfully promoted pro-business Progressivism as the policy with the widest appeal to native and immigrant alike. Fitzgerald's policies included the extension of the city's dock facilities, a promise to set up a commercial high school to provide practical industrial training for the sons and daughters of both Yankee and Irish, and an equitable taxation structure 'so that all sections and all classes may have their share of the burdens of government'.[61] In addition he promised to tackle the grafters 'of every stripe, whether they be Republican architects or Democratic contractors'.[62] Placing himself squarely among the most virtuous, famous and active Progressive mayors in America, he said:

> Our opponents assert that the mayor of Boston can do nothing along the lines I have indicated . . . They forget that Roosevelt settled the coal strike by exercising the moral potency of his office and that a Jones of Toledo and a Johnson of Cleveland occupy a larger place in the life of their communities than the circumscribed area of their official duties.[63]

Fitzgerald's political axiom, a 'bigger, better, and busier Boston', was couched in the rhetoric of reform and it pictured his opponent as the symbol of a Republican caucus that consistently voted against reducing the working hours of women and children, against cutting train fares in and out of the city, against the eight-hour day, against the popular election of senators, against a state sanatorium for consumptives, and against municipal ownership of gas and electric utilities.[64] Fitzgerald was bent on nothing less than transforming the cultural baseline of Progressive and ethnocultural politics in Boston.

Although he widened his electoral appeal, he dared not forget his working-class Irish constituents, with the Boston *Pilot* describing him as 'particularly the friend of the workingman and those who were placed at any disadvantage in the battle for life'.[65] The 1905 campaign was also noted at the time for its ethnic rivalry and the attacks upon the immigrants. The *Pilot* concluded that it was:

time for democrats of Catholic and Irish, yes of Italian, French and Polish blood
to defend themselves and their standard bearer. . . . In the bigger, busier and
more beautiful Boston promised us by Mr. Fitzgerald there will be vastly more
work and no workman will be asked where he goes to Church.[66]

The *Pilot* was impressed by his 'victory over anti–Catholic bigotry'.[67] For
the Boston *Post* the reason for his victory was that 'even under the very
distracting conditions of party politics' Boston 'is a Democratic town'.[68]
Even the Boston *Herald*, one of the newspapers least charitable to
Fitzgerald, acknowledged that his success was a victory over bossism.[69]
The Boston *Globe* saw in his win 'political resourcefulness and sagacity'; he
had 'the experience and capacity to make good'.[70]

His inaugural speech was a landmark in the search for Irish accommodation. As a recent commentator, Doris Kearns Goodwin, has pointed out,
in this speech Fitzgerald addressed both the Yankees and the Irish to allay
the fears of the former and to ask for the latter's greater participation in the
affairs of the city.[71] But his inaugural was also an attempt to lay down the
practical policies that would create a new corporate and community culture
in Boston, to be based upon accommodation and moderation rather than
conflict and extremism. In his speech Fitzgerald spoke to the issues of
economic development and Progressivism that would span the two cultures.[72] His policies were directed toward the Progressive centre ground, to
enlightened business practice and sound finance, equitable taxation, social
reconstruction and philanthropy and the extension of the functions of local
government.

He laid the fears of the Yankee elite by invoking reverence for the past
and inspired the Irish and 'new' immigrants by promising them the future.
'Influences from its [Boston's] glorious history still permeate the mass of
the population. I am confident that the new generations, molding their
ideals to the pattern of the splendid past, will prove worthy of the name
they inherit.' The matching of the ideals of the subordinate immigrant
culture to those of the dominant Yankee elite ensured that he would not be
dividing the civic centre ground. His promotion of 'a prosperous and
contented citizenship' was dependent upon the absorption of the moral, if
not the political, leadership of the elite core culture.

By building his progressive principles into political action he sanitized the
conflicts between the competing cultures.[73] Fitzgerald chose to become the
moderate voice of urban reform, although most Yankees would probably
still have taken some convincing of that on 1 January 1906. Nevertheless,
Fitzgerald was sure the dominant Yankee culture and the practical politics of
the ethnic machine had to be reconciled. He saw this as a process of
arbitration, with himself as the arbiter, and the Democratic Party as its
institutionalization. In effect it was an incorporation, a syncretic process of
political absorption, the intellectual basis of which was a non-ethnic ideology of Progressivism. Fitzgerald's Progressivism was simply an acceptance
by him of the dominant reformist ideology – notably the challenge to
laissez-faire by expanding the functions of city government, the rejection of
Social Darwinism through the implementation of remedial social policies,

which were, however, supported by the efficient application of sound business principles, while all the time maintaining the appeal to traditional moral values. Progressivism in Boston, then, witnessed the creation of a genuine ethnocultural consensus whereby the interests of subordinate and even potentially oppositional social formations were adopted by the dominant and hegemonic class.

As events turned out Fitzgerald needed all his Progressive enterprise and zeal during his first term. He found himself besieged by both the machine and the reform impulse. As Goodwin notes, he quickly discovered the difficulty of reconciling his debts to the machine with his reform rhetoric.[74] The Good Government Association, assiduously led by the reform lawyer Louis Brandeis, uncovered corruption and wasteful practices, particularly in the sewer, street and water departments. The GGA's discovery of graft prompted its call to the state legislature to investigate the financial practices of the city.[75] The idea of a Finance Commission rapidly gained support among the city's reformers, and at the Republican convention in 1906 the demand was made that a commission be established to investigate not only the finances of the city but all municipal affairs. It was difficult for Fitzgerald to ignore these calls, given the weight he had attached to financial probity in his inaugural. Fitzgerald's ideological domestication was complete when he realized it was to his advantage to appropriate the idea.[76]

Fitzgerald's January 1907 address was his opportunity. The public interest would be best served, he said, by the 'creation of a finance commission by the authority of the city government'. He knew this was preferable to an investigation by the state, over which he would have far less influence. Fitzgerald thus heightened his Progressive profile by directing himself in the role of structural reformer. The Finance Commission was finally appointed by him in July 1907, with seven members; five of the seven were known reformers and four of those were members of the GGA.[77]

Before it concluded the first phase of its investigations in January 1909 the Finance Commission had embarked upon the most thorough and wide-ranging investigation of Boston's municipal affairs in the city's history.[78] It condemned the movement toward civic extravagance which it claimed had begun at least a decade earlier, and which could be traced to the weak executive powers in the 1885 city charter as well as the graft and corruption it allowed to grow.[79] The Finance Commission concluded that the only resolution to these problems was a charter revision.[80] It drafted a new charter based upon recommendations of a simplified governmental structure and investing the mayor with genuine executive authority.[81] For the first time there was a concentration of executive authority in the office of mayor. Almost all the heads of department were to be mayoral appointments, and the mayor was given the power of veto over all ordinances of the city council. All spending proposals were to come from the mayor alone. Finally, the power of the office was enhanced by extending the term to four years.[82]

Fitzgerald's next major hurdle was re-election. The election of 1907 was again marked by religious and racial innuendo, and further intra-Democratic Party division. The Boston *Evening Transcript* published two articles by George Kibbe Turner on Fitzgerald in which he characterized 'The Young Napoleon' as hitching his 'political chariot most ingeniously to a great movement of the population of Boston. Beginning with the swarthy hordes . . ., the Jews and then the Italians', Fitzgerald had exploited them for electoral profit.[83] Fitzgerald responded in kind to Turner's attack with the support of the Boston *Pilot*, which claimed he had been 'the target of much unfair criticism. The man with the muckrake [Turner] . . . has been working sedulously to charge up to the present administration every error of every one of its predecessors for the past twenty years.'[84]

In what was to be the last partisan mayoral election, in 1907, Republican Party candidate George Albee Hibbard won by just 2,177 votes. The closeness of the result was partly the consequence of the candidature of an anti-Fitzgerald Democratic candidate, John A. Coulthurst, who polled nearly 16,000 votes. A disgruntled Fitzgerald came second.[85] The Boston *Globe* correctly attributed Fitzgerald's defeat 'mainly to disaffection among his own followers because of his inability to satisfy their demands for patronage and to the revelations of the Finance Commission'.[86] What is significant in the 1907 election result is the fact that had Fitzgerald been able to satisfy the patronage demands of the party, and had Coulthurst not subsequently run, Fitzgerald would probably have enjoyed a stunning electoral success. The Boston *Pilot* concluded, however, that Fitzgerald had 'led a gallant fight' and that 'he deserves and will have from his party two years hence the compliment of another nomination!'[87]

Hibbard's administration was all he promised – he cut municipal costs by $1 million and dispensed with over 1,000 city employees, with the Finance Commission commending his 'business administration'.[88] However, if the Boston GGA expected charter reform to ensure the election of candidates they could freely endorse, then they were disappointed in 1910 in the first election under the new charter, with the re-election of John Fitzgerald. His second election confirmed the changed character of Boston's political culture. Under the new charter, it was possible for a candidate or mayor to attract a city-wide following – the very objective Fitzgerald had been pursuing since his return from Washington a decade earlier.

As expected, the Democratic machine opposed the reforms of the Finance Commission because of the injury to patronage opportunities of a merito-cratic civil service, and at-large council elections that would disrupt ward politics.[89] However, Fitzgerald's Progressivism in the shape of his initiation of the Finance Commission and assault on the Democratic Party was about to pay handsome dividends. He welcomed the clause in the new non-partisan charter that insisted on nomination through petition, and which allowed him simply to dispense with the Democratic machine. The Republicans deemed themselves fortunate in the acceptance of their over-tures by the wealthy Yankee Democrat James Jackson Storrow. He was the dream candidate. A Harvard-educated banker and former President of the Boy Scouts of America, he was a philanthropist and, most important, it was believed, could steal Democratic votes in every ward in the city. Reformist groups like the Committee of One Hundred and Citizens' Municipal League quickly endorsed his candidature.

Faced with Storrow and a Democratic machine in disarray, Fitzgerald knew he had to weld another coalition.[90] He needed the support of Lomasney and the up and coming James Michael Curley. He also needed to split the Storrow vote. To this end he colluded with Lomasney to persuade Hibbard to run again.[91] Although this outlandish manoeuvre did not ultimately affect the result of the election, it prompted the Boston *Evening Transcript* to draw a parallel with 1905 and the intercession of a third candidate that allowed Fitzgerald to win.[92] As usual it was the *Transcript* that led the fight against Fitzgerald, pointing out just prior to the election that the new charter and Fitzgerald's personality could produce corruption on an unprecedented scale.[93] Accusing him of being a 'mountebank' who scatters promises, tunnels and subways and parks and playgrounds where he thinks they will produce the most votes . . .', the *Transcript* was certain that upon his election 'Roman games may be assured.'[94]

The 1910 election was hard-fought and vitriolic. Storrow's platform stressed business efficiency, honesty, civil service reform, the extension of public health facilities and the establishment of a Public Utilities Commission. He borrowed extensively from the Finance Commission report to condemn Fitzgerald.[95] Storrow claimed Fitzgerald's perambulations from ward to ward enabled him to use 'honeyed words' with one ethnic group only to call them 'savages who live in huts' in the next.[96] The ethnic issue finally exploded into the open when ex-Governor Curtis Guild Jr, speaking for Storrow, implied that Fitzgerald had introduced 'the issue of religion' into the campaign.[97] This gave Fitzgerald the boost his run needed and he exploited Guild's attack to the full.

Although the 1,402 majority for Fitzgerald over Storrow in the January 1910 election was marginal, the win indicates the breadth of his appeal to Progressives, businessmen, politicos and immigrants alike. Fitzgerald increased his winning margin in every ward, and even in the traditionally Republican suburban wards his vote rose considerably.[98] His vote was no longer determined by the ethnocultural complexion of the city.[99] As usual the Catholic voice of the city, the Boston *Pilot*, was fulsome in its praise, offering 'hearty congratulations' to a 'Christian Catholic' who, it acknowledged, was 'responsible before a higher tribunal than that of popular election'.[100] Clearly the *Pilot* felt the issue of religion had been seen off by Fitzgerald, and in a very real sense ethnicity – although it remained a historical fact – had ceased to be a political one.

With substantially extended authority, thanks to the Finance Commission, the GGA and the reform impulse, Fitzgerald was able to say that he would give the new charter a fair trial, maintaining, quite accurately, that his election marked 'an important departure in municipal government in America'.[101] His policies were again couched in the ideological rhetoric of Progressive neo-liberalism that had first emerged in 1906: a bigger, better and busier Boston, with a strong emphasis on the Progressive platform of business enterprise, social reconstruction and beautifying the built environment.[102]

His second term was again characterized by his energetic pursuit of cultural cohesion, putting much Yankee reformist liberal thought into practical political action. In his second term he instigated the building of playgrounds, the hospital for consumptives, the commercial high school, the aquarium and the zoo, a pension plan for city employees, the municipal picnic, Saturday half-day holidays for city workers as well as higher salaries; he widened and built new streets and subways, and established social centres, increased the number of sanitary inspectors, set up a corps of nurses to tend the tenement dwellers, replaced horse-drawn ambulances with automobiles, increased the number of public baths, and claimed withal to have lowered the city's tax rate.[103] He was not free from the taunts of political adversaries, of course, and at one point an attempt was made to recall him. It was also the intention of the Strategy Board that Fitzgerald should not serve a third term, but should retire to make way for the new rising Democratic star James Michael Curley.[104] There was much rumour about the state of his health in 1913, although it was reported that he was suffering from nothing more than exhaustion.[105]

In Boston, as in other major cities, the demands of corporate America's Progressive revolution were represented by the creation of a single powerful executive governmental authority. Fitzgerald was not only responsible for the new charter by playing the corporatist–reform card, he also made the system work by creating a unified neo-liberal political culture rather than reiterating the sectarian appeals of the Gilded Age. Fitzgerald was not, however, a transitional figure who presided over the transfer of political power from the Yankee core culture to the Irish and foreign-born. As recent studies have shown, Irish and immigrant Democratic Party partisanship had been in decline since the mid-1890s, well before Fitzgerald's star had risen.[106] Rather it came to Fitzgerald to take this change in the political baseline a stage further, to marry the new culture to the demands of the emergent corporate politics of the new century. He did this in Boston by learning from O'Brien and Collins and by exploiting Progressive appeal to a wider public than any previous mayor. He began the process in his first term, and in his second used the reformed structure of local government to push his policies further into the realm of business efficiency, philanthropy, social reconstruction and education for industrial growth.

After Fitzgerald's two terms ethnocultural politics ceased to be a major fact of political life in the city, and the pursuit of Irish political legitimacy reached its conclusion. Fitzgerald's importance is not merely as a power broker but as a conduit through which flowed the hegemonic cultural stream. This cultural stream became a river that renegotiated Irishness and Catholicism in urban America, and forced open hitherto closed political doors. The most important of these doors were those of the White House, through which Fitzgerald's grandson, John Fitzgerald Kennedy, walked as President some fifty years later.

The final overthrow of Yankee dominance came, then, with the revolution of the Progressive years – America's ideological response to the process of modernization. The need for a new cultural equilibrium demanded the accommodation and incorporation of competing cultures. In Boston as in other major cities a new equilibrium was attempted by Irish leaders like Fitzgerald with the incorporation of all varieties of immigrant cultures.

Fitzgerald, as the new leader of a rising lower-class ethnic community, undertook this process of transformation by the appropriation of Progressivism and its institutionalization within the Democratic Party – and thus established the apparatus of a new political hegemony. When viewed from the perspective of Boston and the career of Fitzgerald, the search for Irish political authority was a significant product of the corporate state.

While to many contemporaries and subsequent generations of historians Fitzgerald appeared to represent the rising Irish classes, he was, as his colonization of the public political discourse reveals, actually the organizer of a new cultural hegemony rooted in the neo-liberal corporate ideology of Progressivism. In terms of practical politics he reconciled the two cultures. He achieved this by recognizing the necessary expansion of the bureaucratic superstructure of local government that overlay the new corporate state. His two terms were a climacteric in the evolution of Boston's political culture and were emblematic of the broader canvas of American-Irish politics. He created a new political environment out of the ethnic and cultural cleavages of the new age. Armed with the ideological shield of the new liberalism, he successfully challenged the residual Yankee value system and, as his grandson's political career shows, incorporated the Irish Catholic into Boston's, Massachusetts's and America's politics. Fitzgerald acknowledged this in his search for Irish political legitimacy, and summarized it in what is one of the classic local formulations of the American corporate and pluralist age, a 'bigger, better and busier Boston'.

Notes

1. The bibliography of Irish politics in corporate America falls into the context of Irish migrationism and assimilation, dealt with elsewhere in this series, and American ethnic politics, specifically Massachusetts's and Boston's Irish politics. The best introduction to the area is J. J. Huthmacher, 'Urban liberalism and the Age of Reform', *Mississippi Valley Historical Review*, 49, September 1962, pp. 231–41. A substantial volume of research into voting behaviour over the past twenty years has indicated the significance of ethnicity in political decision-making. This ethnocultural school of historical analysis is well represented in the following key texts: R. P. McCormick, 'Ethno-cultural interpretations of nineteenth century American voting behavior', *Political Science Quarterly*, 89, June 1974, pp. 351–77; Paul Kleppner, *The Cross of Culture: Social Analysis of Mid-western Politics, 1850–1900*, Free Press, New York, 1970; Michael P. Rogin and John L. Shover, *Critical Elections and Social Movements, 1890–1966*, Greenwood Press, Westport, Conn., 1970; Richard Jensen, *The Winning of the Midwest: Social and Political Conflict, 1888–1896*, University of Chicago Press, Chicago, 1971; Robert P. Swierenga, Ethnocultural Political Analysis: a new Approach to American Ethnic Studies, *Journal of American Studies*, 5, April 1971, pp. 59–79; John M. Allswang, *Bosses. Machines and Urban Voters: an American Symbiosis*, Kennikat Press, New York, 1977; Paul Kleppner, *The Third Electoral System 1853–1892*, University of North Carolina Press, Chapel Hill, N. C., 1979; David Thelen, *Paths of Resistance: Tradition and Dignity in Industrializing Missouri*, Oxford University Press, New York, 1986;

Paul Kleppner, *Continuity and Change in Electoral Politics, 1893–1928*, Greenwood Press, New York, 1987. The Irish and politics in Massachusetts and Boston are also well served by a specialist literature, starting with Arthur Mann, *Yankee Reformers in the Urban Age*, Harvard University Press, Cambridge, Mass., 1954; J. J. Huthmacher, *Massachusetts People and Politics, 1919–1933*, Harvard University Press, Cambridge, Mass., 1959; John H. Cutler, *'Honey Fitz': Three Steps to the White House: the Life and Times of John F. Fitzgerald*, Bobbs–Merrill, New York, 1962; Richard M. Abrams, *Conservatism in a Progressive Era: Massachusetts Politics, 1900–1912*, Harvard University Press, Cambridge, Mass., 1964; Edgar Litt, *The Political Culture of Massachusetts*, Princeton University Press, Princeton, N. J., 1965; Geoffrey Blodgett, *The Gentle Reformers: Massachusetts Democrats in the Cleveland Era*, Harvard University Press, Cambridge, Mass., 1976; Peter K. Eisinger, 'Ethnic political transition in Boston, 1884–1933: some lessons for contemporary cities', *Political Science Quarterly*, 93, summer 1978, pp. 217–39; Dennis P. Ryan, *Beyond the Ballot Box: a Social History of the Boston Irish, 1845–1917*, University of Massachusetts Press, East Brunswick, Mass., 1983; Ronald P. Formisano and Constance K. Burns, eds., *Boston 1700–1980: the Evolution of Urban Politics*, Greenwood Press, Westport, Conn., 1984; Alun Munslow, 'The decline of ethnic politics in Boston, 1882–1921', *Proceedings of the Massachusetts Historical Society*, 98, 1986, pp. 116–34; Doris Kearns Goodwin, *The Fitzgeralds and the Kennedys*, Simon & Schuster, New York, 1987.
2. Charles H. Trout, 'Curley of Boston: the search for Irish legitimacy', in Formisano and Burns, *Boston*, pp. 165–95.
3. R. F. Foster, *Modern Ireland, 1600–1972*, Penguin, London, 1988, p. 355.
4. David N. Doyle, 'Catholicism, politics and Irish America since the 1890's: some critical considerations', in P. J. Drudy, ed. *The Irish in America: Emigration, Assimilation and Impact*, Cambridge University Press, Cambridge, 1985, p. 191.
5. Foster, *Modern Ireland*, p. 357; David Fitzpatrick, *Irish Emigration, 1801–1921*, Studies in Irish Economic and Social History, 1, Trinity History Workshop, Dundalk, 1984, p. 32; D. H. Akenson, *The United States and Ireland*, Harvard University Press, Cambridge, Mass., 1973, pp. 69–71, and 'An agnostic view of the historiography of the Irish-Americans', *Labour*, 14, 1984, pp. 127–8.
6. *Ninth United States Census*, 1, table 8, Washington, D. C., Government Printing Office, 1872, pp. 386–91.
7. *Thirteenth United States Census*, 1, *Population*, tables 34, 36, Washington, D. C., Government Printing Office, 1912, pp. 942–5; Morton D. Winsberg, 'Irish settlement in the United States, 1850–1980', *Eire-Ireland*, 20, Spring 1985, pp. 10–11.
8. *Fourteenth United States Census*, *Abstract*, table 75, Washington, D. C., Government Printing Office, 1923, pp. 312–15.
9. Akenson, *The United States and Ireland*; Doyle, 'The Regional Bibliography of Irish-America, A review and an addendum'. *Irish Historical Studies*, xxiii, 1983, p. 254. Morton D. Winsberg, 'The suburbanization of the Irish in Boston, Chicago and New York', *Eire-Ireland*, 21, Fall 1986, pp. 90–91.
10. Kerby Miller, *Emigrants and Exiles: Ireland and the Irish Exodus to North America*, Oxford University Press, Oxford, 1985, and 'Emigrants and exiles: Irish cultures and Irish emigration to North America, 1790–1922', *Irish Historical Studies*, 22, September 1980, pp. 97–125
11. Miller, *Emigrants and Exiles*, p. 493.
12. Miller, *Emigrants and Exiles*, p. 493.

13. Lawrence McCaffrey, 'A profile of Irish America', in D. N. Doyle and Owen Dudley Edwards, eds., *America and Ireland, 1776–1976: the American Identity and the Irish Connection*, Greenwood Press, Westport, Conn., 1980, pp. 81, 83.
14. James Bryce, *The American Commonwealth*, Macmillan, London, 1893, reprinted 1917, II, p. 36.
15. John Paul Bocock, 'The Irish conquest of our cities', *Forum*, 17, April 1894, pp. 186–7.
16. To produce an exhaustive listing of the interpretations of Progressivism would be inappropriate here; however, the major historiographical landmarks are well known: Eric F. Goldman, *Rendezvous with Destiny: a History of Modern American Reform*, Random House, New York, 1952; Richard Hofstadter, *The Age of Reform*, Vintage, New York, 1955; Robert Wiebe, *The Search for Order, 1877–1920*, Greenwood Press, New York, 1967; James Weinstein, *The Corporate Ideal in the Liberal State*, Beacon Press, Boston, Mass., 1968; David Thelen, *The New Citizenship: Origins of Progressivism in Wisconsin, 1885–1900*, University of Missouri Press, Columbia, Mo, 1972; Paul Boyer, *Urban Masses and Moral Order in America, 1820–1920*, Harvard University Press, Cambridge, Mass., and London, 1978; although not dealing strictly with the Progressive era, T. J. Jackson Lears, 'The concept of cultural hegemony: problems and possibilities', *American Historical Review*, 90, 5, June 1985, pp. 567–93, is methodologically important. Also of significance recently have been Daniel T. Rodgers, 'In search of Progressivism', *Reviews in American History*, 10, 1982, pp. 113–32; A. S. Link and Richard L. McCormick, *Progressivism*, Harlan Davidson, Arlington Heights, Ill., 1983; James T. Kloppenberg, *Uncertain Victory: Democracy and Progressivism in Europe and America, 1870–1920*, Oxford University Press, New York, 1986; John Milton Cooper, *Pivotal Decades: the United States, 1900–1920*, Norton, New York, 1990.
17. In *Selections from Prison Notebooks*, Lawrence & Wishart, London, 1982, Antonio Gramsci explores the character of cultural hegemony by noting the central role of the intellectual, operating as the dominant group's subaltern in the dispersion of cultural values, but especially in the field of political government, to organize the 'spontaneous' consent of the masses – not least among potentially oppositional cultural groups (p. 12).
18. Eisinger, 'Ethnic political transition'; Formisano and Burns, *Boston*; elsewhere I have suggested that ethnocultural politics in the city were in substantial decay before the turn of the century, see Munslow, 'The decline of ethnic politics'.
19. Gramsci, *Prison Notebooks*, p. 5. The function of the cultural and political leaders, what Gramsci calls organic intellectuals, is to articulate and diffuse an ideological position throughout the institutions of society – the schools, Churches, the press, political parties, and even the built environment. See Alun Munslow, 'Andrew Carnegie and the discourse of cultural hegemony', *Journal of American Studies*, 22, 2, 1988, pp. 213–24, for a more detailed application of this model to the role of the organic intellectual in American history.
20. Gramsci, *Prison Notebooks*, pp. 56–7; John D. Buenker, *Urban Liberalism, and Progressive Reform*, Oxford University Press, Oxford, 1978, p. 10.
21. Thelen, *The New Citizenship* and *Paths of Resistance*, and Rogin and Shover, *Critical Elections*. See also the local examinations of urban bossism which have noted the character of the boss – immigrant relationship, representative of which is Zane L. Miller, *Boss Cox's Cincinnati: Urban Politics in the Progressive Era*, Oxford University Press, New York, 1968, pp. 219–41.
22. Hoftsadter, *The Age of Reform*, p. 181.

23. Hofstadter, *The Age of Reform*, p. 182.
24. Gramsci, *Prison Notebooks*, pp. 323–6; Hofstadter, *The Age of Reform*, p. 182.
25. Thomas N. Brown, 'The political Irish: politicians and rebels', in Doyle and Edwards *America and Ireland*, p. 135.
26. Daniel P. Moynihan, 'The Irish', in Daniel P. Moynihan and Nathan Glazer, eds., *Beyond the Melting Pot*, Harvard University Press, Cambridge, Mass., 1963, p. 229.
27. Brown, 'The political Irish', p. 134.
28. Melvin G. Holli and Peter d'A. Jones, eds., *Biographical Dictionary of American Mayors, 1820–1980*, Greenwood Press, Westport, Conn., 1981, p. 249; John T. Galvin, 'Patrick J. McGuire Boston's last Democratic boss', *New England Quarterly*, 55, 1982, 402–4.
29. Geoffrey Blodgett, 'Yankee leadership in a divided city, 1860–1910', in Formisano and Burns, *Boston*, p. 99.
30. Munslow, 'The decline of ethnic politics', p. 131.
31. Cutler, *'Honey Fitz'*; Goodwin, *Fitzgeralds and Kennedys*, pp. 110–17; Holli and d'A. Jones, *Biographical Dictionary*, pp. 116–17; William V. Shannon, *The American Irish* (rev. edn), Macmillan, Chicago, 1966, p. 208.
32. Joseph F. Dineen, *The Purple Shamrock*, New York, 1949, quoted in Shannon, p. 210.
33. John R. Barrett, *Work and Community in the Jungle: Chicago and Packinghouse Workers, 1894–1922*, Illinois University Press, Urbana and Chicago, 1987, introduction.
34. Goodwin, *Fitzgeralds and Kennedys*, pp. 93–4.
35. Goodwin, *Fitzgeralds and Kennedys*, pp. 94–6.
36. Goodwin, *Fitzgeralds and Kennedys*, pp. 96–8.
37. Cutler, *'Honey Fitz'*, p. 56.
38. Boston *Evening Transcript*, 16 December 1891, p. 4.
39. Blodgett, *The Gentle Reformers*, pp. 226, 240–2.
40. Goodwin, *Fitzgeralds and Kennedys*, pp. 96–7; Cutler, *'Honey Fitz'*, pp. 60–63.
41. Goodwin, *Fitzgeralds and Kennedys*, pp. 96–8.
42. Boston *Pilot*, 11 July 1896, p. 4.
43. Walsh, pp. 21–2.
44. Goodwin, *Fitzgeralds and Kennedys*, p. 101.
45. Boston *Herald*, 2 December 1899, p. 6.
46. Munslow, 'The decline of ethnic politics', p. 131.
47. *Annual Report of the Board of Election Commissioners*, Boston, Mass., 1899, pp. 54–7.
48. Boston *Herald*, 13 December 1899, p. 1.
49. Munslow, 'The decline of ethnic politics', pp. 130–1.
50. Boston *Pilot*, 21 December 1901, p. 4.
51. A process echoed in other American cities at the time; see Miller, *Boss Cox's Cincinnati*.
52. Goodwin, *Fitzgeralds and Kennedys*, p. 106.
53. Boston *Herald*, 16 November 1905, p. 1.
54. Cutler, *'Honey Fitz'*, p. 92.
55. Boston *Post*, 2 November 1905, p. 1.
56. Boston *Post*, 9 November 1905, p. 9.
57. Boston *Post*, 17 November 1905, p. 6.
58. Boston *Evening Transcript*, 5 December 1905, p. 8.
59. Boston *Post*, 6 December 1905, p. 1; *Annual Report of the Board of Election Commissioners*, Boston, Mass., 1905, pp. 165–71.

60. Boston *Globe*, 5 December 1905, p. 8.
61. Boston *Globe*, 5 December 1905, p. 8.
62. Boston *Globe*, 5 December 1905, p. 8.
63. Boston *Globe*, 5 December 1905, p. 8.
64. Boston *Globe*, 5 December 1905, p. 8.
65. Boston *Pilot*, 9 December 1905, p. 4.
66. Boston *Pilot*, 9 December 1905, p. 4.
67. Boston *Pilot*, 16 December 1905, p. 4.
68. Boston *Post*, 13 December 1905, p. 1.
69. Boston *Herald*, 13 December 1905, p. 6.
70. Boston *Globe*, 13 December 1905, p. 10.
71. Goodwin, *Fitzgeralds and Kennedys*, pp. 111–12.
72. See the Boston *Globe* 1 January 1906, p. 1, for all quotations from Fitzgerald's inaugural.
73. Boston *Globe*, 2 January 1906, p. 6.
74. Goodwin, *Fitzgeralds and Kennedys*, p. 117.
75. Cutler, '*Honey Fitz*', p. 106.
76. Boston *Evening Transcript*, 13 December 1906, p. 2.
77. Cutler, '*Honey Fitz*', p. 110; Chester A. Hanford, 'The government of the city of Boston, 1880–1930', in *Fifty Years of Boston: a Memorial Volume*, ed. Tercentenary Committee, Boston, Mass., 1930, pp. 84–115.
78. George R. Nutter, 'The Boston City Charter', *National Municipal Review*, 2, 4, October 1913, p. 584.
79. Hanford, in *Fifty Years of Boston*, p. 101; Boston *Globe*, 5 December 1907, p. 6.
80. Cutler, '*Honey Fitz*', pp. 112–13.
81. Hanford, *Fifty Years of Boston*, p. 102.
82. Cutler, '*Honey Fitz*', p. 118.
83. Boston *Evening Transcript*, 5 November 1907, p. 9.
84. Boston *Pilot*, 30 November 1907, p. 4.
85. *Annual Report of the Board of Election Commissioners*, Boston, Mass., 1907, pp. 205–10.
86. Boston *Globe*, 11 December 1907, p. 1.
87. Boston *Pilot*, 14 December 1907, p. 4.
88. Cutler, '*Honey Fitz*', p. 119.
89. Cutler, '*Honey Fitz*', p. 121.
90. Cutler, '*Honey Fitz*', p. 126; Boston *Evening Transcript*, 5 November 1909, p. 1.
91. Boston *Evening Transcript*, 29 November 1909, p. 1.
92. Boston *Evening Transcript*, 29 November 1909, p. 1.
93. Boston *Evening Transcript*, 29 November 1909, p. 1; 14 December 1909, p. 12.
94. Boston *Evening Transcript*, 14 December 1909, p. 12.
95. See, for example, the Boston *Post*, 3 January 1910, p. 4; 4 January 1910, p. 5; 8 January 1910, p. 8.
96. Cutler, '*Honey Fitz*', p. 136.
97. Cutler, '*Honey Fitz*', p. 137.
98. *Annual Report of the Board of Election Commissioners*, Boston, Mass., 1910, pp. 135–142.
99. *Thirteenth United States Census*, 2, *Population*, table V, p. 890; Munslow, 'The decline of ethnic politics in Boston'.
100. Boston *Pilot*, 15 January 1910, p. 4.
101. Boston *Globe*, 7 February 1910, p. 1.
102. Boston *Globe*, 7 February 1910, p. 1.

103. Boston *Globe*, 7 February 1910, p. 1.; 6 February 1911, p. 1; 3 February 1913, p. 5.
104. Holli and d'A. Jones, *Biographical Dictionary*, p. 117.
105. Boston *Evening Transcript*, 9 December 1913, p. 2.
106. Munslow, 'The decline of ethnic politics', pp. 127–34.

7 The Irish childhood and youth of a Canadian capitalist

T. D. Regehr

Sir Herbert Samuel Holt was one of Canada's most influential businessmen. During the first three decades of the twentieth century, he masterminded the growth and development of one of Canada's largest chartered banks, created the country's largest privately owned hydro–electric power company, and merged numerous competing companies to form the country's largest pulp and paper manufacturing conglomerate. He was involved in huge textile, fur, coal, iron, steel, street and steam railway, trust and insurance, communications, movie and sports corporations, serving as director of hundreds of major Canadian and international corporations.[1]

The influence of this man seemed to be everywhere in the Canadian corporate world. His strategy and policies nevertheless perplexed his contemporaries, as they have puzzled business writers and historians of more recent times. During his lifetime an aura of mystery, aloofness and power hung over his austere but spacious office in Montreal's Power Building.[2] Since his death in 1941, historians have largely ignored his influence and achievements, particularly in Quebec. Attention has instead been devoted to the nationalization of Holt's most profitable creation, the Montreal Light, Heat and Power Consolidated, and of French Canadian success in making the new Quebec Hydro a modern, technologically advanced corporation in which French was the working language.[3] The fact that Sir Herbert left no personal papers, and tried to destroy all documentary evidence related to his career, has made the task of the historian and biographer very difficult.[4]

Some interesting and revealing insights into the personality, policies and ideas of this Canadian businessman can be gained through a study of his difficult childhood and youth in Ireland. He came from a farming family, and was trained to be a farmer, but he also learned much about business and modern technology. Personal and family misfortunes eventually forced him to abandon all hope of becoming a progressive gentleman farmer in Ireland, and instead to seek his fortune in the New World.

Holt himself said very little about his Irish childhood and youth, and made no effort to correct serious factual errors by journalists and business writers. Thus, for example, the various obituary notices published immediately after his death, and Peter C. Newman's biographical sketch published many years later, seemingly copied one another when they reported that Herbert Holt had migrated from Ireland in 1875 when he was nineteen years old.[5] He had in fact come to Canada in August of 1873, beginning work as an engineering assistant with the Toronto Water Works in September of that year.[6] There are similar errors pertaining to the circumstances of his family in Ireland, and to the education he received before coming to Canada.[7]

This article, based on extensive new primary research in Ireland,[8] provides new information on Herbert Holt's early life in Ireland. It also indicates how those early Irish experiences influenced Sir Herbert's subsequent Canadian business career.

Herbert Samuel Holt was born on 12 February 1855 at Geashill, King's County, now County Offaly, Ireland. He was baptised on 26 April 1855 in St Mary's Parish Church, Church of Ireland, in Geashill. The small town of Geashill lies approximately sixty-five kilometres west and slightly south of Dublin. Herbert Holt's parents were William Robert Grattan Holt and Jane Hannon Holt. An older brother, Thomas Grattan Holt, was born on 7 August 1853, and two younger sisters, Adelaide Mary, and Henrietta Jane, were born 14 March 1856 and 19 November 1857 respectively.[9]

Members of the Holt family had lived in the Carbury or Castle Carbre area, located approximately ten kilometers from Geashill, for centuries. The ancestral home was a farm known locally as Coolavacoose (House of the Caves). This farm lies very close to the medieval Clonkeen Castle which stood on a small hill overlooking the plain on which the Boyne River has its origin. Coolavacoose was first leased by a member of the Holt family in the 1640s, and has been occupied by Holts in continuous succession ever since.[10] A member of the family still had the farm in 1985, and his young son indicated that he planned to take over in the normal course of affairs.[11]

The Holts of Coolavacoose became prosperous tenant farmers, and in 1811, or shortly thereafter, a younger son named Samuel, who had married in 1811 into the Irish patriot Grattan family, acquired the lease to a second farm in the area. This farm, comprising 175 acres of land, a poorly maintained house and several dilapidated outbuildings, was locally known as the Carberry Farm. The first Samuel Holt to hold the lease to it had married Ann Grattan Holt. This family prospered and made numerous expensive improvements, including the construction of an unusually large house which allegedly cost more than £4,000 to build in the 1840s. The land owner, John James Pomeroy, (Viscount Harberton in the peerage of Ireland),[12] was so pleased with the improvements made by Samuel and Ann Grattan Holt that he offered them the lease to another, larger farm – the Haggart Farms which comprised 277 acres of land.[13] Thereafter the Carberry and Haggart Farms were operated as single farming unit by Samuel Holt, and after 1844 by his son who was also named Samuel Holt.

The Holts of Coolavacoose, and those of Carberry/Haggart, lived close together and maintained close family ties. They were gentlemen farmers who survived the disasters of the famine in the 1840s, but family correspondence at Coolavacoose indicates that some of the peasant subtenants and workers starved during the famine, and several younger family members migrated to the United States or to Australia during those difficult years.[14]

Samuel and Ann Grattan Holt, who had enjoyed exceptional success on the Carberry and Haggart farms reassigned their lease to both farms to their son, another Samuel, in 1844.[15] The landlord, Viscount Harberton, readily granted the new leasee a new 21-year to life lease.[16] He was delighted with the various improvements the elder Samuel Holt had made, and agreed to hold the rent to a very modest £318. The two Samuel Holts, father and son, who leased and operated the Carberry and Haggart farms in the nineteenth century, until 1873, were the paternal grandfather and uncle of the Canadian entrepreneur Herbert Samuel Holt.

The father of Herbert Holt, William Robert Grattan Holt, was a younger son of Samuel and Ann Holt, and a brother of the Samuel Holt who obtained the Carberry/Haggart leases in 1844. There was apparently some bad blood between William and his brother Samuel, although the details are no longer known. It is clear, however, that after 1844 the younger brother did not find a place suited to his interests and talents on the Carberry/Haggart farms.[17] William's activities from 1844 until 1851 are not given in the surviving documents, but in 1851 he married Jane Hannon of Prumpleston Mills and secured the lease of a 291-acre grazing farm near Geashill, known locally as Ballycrystal.

Geashill was approximately ten kilometres from the established Holt leased Coolavacoose, Carberry and Haggart farms. It is described in contemporary sources as 'an inconsiderable village, mostly composed of thatched cabins'. The roads to and from the village, over which produce from the farm had to pass to market, were 'shamefully bad, and at times almost impassable . . . in a lamentable state of neglect'.[18]

The Ballycrystal farm itself had several impressive buildings. The house was a long two storey building. Convenient to it was an enclosed yard built on three sides with slated barn, stable and cattle sheds. Nearby was a small shepherd's hut which, together with a small garden plot, was sub-leased by William Holt to the shepherd Philip Greene for a small fee. The Ballycrystal farm comprised a total of 291 acres, 172 of which were described as deep brown loam, 66 as adhesive clay and dry moor, and 50 as wet, worn moor. The farm was devoted entirely to grazing during the years that William Robert Grattan Holt held the lease, but later Irish Land Commission records noted that 'The farm would lend itself better to mixed husbandry than to exclusive grazing. It has been overstocked in winter and much cut up. The land digs better than its herbiage indicates. The moor land is deteriorating from want of top dress when in meadow.'[19]

The annual rent paid by William Robert Grattan Holt was £215.[20] It was a higher rent than the productive capacity of a farm which could sustain only one hundred cattle in summer and fifty in winter.[21] Ballycrystal was owned by Lord Viscount Digby, eighth Baron of Geashill, an absentee landowner whose administrators and agents followed short-sighted and exploitative leasing policies. Expenditures by Lord Digby for improvements were allegedly reduced as much as possible.[22] The length of leases was shortened as much as possible, and farms and lands covered under expiring leases were thrown open to competitive bidding. Tenants who made improvements found they had to pay higher rents if they wished to renew their leases. Tenants and agricultural spokesmen alike complained about the results of such policies by absentee landowners.

> In England, perhaps, those short leases may answer, but here, it is presumed, 'tis a mistaken policy, as certainly there is no encouragement to lay down the ground well, as above half of the period of the term must be spent in preparing the land in proper heart for grass, and, by the time the farmer begins to enjoy the fruit of his labour, his lease expires; but here the vitals of the soil are exhausted by constant tillage, and, at the high rents which these lands are leased, no man can make much profit, except he holds the plough himself, and has a son to drive it; for there is no want of bidder to every farm out of lease, and the highest gets the preference . . . Where such short leases only are granted, little real improvement can be expected; the tenant is discouraged from it, lest he should have his rent raised in his next tenure, to the value of his improvements, which he is fairly apprized of; the highest bidder always having the preference. When the peasantry become more civilized, perhaps this rigorous mode will be abandoned, and real solvent tenants may be granted encouragement, proportionate to their abilities and industry.[23]

Short-sighted and exploitative leasing policies, resulting in serious over-grazing and other poor farming practices, were aggravated by serious marketing problems. The cattle and smaller numbers of sheep and pigs raised at Ballycrystal were destined almost entirely for local and domestic markets in the 1850s. Some of the produce was taken to the Grand Canal and then sent to markets in the larger county town of Tullamore, but the roads made land transportation very difficult. Canal shipping costs were high, and inadequate care of animals loaded onto canal barges resulted in frequent losses.

The marketing of Irish agricultural produce in the 1850s was further seriously affected by trade disruptions due to the famine and the abolition of the British Corn Laws and Navigation Acts. The trade reforms were desperately needed to meet the needs of the starving Irish peasantry, but they also undercut and threatened to destroy local markets for Irish agricultural produce. The ability of people to pay for needed agricultural products was, in any case, very limited, and Irish farmers dependent on local markets for their survival fared very poorly. Massive rural depopulation during and immediately after the famine, due both to starvation and emigration, further weakened local agricultural markets.[24]

The terms of William Robert Grattan Holt's lease, and the state of Irish agriculture at the time, made it virtually impossible for the newly married lessee to sustain himself as a gentleman farmer. His lease was for a five-year period. It expired in 1856 and, like many other local leases, was thrown open for competitive bidding. The family of William and Jane Holt was not able to renew the lease, and was forced to move to a much smaller farm at nearby Alderboro where they had to do most of the manual farm labour themselves.

The move from Ballycrystal to the small farm at Alderboro sharply reduced the social status of the family. At Ballycrystal William Holt was an

'Esquire' and a 'gentleman farmer'. At Alderboro he was simply a 'farmer', and some regarded him as a 'peasant'. The local parish registers, in which the births of the four Holt children were recorded, tell the story of this decline. When the oldest child, Thomas Grattan Holt, was born in 1853 the occupation of his father was listed as 'gentleman and farmer'. William Holt was listed proudly and simply as a 'gentleman' when his next two children, Herbert and Mary, were born, but merely as a 'farmer' when the birth of his youngest daughter, Henrietta, was recorded after the family had lost the Ballycrystal lease. This loss of social status was more difficult to bear because the relatives on the Coolavacoose, Carbury and Haggart farms continued to do well and to make substantial improvements, and they enjoyed much more reasonable rents than those William Holt had been obliged to pay at Ballycrystal.

The loss of Ballycrystal occurred when Herbert Holt was only a year old. It must, nevertheless, have become a matter of subsequent family lore. All of Herbert Holt's schooling in Ireland after the loss of Ballycrystal was, as will be shown below, designed to prepare him for a career as a progressive and scientific gentleman farmer. That career was not ultimately available to Herbert Holt, but much later in life, after he had made his fortune in Canada, Sir Herbert built a palatial summer retreat in the Bahamas. It was named Ballycrystal, as was a racehorse owned by Sir Herbert's eldest son.

Sensitivity about the loss of social status also manifest itself in other ways. Early in his own business career, Herbert Holt insisted that he be addressed as an 'Esquire' and even added the letters 'Esq.' to his signature during the time when he served as Superintendent of Construction on the Rocky Mountain section of the Canadian Pacific Railway mainline. Retrieval of the respect and social status that the family had lost with the Ballycrystal lease was an obvious matter of concern to Herbert Holt as he built his Canadian business empire.

The economic and social status of the William and Jane Holt family after the loss of the Ballycrystal lease remained unstable throughout the 1850s, but they became absolutely desperate in the 1860s. William Robert Grattan Holt died in late December 1862, and was buried in the cemetery of St Mary's Church, Carbury, on 3 January 1863. He was 35 years old. His wife and four small children were left destitute. Herbert was not quite eight years old when his father died.[25]

Jane Hannon Holt left the Alderboro farm and moved to the nearby larger market town of Portarlington immediately after her husband's death. In Portarlington she eked out a living working as a seamstress and doing other odd jobs including work as a domestic maid or housekeeper. The two boys, then eight and nine years of age, were entrusted to the care of their maternal grandfather, John Hannon, who ensured that they got a good education.

The educational system of Ireland was significantly altered as a result of the Irish Famine of the 1840s. The Famine was, above all else, an agricultural disaster, and many in Ireland insisted that students must be taught progressive and scientific methods if Ireland was ever to feed itself again. Many absentee Irish landlords, including the Ninth Baron of Geashill who inherited his title in 1856, made determined efforts to modernize farming methods on their estates. Toward that end new National Schools were established in many rural communities. One of these new schools, funded by the Ninth Baron, was built in Geashill.

The work of the new National Schools was enhanced by the establishment of Model Schools, to which a model farm was often attached. The Model Schools taught pupils who were expected either to become gentlemen farmers, or who would become teachers in the National Schools. At the top of the new system of more progressive and scientific education there stood the Albert Agricultural College, Glasnevin, which later became the Faculty of Agriculture of Trinity College, Dublin.[26] It too had a large (at least large by Irish standards) model farm, offering the best instruction for intending farmers and for teachers in the rural National Schools.

Thomas and Herbert Holt, with the financial support and encouragement of their maternal grandfather and uncles, were the beneficiaries of this new Irish rural and agricultural educational system. Both boys began school, in the new Geashill National School before the death of their father.[27] This school, although funded by the Ninth Baron of Geashill, was administered by the local Established Church clergyman. It nevertheless attracted almost equal numbers of Established Church and Roman Catholic pupils.[28]

Students normally began to attend school at the age of six, and Herbert Holt attended the Geashill National School for one and a half years. He left in January of 1863, immediately after his father's death. His maternal relatives then placed the two Holt boys in an agricultural model school – the Dundalk Institute – where several of the Hannon cousins also attended. Herbert Holt spent two years at this institute, after which he spent an additional one and a half years at the Athy Model School. The move to Athy was apparently prompted by the purchase by their uncles, James and Henry Hannon, of a large mill and of Ardleigh House, both located on or near the Grand Canal in Athy. A later Principal of the Athy Model School wrote as follows about the attendance of Thomas and Herbert Holt at that school.

> The Holt family were left not very well provided for. A kinsman, H. H. Hannon, father of a John Alexander Hannon of Ardleigh House, Athy, took Herbert Holt and his brother Tom Holt and they attended Athy Model School, then connected with the Model Farm next door.
>
> Boarders were kept in Athy Model School then, those acting as monitors, and what would be now known as 'Agricultural Students' who attended the Model Farm also for Practice and Theory.
>
> Only two years ago a press was in existence in the old dormitory with 'H. Holt' carved on it and several places with 'H H'.
>
> The story goes that after being in Glasnevin Herbert Holt, with his brother Tom, was handed £100 by H. H. Hannon and told to make his fortune in Canada – which he proceeded to do![29]

The main purpose of the Model Agricultural Schools, such as that at Athy in the 1860s, was to train future farmers and future school teachers who would carry the message of progressive and scientific agriculture to the

National Schools throughout the country. There was, however, a higher institution of agricultural training in Ireland. That was the Albert Agricultural College and Model Farm at Glasnevin, immediately north of the then city limits of Dublin. This was the capstone of the Board of Education's attempt to improve training in, and the practice of, agriculture in Ireland. It had been established in 1838 as 'a School for Industry in the immediate neighbourhood of Dublin with workrooms and a farm of from forty to fifty acres annexed to it; and . . . those who attend it shall be practiced, at stated times, in different descriptions of manual work, and in the general business of agriculture.'[30]

The primary purpose of the new College was to train progressive farmers who would run their own or large leased farms in a model or exemplary way. The college was also designed to train teachers who would then take up positions in the various Model and National Schools strategically located throughout the country.[31] It had boarding facilities which, in 1871, accommodated approximately fifty students. Students were only admitted to the Albert Agricultural College, Glasnevin, on the personal recommendation of the principal of one of the Model Schools, and after sitting a rigorous series of written and oral examinations in reading, penmanship, spelling, grammar, geography, arithmetic, book-keeping, geology and minerology. In addition to these examinations, prospective students had to demonstrate their aptitude for the practical work on the model farm. They were first admitted only on a provisional basis, but after a period of about two weeks those deemed best suited to the program were admitted while the others were sent home.

Herbert Holt entered the Albert Training Institute on 11 January 1871 for examination and observation of his work on the farm. Two weeks later the college records include a list of 'those who were considered unfit for the place'.[32] The list included the name of Herbert Holt. It was customary, however, for students to leave at various times during the year, and also for some to be expelled for disciplinary reasons. As vacancies arose students who had not been admitted, but had placed sufficiently high in the examinations and in the practical farm work were invited to return to take up the vacant positions. Thus, a notation on 8 May 1871 stated that Herbert Holt was once again admitted on trial. His probationary period ended in June, after a series of examinations which left him sick in bed for at least four days. He was one of twenty-six candidates sitting the examinations, gaining ninth place and with it admission to the Albert Training Institute.[33]

Those admitted to the programme had to follow a rigorous work and study schedule. The following was a fairly typical day:

At 6 o'clock	The pupils rise
6:00 to 6:30 a.m.	They dress and say prayers
6:30 to 7:00 a.m.	Feed & clean horses, cattle, etc.
7:00 to 8:00 a.m.	Lecture on Agriculture
8:00 to 9:00 a.m.	Lecture on Agricultural Chemistry, Botany or Veterinary Medicine.
9:00 to 9:30 a.m.	Breakfast

9:30 to 2:00 p.m.	All pupils work on the land
2:00 to 3:00 p.m.	Dinner and recreation
3:00 to 6:00 p.m.	Half the students to farm, and the other half to literary instruction. In winter, farm work till dusk only, remainder literary instruction
6:00 to 8:30 p.m.	Literary subjects. During this period a limited number of junior pupils assist in their turn in the stable, cowhouse, etc.
8:30 to 9:00 p.m.	Supper
9:00 to 9:30 p.m.	Attend horses, cattle, etc.
9:30 to 10:15 p.m.	Retire to dormitories and say prayers
10:15	Lights out.[34]

Like many other dormitory schools of its day, the Albert Institute had a long list of house rules and regulations. There were roll calls for all lectures and any absences had to be arranged in writing. The discipline was, according to one official history, 'maintained with great firmness' but also with 'as much kindness as it is possible to blend with the requisite degree of firmness'.[35]

With the written application of a parent or guardian students could dine out, or leave the college for other reasons, but all such approved applications were carefully recorded in the college records. There is no record that Herbert Holt was ever invited to dine out during the two years he spent at the college, or that he left the college for any other reason than for two Christmas vactions and during the summer.

The college records also note the occasions when students were absent from work or lectures due to illness, and in this regard Herbert Holt's name appears on the records forty-two times. There were a number of others who were frequently sick, but Holt's record in that regard was well above normal. Illness also resulted in the only recorded disciplinary action against Herbert Holt. The reference in this regard, dated 4 July 1872, reads as follows:

> On calling the roll for Literary Instruction at three o'clock I missed three pupils – Herbert Holt, W. Walpole, and I. Keenan. I was told on making enquires that they went to bed ill a few minutes before three o'clock. I went to the dormitories immediately, and on going into H. Holt's room, he was in bed, but reading some book or newspaper.
>
> He immediately placed it under his person and I asked him what did he complain of. He said he was suffering from headache. He had no appearance of illness and I requested to see the book he was reading, he refused saying it was a religious work, and he could not show it.
>
> I have never known a pupil to refuse a similar request to any officer of the establishment and I fear that instead of a religious work, he was perusing one of an objectionable character.[36]

This incident brought further investigation and inquiry by the principal of the school, who noted that 'Holt says the book was his Bible. I have admonished him for not showing it when asked'. This incident, or perhaps the general methods of enforcing discipline at Glasnevin, apparently left a peculiar legacy. Several writers many years later commented about the unusual and intimidating arrangement of Sir Herbert Holt's office atop the aptly named Power Building in Montreal. 'This man Holt seemed to inhabit a world absolutely foreign. He sat behind a desk at the end of a long office, so that everybody coming to talk to him was inspected en route. He spoke like a high priest, and convinced me I should never like to be his secretary'.[37] Holt's old office in the Power Building was renovated long ago, but this description has a remarkable similarity to what the old office, and the occupant, of the Principal's Office at Glasnevin must have looked like to a young transgressor.

The normal course of training at the Albert Agricultural College did not depend a great deal on examinations, other than those for purposes of admission. Students followed the prescribed course of instruction and work, and most left without writing any formal final examinations. The length of the program at that time was two years, and Herbert Holt stayed the two years. There is no reference that he wrote any final examinations or passed some other hurdles to indicate that he had completed the course of study. The official records only have a simple notation, dated 5 June 1873, that 'Herbert Holt left the Institution'. The Registry of Pupils has a some-what more complete assessment of Holt's two year sojourn.

He is active and intelligent, and applied himself diligently to his studies. He was careful in the performance of all duties that devolved on him. He was promoted to the practical agr. class on 1st Sept. 1872. He has acquired a good knowledge of the science and practice of agriculture as taught and exemplified at Glasnevin. He understands land surveying, levelling and mapping. I believe him to be a young man of very excellent character.[38]

Herbert Holt had received the best agricultural education available in Ireland in the 1870s. Most of what he had learned at the Albert Agricultural College, however, would prove of little use to him in his later Canadian business career. He did not become a farmer or an agricultural teacher. The agricultural surveying, land levelling and mapping skills he learned at Glasnevin could be, and were, applied with great success to work he did in railway construction and contracting work, but the most important things Herbert Holt learned in Ireland, and later applied in Canada, were not learned in school. They were the business practices followed by his maternal grandfather, uncles and cousins.

Herbert Holt's grandfather, John Hannon of Prumplestown Mills and later of Athy, owned and operated the old water-powered flour and grist mill after whom the small community of Prumplestown Mills was named. This large old mill served the needs of the local farmers, and the Hannons combined the craft of milling with farming activities. The Prumplestown Mill faced serious competition when the Barrow Navigation Project of Grand Canal opened up shipping from Dublin, via Athy, Carlow and New Ross, to the southern coast of Ireland at Waterford.[39] The new canal provided admirable sites for the development of water power, and large new mills were built at Athy and Carlow.

The Hannons of Prumplestown Mills did not have the necessary funds, and apparently were denied adequate loans, to build new mills on the sites along the Grand Canal. Instead they slowly and painfully built up the business at Prumplestown Mills and then fought to defend it against competitive onslaughts by newer, more efficient but also more indebted rivals on the new canal. During the disastrous economic upheavals of the 1840s the Hannon mill survived because it had no heavy debts. The rival mills at Athy and Carlow failed, and were eventually acquired by the Hannons at a fraction of their original construction costs. The Hannons thus gained effective control, though not a complete monopoly, over the rural milling enterprizes along the Barrow Navigation project. But the exceedingly cautious debt or capitalization policies of the family continued. As late as 1905 family funds were so fully committed to the business that Henry Plewman Hannon felt he could not endanger the venture by providing an appropriate dowry for his daughter. 'It is a strange situation', he wrote in his will, 'that with what means I have locked up in business I cannot provide a reasonable dowry for the girl.'[40]

The business policies of the Hannon family became the policies on which Sir Herbert Holt built his Canadian business career. He was not a person who went heavily into debt to finance a major new venture. He preferred to let others take such risks, and to take over what they had built if and when they got into trouble. In the late 1920s, for example, Herbert Holt masterminded a series of pulp and paper company mergers which left his company, the Canada Power and Paper Company, as the largest newsprint company in Canada. But he said later that neither he nor any of the pulp and paper companies under his control had ever built a new mill, nor had he ever borrowed money from the Royal Bank of which he was President to finance his pulp and paper ventures. He created and expanded the Canada Power and Paper Company by taking over rivals who had gotten into trouble, often thanks to loans made to those rivals by the Royal Bank. He startled an enquiring parliamentary committee, and prompted loud expressions of disbelief, when he told them that neither he nor the pulp and paper companies he controlled had ever borrowed money from the Royal Bank, or from any other Canadian bank. He stated emphatically that it was not his policy to borrow money – he was in the business of loaning it to others. The strategy which had worked, albeit inadvertently, for his relatives in Ireland was refined and implemented with great success in Canada.

The struggle between the several Irish mills near the Barrow Navigation project, and their eventual consolidation into a Hannon-controlled venture also provided valuable insights into the problems that competition can cause, and how consolidation and the establishment of near-monopoly conditions could ensure a more stable business environment. Neither the mill at Prumplestown Mills nor those on the Grand Canal had prospered while competing vigorously with one another. The Hannons were able to stabilize the situation once they gained control of the situation and for a time closed one of the large mills since there was not really enough business for all of them. Similarly, Herbert Holt's answer to a messy and unprofitable competitive situation was always to work for a consolidation which would eliminate the unfortunate aspects of such competition. Nowhere did he succeed better in this than in the generation, transmission and distribution of hydro-electric power on the Island of Montreal. Montreal Light, Heat and Power Consolidated became a classic and inordinately profitable Canadian monopoly company.

The summers and Christmas holidays Herbert Holt spent with his Hannon relatives had an additional benefit. The use of water-power to drive flour and grist mills was not entirely new in the 1860s, but new technological improvements were being made constantly. The most dramatic of the new improvements was the use of waterpower to generate electricity. Herbert Holt almost certainly learned most of what he knew about electricity only after he came to Canada, and only after he had spent at least fifteen years building track for steam railways. The knowledge he had gained in Ireland, however, made it possible for him to realize more quickly than most the potential that lay in converting old water-power driven works to the generation of electricity. He first became involved in Canadian electricity projects by accident. After completing a series of steam railway construction contracts, he obtained a construction contract to built a small electric tramway in Montreal. When the promoters were unable to pay him for construction services rendered, Holt took over the tramway company.

The electricity used in the City of Montreal in the 1890s was generated by coal-fired plants. Herbert Holt had sufficient knowledge of electrical engineering to prepare one of the first studies of the feasibility of generating electric power at the locks of the nearby Chambly Canal. The construction and early operation of the Chambly power plant was fraught with major technological and entrepreneurial difficulties, but in 1901, after a tense boardroom battle, the Chambly power company was merged with Montreal Gas and Royal Electric to form Montreal Light, Heat and Power.

Herbert Holt had come to Canada in 1873 with a practical knowledge of the effective use of capital, and of the basic principles of competition and monopoly practices. He also had a basic familiarity with the application of water-power. He learned these things while preparing himself for a farming career in Ireland.

The surviving documents do not give a clear reason why Herbert Holt left Ireland for Canada immediately after completing the agricultural course at Glasnevin. It seems probable, however, that a major family disaster in 1871 contributed substantially to the decision to emigrate. The disaster involved the Samuel Holt family which held the leases to the Carbury and Haggart Farms. The family had, as was noted earlier, made very substantial improvements on both farms. In 1870 a new Irish Land Act was passed. Under Section 6 of this Act it was provided that major improvements made by a tenant during his occupancy legally belonged to that tenant and could be registered as an encumbrance against the title to that land. Samuel Holt of Carbury and Haggart was one of the first to come forward to register improvements he and his father had made, which he valued at more than £8,000.

The claim was contested by agents of the landlord, Lord Harberton, and came before Judge Lefroy, Chairman of the Quarter Sessions, County Kildare, sitting at Maynooth on 5 January 1871. The major item in dispute was the large and very well built house built just below Carbury Hill, which was valued at £4,000. In addition, major claims were made by the Holts for the building of fences, for the drainage of marshy land, the construction of other farm buildings, and the removal of old and non-functional buildings once new and more modern buildings were erected.[41]

Lord Harberton's agents challenged Samuel Holt's claim to ownership, or compensation for the various improvements they had made. They argued that historically all improvements belonged to the landlord, and that in setting rents for the property Lord Harberton had taken fully into account the various improvements made, or about to be made. The Holts had been granted exceptionally low rental fees because they were making various improvements which would be the property of the landlord. Lord Harberton's agents also argued that since the new provisions had only come into force in 1870 they should apply only to improvements made after that date. But even they admitted that the wording of the Act clearly suggested that at least some prior improvements should be included. It was, however, by no means clear whether improvements made by the current leaseholder's father could be included. Most of the disputed improvements had been made before the elder Samuel Holt had turned the lease over to his son, Samuel, in 1844.

The hearings were protracted, and a decision was not reached until April 1871. The final ruling, however, was a severe defeat for the Holts. Judge Lefroy ruled that some of the drainage, fencing and reclamation work could be registered as the property of the tenant, but that the large and expensive house and most of the other buildings belonged to the landlord. This defeat prompted Samuel Holt of Carbury/Haggart to reassign the lease to his brother-in-law, Henry Barker, and to depart for the United States where, reportedly, he made and lost another fortune.

The litigation and associated problems related to the Carbury and Haggart farms took place at the time when Herbert Holt was just beginning his studies at the Albert Agricultural College. The earlier failure of his father on the Ballycrystal farm, and now the loss of the Carbury and Haggart farms case by his uncle could hardly have encouraged Herbert Holt to take up a farming career in Ireland. While there is no documentary evidence to show that Herbert Holt was preparing himself to take over some or all of the farming operations at Carbury/Haggart, or perhaps some of the farming ventures of his Hannon relatives who were becoming more and more involved in the milling business, it is clear that all his training, up to the time when he left for Canada, pointed in such a direction.

The Carbury/Haggart fiasco probably added one further lesson which Herbert Holt would later apply, often with a vengeance, in Canada. The case demonstrated the power and influence of the law, and of the lawyers who worked very effectively for Lord Harberton. It seemed to reporters of the time, and probably to members of the Holt family as well, that the case was not lost because it was weak, but rather because Lord Harberton could afford to hire the best lawyers to fight the case for him. In later life Sir Herbert found many occasions when good lawyers served him very well. Lawyers and protracted suits became effective instruments whereby Herbert Holt advanced his later business interests in Canada.

Herbert Holt's Irish childhood and youth were not easy. The Holt family had lived in the Carbury area for centuries, but Herbert Holt's father failed as a farmer and died young and destitute, leaving Herbert and his older brother to the care of their maternal relatives. Herbert Holt received the best available agricultural training, but the business careers of his maternal grandfather and uncles, an understanding of their financial, competitive policies and technological innovations, and the lessons learned about the legal system in the case in which the paternal family home was lost, proved of far greater relevance than the things he learned in school. Twelve years after arriving in Canada, Herbert Holt had become a successful and moderately wealthy railway contractor. In the year marking the successful completion of the transcontinental Canadian Pacific Railway, in whose construction Herbert Holt played a prominent role, he received word that his mother had died in Ireland. She bequeathed to her son Thomas Grattan Holt 'the sum of £5 as a token of my love and remembrance' and to her son Herbert Samuel Holt, 'the sum of £5 in token of remembrance wishing it was more.'[42] Jane Hannon Holt may not have known it at the time of her death, but her two sons were putting into practice in Canada the sentiments expressed in her will. Thomas was a jovial, and many would say loveable, railway contractor who loved the comraderie of the construction camps. Herbert, on the other hand was putting into practices some of the hard and practical lessons he had learned in Ireland, amassing financial resources and power which ensured that his estate would exceed Jane Holt's wildest dreams or hopes.

Notes

1. No complete list of all the corporate directorships held by Sir Herbert Holt has ever been prepared. Various issues of *Who's Who in Canada* list many, but not all, the Holt directorships.
2. See for example, M. Grattan O'Leary, 'Holt vs. Jones. Twin word sketches of the principals in a colossal struggle for control of Canada's most stupendous asset – hydro-electric power', *Maclean's*, 15 March 1929.
3. Clarence Hogue *et al.*, *Quebec: Un siecle d'electricite*, Montreal, Libre Expression, 1979.
4. The most detailed published biographical study of Sir Herbert Holt is the first chapter in Peter C. Newman, *Flame of Power*, London, 1959. Newman's work, however, has numerous factual errors. It is based, in part at least, on rumour and gossip in the Canadian political and business community.
5. *The Gazette, Montreal*, and *The Montreal Daily Star*, 29 September 1941.
6. Herbert Holt provided a detailed chronology of all the jobs he had held in Canada, from September of 1873 until the summer of 1888, in his 1888 application for membership in the Canadian Society of Civil Engineers. The application is in NAC. *MG 28. I. 277*

7. Peter C. Newman in *Flame of Power* repeated the mistaken claim that Herbert Holt had been trained at Trinity College, Dublin, as a civil engineer. In fact, as will be shown in this paper, Holt studied agriculture at Glasnevin, not engineering at Trinity College, and he migrated to Canada at age 17, not 19 as Newman and others have claimed.

8. This research has been expedited by the work done by Professor John Carroll, former Dean of the Faculty of Agriculture, Trinity College, Dublin, and by J. F. Clarke of Toronto, both of whom gathered relevant information about Herbert Holt's education and family background in Ireland. These two gentlemen graciously made the results of their research available to me. I checked all the relevant sources in Ireland, and also consulted other relevant primary and archival sources, in a research trip to Ireland in 1985.

9. Register of Baptisms, 1846–1905, St Mary's Church, Church of Ireland, Parish of Geashill, King's County. This register was still in the custody of St Mary's Church when I saw it in 1985. In the Register the name of the child is given as Samuel Herbert Holt, but he was always known as Herbert Holt or as Herbert Samuel Holt.

10. Detailed geneological notes and family trees of the Holts of Coolavacoose have been prepared. Family members made copies of these available to me when I visited the farm in 1985.

11. The Samuel Holt family which occupied the Coolavacoose farm in 1985 had in their possession a local history and several newspaper accounts giving some of the colourful details of Castle Carbre. The Castle, sometimes referred to as the Manor House, fell into ruins when one of the female heirs became embroiled in a legal suit. She lost the case, but before her eviction she gave instructions to have the roof torn off the building, which quickly fell into ruin when this was done.

12. Biographical details on the Pomeroy family are given in Sir Bernard Burke's 1862 edition of the *Dictionary of the Peerage and Baronetage of the British Empire*, p. 514.

13. Details about the acreage, buildings and valuation of these farms are given in Richard Griffith, Commissioner of Valuation, *General Valuation of Rateable Property in Ireland, Act 15 and 16 Victoria, Cap. 53. County of Kildare. Valuations of the Several Tenements comprising that portion of the Union of Edenderry, Situate in the County above named*, (Dublin: Board of Guardians of the Edenderry Union 1853). Additional information is available in Irish Land Commission, Register of Freeholders, Folio 1414, and in the Irish Land Commission, Order fixing fair rent, No. 2486 which indicates that Samuel Holt paid an annual rent of £321 5s 8d for the Haggard and Carbury farms which together comprised 453 acres of land. The various improvements made by Samuel and Ann Grattan Holt, and by their son Samuel, are described in great detail in an article entitled 'The Land Act and Its Working', published in *The Irish Builder*, 15 January 1971, p. 16–17, and in a series of articles in the *Leinster Express*, 7 and 14 January 1871 and 15 April 1871.

14. Two letters in the possession of Samuel Holt of Coolavacoose give details of family members who emigrated: Thomas Holt, Wellesley, Ontario to Samuel Holt, 28 January 1870, and Thomas Holt, New Haven, Connecticut, to Sam Holt, Coolavacoose, 1 December 1873. A cousin of Sir Herbert Holt visited Montreal in 1936 and wrote of his impressions of his cousin whom he describes as 'a big man in the Dominion. William Grattan Holt, Kansas City, Missouri, to Samuel C. Holt, Coolavacoose, 5 November 1936.

15. Details of the lease reassigned by Samuel Holt to his son, another Samuel Holt,

are given in Irish Land Commission, Order fixing fair rent No. 2486.

16. The terms of the lease were for twenty-one years, or for the life of the leasee, whichever came first.

17. No one in the family now seems to know the precise nature of the problem between Samuel Holt of Carbury and Haggart farms and his brother William, but several family members remembered hearing that the affairs of the William Robert Grattan Holt family would not stand up to close scrutiny. There were four sons and one daughter in the family of Samuel and Ann Grattan Holt. According to the family pedigree GO 576, p. 106 and the *Alumni Dubliniensis*, the eldest son, Thomas Grattan Holt, obtained both a B. A. and an M. A. degree at Trinity College, Dublin. The records of the Institute of Civil Engineers of Ireland show that another son, Edward Grattan Holt, received an engineering degree from Trinity College, Dublin. Samuel, the second son of Samuel and Ann Grattan Holt, who took over the leases to the Carbury and Haggart farms in 1844, and William Robert Grattan, the youngest son and later the father of Sir Herbert Holt, apparently had no advanced schooling. The youngest member of the family was a girl named Anne who married Henry Barker of Celbridge. The Barkers' son, John Edward, took over the lease to the Carbury and Haggart farms in 1873 after her brother Samuel lost an important land law case and left for the United States, although at some time between 1873 and 1903 Barker leased the farms to William F. Pilkington. Pilkington applied to the Irish Land Commission for an Order Fixing Fair rent in 1903, at which time the rent was reduced from £318 to £281. The following year the farms were sold for £7028 to the sub-leasee, William H. Pilkington. The Irish Land Commission provided an advance of £7,000. The purchaser agreed to make annual payments of £227 until the debt was retired. Documentation is available in the records of the Irish Land Commission. Agreement between Vendor and a Tenant for Sale of a Holding, dated 10 February 1904, between E. A. G. Pomeroy and William H. Pilkington.

18. Sir Charles Coote, *General View of the Agriculture and Manufactures of the King's County, with Observations on the means of their improvement*, Dublin, Graisberry & Campbell, 1801.

19. The Ballycrystal farm is described in some detail in Richard Griffith, *General Valuation of Rateable Property in Ireland, King's County and County Westmeath. Valuation of the several Tenements in the Union of Tullamore situate in the Counties above named*, Dublin, Alexander Thom and Sons, 1854, p. 28. See also Irish Land Commission Records, Schedule attached to Order No. 1718, Order Fixing Fair Rent, 5 July 1904; Irish Land Commission Records, Agreement between Vendor and Tenant for Sale of a Holding, 26 October 1908, and Land Registry of Ireland, Register of Freeholders, County Kings, Folio 5732.

20. Griffith *1854 Valuation*, p. 28

21. For more information on the productive capacity of the Ballycrystal farm see Irish Land Commission, Schedule attached to Order Fixing Fair Rent, No 1718, 5 July 1904.

22. For specific details see Dorset Record Office, Wingfield-Digby Ireland files, 'Report of Works of Land Improvement executed Between the year 1847 and the present time in the Barony of Geashill, the property of Earl Digby, November 1853' and the 'Geashill Manor Account for Year ended on the 25th March 1854'. These documents indicate that Lord Digby was willing to make loans available to tenants who wished to make improvements, but that he made few substantial improvements on his own account.

23. Coote, *Agriculture and Manufactures of the King's County*. The description given

here is for 1801, fifty years before William Grattan Holt leased Ballycrystal, but other evidence suggests no substantial improvements or changes were made until 1856 when the Eighth Baron of Geashill died and was succeeded by his much more progressive and far-sighted son who initiated new rental policies and made numerous other improvements. The extent of the improvements after 1856, the year in which William Robert Grattan Holt lost his lease to Ballycrystal, is discussed in *The King's County Directory. First Year, 1890, including a Short History, together with Coloured Map, Almanac and Calendar,* Parsontown, King's County Chronicle, 1891, p. 213–214.

24. R. D. Crotty, *Irish Agricultural Production: Its Volume and Structure,* Cork, 1966.
25. No documentation seems to remain which explains the circumstances of William Robert Grattan Holt's death, but surviving and transmitted family gossip at Coolavacoose hints at, but does not document or explain, dubious circumstances.
26. The name of the Albert Agricultural College at Glasnevin changed over the years. I shall use the most commonly used name throughout, although in the early years it was often referred to simply as the Albert Training Institute or the Albert Agricultural Training Institute. The history of the college is given in a special publication celebrating the centennial of the college and entitled, *The Albert Agricultural College, Glasnevin, 1838–1939,* a copy of which is available in the Library on the new campus of the Faculty of Agriculture, Trinity College, Dublin.
27. *The King's County Directory,* p. 213.
28. The pupil registers, giving among other facts the religious affiliation of each pupil, were being stored in the furnace room of the new Geashill school when I visited it in 1985. The National School which Herbert Holt attended still stood, but was in process of extensive renovation and at least partial demolition.
29. Copy of a letter received from Ellis Kemp, Principal, Athy Model National School, County Kildare. This letter was sent to Professor John Carroll, former Dean, Faculty of Agriculture, Trinity College, Dublin, who kindly made it available to me. A copy is also available in the Holt file in the archives of the Royal Bank of Canada, in Montreal.
30. *The Albert Agricultural College, 1838–1938,* p. 12. Details pertaining to the curriculum and to some of the distinguished agriculturalists and scientists who taught at the Albert Agricultural College during the years when Herbert Holt attended the college are given on pages 34 and 35 of this centennial history.
31. According to the college's centennial history 848 pupils attended the school in the first thirty years of its existence. Of these, 189 reportedly became farmers on their own account, 204 worked as land stewards, agents and gardeners, 107 became teachers of agriculture and other subjects, 55 were engaged in other industrial pursuits connected with farming, 52 had emigrated to become planters in the Caribbean or in Canada, while the later career of the others was either unknown or not directly related to agriculture. *Albert Agricultural College, 1838–1938,* p. 30.
32. 'Register of the Albert Training Institute', now at the Faculty of Agriculture, Trinity College, Dublin.
33. *Ibid.*
34. *The Albert Agricultural College, 1838–1938,* pp. 35–6.
35. *Ibid.*
36. Copied from the records of the Albert Training Institute, Faculty of Agriculture, Trinity College, Dublin.
37. As quoted in Newman, *Flame of Power,* p. 31.

38. Register of Pupils, Albert Agricultural College, Glasnevin, held at the Faculty of Agriculture, Trinity College, Dublin.
39. The Grand Canal ran westward from Dublin for approximately 45 kilometres. Then it split into two major projects. One major canal system, often referred to as the Barrow Canal project, followed the Barrow River southward via Athy, Carlow and New Ross to provide water communication with the south coast at Waterford. The second branch was the Shannon Navigation project. It continued westward until it intersected the Shannon River and Lakes system which offered navigation south-westward to Limerick.
40. Irish Public Record Office, Probate of the Will of Henry Plewman Hannon, 1905.
41. According to officials in the Irish Public Record Office, and the Irish Land Registry Office, the original transcripts of this trial were destroyed during the civil war in 1922. The case was, however written up in detail in both *The Irish Builder* and *The Leinster Express*. The account given here is based on the reports in those two papers.
42. Public Record Office of Ireland, *Wills and Administration, 1885*, and *Will Book, Probate Division, District Registry at Kilkenny*, 1885, p. 58. The wording of the will is unusual, but highly appropriate. Thomas Grattan Holt was a warm and gregarious individual. He was the jovial storekeeper in the Rockies after whom the temporary Canadian Pacific Railway construction town of Holt City was named. He was a person to whom a mother, or others who had known him, might extend their love. Herbert got only the more appropriate wish that the inheritance might have been larger. Thomas spent most of his adult life as a railway contractor, first for the Canadian Pacific Railway and later for the Canadian Northern Railway. He loved the cameraderie of the construction camps. Herbert was a loner.

8 Friendship patterns and social networks among post-war Irish migrants in Sydney

Seamus Grimes

While considerable attention has been paid to analysing the settlement patterns of particular migrant groups such as the southern Europeans, and more recently the Indochinese refugees, in Australia's large cities, Irish migrants have given rise to very little study. Among the reasons which may account for this is the miniscule size of the Irish migrant population during the period since the Second World War. Another important reason is the general consensus in Australia that the Irish have been an essential part of the foundational European settlement, and their cultural closeness to the Australian identity would suggest that Irish migrants had little difficulty in adapting to their new society. This chapter, however, sets out to show that this view of Irish migrant settlement is rather facile, and that there is a greater need to appreciate the intricacies of migrant adaptation in a new urban society. To illustrate some of the processes involved, a detailed analysis was undertaken of the formation of friendship patterns and social networks among a small sample of the Irish migrant population in Sydney.

The postwar period was one of major expansion in the Australian migrant population, resulting in a huge influx from a variety of sources. Initially, displaced refugees, mainly from Eastern Europe, obtained a home in Australia. Later on, the largest inflow of post-war migrants began arriving from southern Europe, particularly from Italy and Greece. Since the 1970s, however, the admittance of more than 120,000 Indochinese refugees has signalled a significant shift in migration policy from the days of 'White Australia'. It was not until 1972 that preferential treatment of 'British subjects' regarding visas and permanent residence was removed from Australian policy. Preferential treatment also extended to the assisted passage scheme, with 84 per cent of British migrants who arrived between 1947 and 1969 being assisted, compared with only 24·5 per cent of southern Europeans.[1] The term 'British subject' also referred to Irish persons who were born before 1949, when Ireland left the Commonwealth.

Despite this favourable treatment, however, the post-war Irish influx formed only a miniscule part of the total migrant population. The Irish proportion of the foreign-born fell from 20 per cent in 1901, when the Irish were the second largest migrant group after the English, to 6 per cent in 1947 and to 2·2 per cent in 1981. It is within the context, therefore, of a diminishing Irish presence in a society which was increasingly taking on a multicultural complexion that the adaptation of post-war Irish migrants to Sydney is investigated. Their adaptation is examined in terms of the spatial dimension of their social interaction within the Sydney metropolitan area.

Migrant studies to date both in Australia and elsewhere have been strongly influenced by the findings of Duncan and Lieberson, which demonstrated an inverse relationship between the residential concentration of migrants and their assimilation.[2] In the larger Australian cities of Sydney and Melbourne these findings have been substantiated by a number of studies.[3] Much of this Australian work has demonstrated a range of assimilation levels, varying from the high levels of the 'British and Irish-born' to intermediate levels of north-west Europeans, down to the low levels of southern Europeans. Because of the particular historical background of the Irish in Australia, and because of their numerical insignificance in recent years, the Australian census unfortunately groups the Irish in the same category as the British. While making access to Irish birthplace data more difficult, it partly reflects the official view regarding the relative homogeneity of this grouping. In addition, the general consensus emanating from the Australian literature to date suggests that the Irish, like the British, are the closest, both socially and culturally, to the Australian host society, and that their residential dispersal reflects a high level of assimilation.

While the census data support this general consensus, this study challenges a simplistic interpretation based on secondary data which are totally residence-based. The significance of residence alone in the context of migrant adaptation has been greatly overemphasized, largely because of the availability of census data, and because of the difficulties associated with analysing the more complex – although more relevant – phenomenon of social interaction. While there has been growing awareness in the literature of the need to focus on social interaction, migrant studies to date have shown little evidence of the extensive fieldwork necessary for this approach.[4]

Although the use of census data is an essential part of analysing migrant adaptation, it is merely an initial stage in the analysis, and in isolation it can give an inaccurate view of assimilation. Part of the initial analysis involves the identification of social and spatial differences within the migrant population in relation to period of residence, realizing that the adaptation process has both a temporal and a spatial pattern associated with it.

Migrant adaptation can be conceptualized in terms of the need for immigrants who have been cut off from former kin and friendship networks to construct new social networks in their adopted environment. The construction of such networks may involve a radically new experience for migrants, in an environment which is both culturally and spatially quite different from their previous experience. The main focus of this study is the construction of such networks within a spatial context.

Upon entering the new environment a myriad of social and spatial factors will influence the construction of migrant networks. The nature of the migration process itself, which tends to be very selective in terms of age, sex and social background, needs to be examined. The inflow of a migrant group and their eventual distribution throughout a metropolis is affected by such factors.

In examining social interaction in a metropolis with a considerable migrant population, it is essential at the outset to differentiate between the native and non-native populations, and also, because of varying migration experiences, between different migrant groups. While the non-native population may have many social and demographic characteristics which are different from the native population, an essential difference is the reduced access of the non-native population to kin relations. This latter characteristic, however, will vary between migrant groups, depending on their migration history.

In the context of Australian migration, groups such as the Greeks and Italians appear to have considerable kinship relations, resulting from chain migration operating within a traditional society, characterized by an extended family structure.[5] The Irish, however, who, like the British, have benefited significantly from the assisted passage scheme, have been characterized by a migration experience dominated by single persons and young married couples, although migrants from Northern Ireland appear to have been more commonly part of a nuclear family structure upon arrival. In an excellent study of post-war Irish migration to Britain, where kinship networks did play an important role, Walter described the main structural characteristics of migrants as including youth, single status, low socio-economic group and rural background.[6] While the Irish in Sydney also shared such background characteristics, many of them found it necessary to substitute former kinship relations with new networks based on friendship.

Post-war Irish migrants

The population censuses of 1954 and 1981 have been examined to obtain some indication of the main demographic and social characteristics of post-war Irish migrants, and in particular to analyse their distribution within the Sydney metropolitan area. Table 8.1 illustrates the Irish population of New South Wales in 1981 by period of residence. A quarter of the 21,673 persons antedated 1952 and another quarter arrived during the 1970s. The remaining half were unevenly divided between the 1950s and the 1960s, with 1953–59 accounting for only 10·5 per cent of the total.

The 1954 census reveals that few Irish migrants had brought children with them to Australia.[7] The ratio of persons under twenty years of age per thousand females (twenty to forty-nine) had the following values: 95 for 'Ireland' and the Irish Republic, 268 for Northern Ireland and 389 for European migrants. The Irish population also had a high male ratio, which increased from 112 in 1921 to 132 in 1954. Occupationally the main contrasting feature was the high proportion of males from the republic in

Table 8.1 The Irish population of New South Wales, by length of residence, 1981 (%)

Pre-1953	24·3
1953–1959	10·5
1960–1971	37·7
1972–1981	25·3
Not stated	2·2
Total population (1981): 21,673	

Source: Census of population, 1981.

'Building and Transport' (32·5 per cent, compared with 19 per cent for Australian males, and 22 per cent for males from Northern Ireland).

By 1981 the Irish migrant population had undergone some changes in composition, yet some of the contrasts with the host population remained. The number of married couples coming to Australia with Irish-born children increased, yet the number from the republic remained relatively small compared with those from Northern Ireland and England. The ratio of persons under twenty years per thousand females (twenty to forty-nine) in New South Wales had the following values: 289 for the Irish Republic, 497 for Northern Ireland and 550 for England.

By 1981 the male/female ratio for under thirty-year-olds was now quite even, but it increased with increasing age: thirty to thirty-four years (112), thirty-five to thirty-nine years (117), forty to forty-four years (115) and forty-five to sixty-four years (136). An examination of the marriage rate for different age groups points towards the end of the 'European marriage pattern' – which had long characterized Irish demography – for young Irish migrants, with 25 per cent of twenty-to-twenty-four-year-old males married, compared with only 9 per cent of the same age group in Ireland. However, from twenty-five years of age upwards, both males and females from the republic had the lowest marriage rate in each age group, while Northern Ireland's proportion was higher than for the Australian population. Very low marriage rates characterized migrants from the republic, particularly, in the 'Professional, Technical and Related' occupations, which may have been influenced by the number of Irish priests and religious in Australia.

Occupationally, the contrast between the two populations had diminished since the 1950s (Table 8.2). The main difference for males was the higher proportion in the 'Tradesmen, Process Workers and Labourers' category (46 per cent, compared with 37 per cent for Australian males). The Irish female labour force, on the other hand, had a higher status profile compared with Australian females, with a quarter of those from the republic in the 'Professional, Technical and Related' category, compared with only 18 per cent of Australian and 16·7 per cent of Northern Ireland females. In addition to having a more youthful composition, therefore, because of the relatively larger number of children accompanying parents, compared with those from the republic, the Northern Ireland population also had a more working-class occupational profile in 1981.

Table 8.2 Labour force in Australia, by birthplace, 1981 (%)

	Australia	Northern Ireland	Irish Republic including Ireland undefined
Males			
Tradesmen, Process workers, Labourers	37·0	46·8	46·2
Professional and related	12·0	11·2	11·9
Farmers, Fishermen and related	9·4	2·9	3·0
Clerical	9·2	7·8	6·9
Administration	7·4	6·9	6·8
Transport/Communications	7·1	6·0	7·1
Service/Sport	4·9	7·0	6·8
Sales	7·0	6·8	6·0
Remainder	6·0	4·6	5·4
Females			
Clerical	33·9	32·2	27·3
Professional, Technical and related	18·0	16·7	25·1
Service/Sport	12·9	19·1	18·2
Sales	11·9	10·8	8·7
Trades	6·1	10·4	8·4
Remainder	17·2	10·8	12·3

Source: Census of population, 1981.

Table 8.3 The Irish-born and total populations of Sydney statistical subdivisions, 1981 (%)

Statistical subdivision	Total population		Northern Ireland		Irish Republic	
	Male	Female	Male	Female	Male	Female
Central Sydney	14·2	14·0	12·3	10·9	17·1	17·8
Inner Western	4·6	4·8	2·9	2·2	5·6	5·3
Southern Sydney	21·0	21·0	17·2	16·7	18·8	17·3
South Western Sydney	7·0	6·8	10·8	11·8	7·9	6·7
Western Sydney	27·3	26·6	35·6	35·3	31·7	27·6
Northern Sydney	20·7	21·6	17·3	19·4	18·2	21·4
Gosford–Wyong	5·0	5·1	3·8	3·6	3·7	3·7

Source: Census of population, 1981.

The Irish in Sydney

In 1981 more than a quarter of Australia's 67,738 Irish migrants lived in Sydney, constituting a mere 0·5 per cent of the metropolitan population. Table 8.3 indicates that the Irish were well dispersed residentially. The main difference between them and the remainder of the population was their higher representation in the lower-status western subdivisions, and their lower representation in the higher-status northern and southern subdivisions. Interesting differences were also evident between the distribution of the Northern Irish population and the Irish from the republic. The Northern Irish were more strongly represented in the two western divisions, where the Irish Republic's population was closer to the total population. Migrants from the republic, on the other hand, had higher

Table 8.4 Selected dissimilarity indices at the local government area level in Sydney, 1966 and 1981

Year	Population	Index	
		Males	Females
1966	Total: Irish-born	11·6	10·1
1981	Total: Irish Republic	10·3	14·6
	Total: North Ireland	14·7	14·6
	North Ireland: Irish Republic	14·2	15·6
	Total: Irish-born, five years' residence	21·1	18·2
	Total: Irish, five years' residence	11·0	12·2

proportions than either the total population or the Northern Ireland population in the Inner West and Central subdivisions.

These differences are further summarized in Table 8.4 in the form of dissimilarity indices. The index of dissimilarity is the percentage of a birthplace group that would have to redistribute itself by spatial units to have the same percentage distribution as the host society (Australian-born) population. The Irish index was relatively small in 1966 and it remained little changed by 1981. Indices for non-English-speaking migrants in 1966 varied between 25 for Germans and 55·3 for Greeks. The Northern Irish had a higher index both in relation to the total population and in relation to Irish persons from the republic. Also, recent arrivals had an index twice as large as the general migrant population.

A more detailed analysis of the Irish population at the census collector's district level in 1971 (Fig. 8.1) revealed a number of clusters of Irish persons living in contiguous collector's districts in the western suburbs, the inner city and the mid-western suburbs. Within these clusters the Irish population was more concentrated than the remainder of the population and it was also characterized by a strong male bias. Indeed, one of the main contrasts between the Irish-born and the total population was in relation to the sex ratio (Table 8.5). A male deficit characterized the total population for all areas apart from the western and south-western subdivisions, whereas this was true only of the Irish-born in north Sydney. Elsewhere the number of males per hundred females ranged between 104 and 122. Despite the reduction in the male/female ratio since the 1950s, the Irish population's residential distribution in 1981 was still marked by a strong male bias.

In keeping with its widely dispersed residential pattern throughout the metropolitan area, the Irish population had a considerably differentiated socio-economic composition. A non-randomly selected sample of 620 Irish persons taken from a wide variety of Irish social events in the city indicated that the inner, eastern and mid-western suburbs acted as receiving areas for the most recent arrivals, while the outer suburban areas had a more settled and established migrant population.[8] The Irish in the mid-western suburbs were predominantly in lower-status occupations, had lower levels of home and car ownership, and more than half of them did not consider themselves as permanently settled in Australia. In the low-status far western suburbs three-quarters of the Irish were married, they had four or more children and

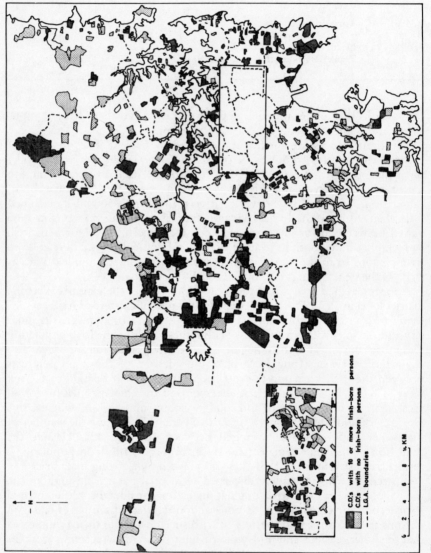

Figure 8.1 Distribution of the Irish-born population of Sydney, 1971. *C.D.* Census collector's district. *L.G.A.* Local government area

Table 8.5 Sex ratios of the Irish and total populations of Sydney, 1981: number of males per hundred females

Statistical subdivision	Total population	Northern Ireland	Irish Republic	All Ireland
Central Sydney	85	119	109	111
Inner Western	93	139	119	122
Southern Sydney	97	109	118	108
South Western Sydney	100	97	109	104
Western Sydney	100	107	114	112
Northern Sydney	93	95	96	95
Gosford Wyong	96	111	114	113

Source: 1981 census.

the majority of them were home owners. The northern suburbs, on the other hand, had the highest proportion of Irish in professional and service occupations, and few of them had an Irish spouse.

There was evidence of considerable residential movement within the metropolitan area, predominantly from inner transient to outer suburban neighbourhoods. Much of the movement was associated with marriage and the acquisition of a home, the major flow being in the direction of the relatively less expensive far western suburbs. Such moves frequently involved distances of more than 20 km, placing considerable strain on efforts to maintain contact with Irish friends in the former area of residence. There were also frequent short-distance moves between flats among the transient Irish population.

Analysis of the Irish club membership files for 1975, representing about 10 per cent of the migrant population, revealed that the largest concentration of club members (32 per cent) was in the mid-western suburbs. The Burwood area had a particular significance for those involved in construction work. Their residential pattern indicated a preference for home unit blocks located close to the two main railway lines, and it also demonstrated a definite pattern of flat-sharing. The area also had a remarkable concentration of labourers, semi-skilled workers and tradesmen, frequently mentioned occupations being 'plant operator', 'drainer' and 'pipe layer', indicating the near monopoly by the Irish of underground cable installation since the 1960s.

Irish migrants of the mid-western suburbs

Since there was no base population from which to draw a random sample, a network approach was used to build up a snowball sample. Background research based on the reconnaissance survey of Irish social activities, the analysis of Irish club membership files and the spatial distribution of the 1971 Irish population at the collector's district level suggested the mid-western suburbs as the most likely part of the metropolitan area in which to obtain a reasonable number of contacts within a short period. A sample of 100 households with an Irish head were interviewed, and information concerning their 484 friends throughout the metropolitan area was also obtained.

The data, therefore, allowed a detailed analysis of local contact patterns within the study area and a more superficial examination of patterns within the metropolitan area as a whole. Friendships with persons of any nationality were included. Since the addresses of all interviewees and their friends were obtained, together with information on socializing nodes, it was possible to carry out a detailed examination both of the spatial structure of friendship patterns and of the social processes underlying them. A further aim was to trace the extent of interconnectedness of friendship patterns, particularly within the interview area.

Considerable difficulty was encountered in tracing the sample. The procedure began with a small number of contacts from the reconnaissance survey and gradually a list of potential respondents living in the area between Stanmore and Flemington was compiled. After each interview further contacts were sought, and interviewing proceeded on a daily basis for five months. A bias towards married migrants developed because of difficulties in gaining entry to the close-knit networks of single males in the Burwood area.

Problems also arose regarding the confidentiality of the information being requested, such as the names and addresses of friends. Because friends of friends were being traced in many instances, however, a greater level of acceptance was gradually achieved. The network approach also had the advantage that gaps in the information were filled in by subsequent respondents. The data collection method, however, resulted in a study that was more akin to a participant observation approach than to the orthodox random sample. While the more conventional method would have had the important advantage of being representative of the total migrant population, it is unlikely that it would have contributed the insights into the processes underlying interconnections between migrants which were provided by network analysis.

The study area

Between 1921 and 1971 the mid-western suburbs were a downwardly mobile area, with the local government areas of Ashfield, Marrickville and Burwood falling by two quartiles in socio-economic status.[9] During the post-war period the older part of these suburbs experienced considerable migrant settlement, with southern Europeans accounting for between 44 and 74 per cent of migrant movement into the local government areas of Ashfield, Concord and Marrickville between 1947 and 1966. Because of the unfortunate census practice of grouping UK and Irish-born migrants together, the census atlas of 1971 noted a marked absence of UK and Irish-born migrants from the inner western suburbs favoured by Greeks and Italians.

The mid-western suburbs were well provided for by public transport, with two railway lines giving ease of access to the central business district,

Table 8.6 Characteristics of interviewees and their friends (%)

Interviewees (n=100)	%	Friends (n=484)	%
Abroad ten years or more	57	Friend type:	
Not settled in Australia	34	Family	42
Unskilled/Semi-skilled/Skilled	68	Drinking	24
Three years or less in present job	60	Other	34
Work with the Irish	42	Socializing place:	
Changeable job location	34	Hotel	26
Work trip thirty minutes or more	31	Home	47
One or more cars	76	Other	27
Under two years in precious residence	48	Occupational status:	
Flat or home unit	48	Unskilled/semi-skilled	36
Renting accommodation	59	Skilled	31
Plan to move from present residence	48	Small business/Professional	33
Regular contact with family in Ireland	58	Nationality of friends: Irish	76
Contact with kin in Sydney	17	Nationality of friend's spouse: Irish	45
Contact with in-laws in Sydney	22	Marital status: married	72
Naturalization – desirable	21	Mode of contact: exchange home visits	60
Attend Irish Centre/functions	25	Duration of friendship:	
Read Irish newpapers	40	Under 4 years	34
No Australian friends	41	4–9 years	34
		9 years and over	31
		Distance to residence of friend:	
		under 4.3 km	55
		4.3–11.6 km	24
		11.6 km and over	21
		Frequency of contact: at least weekly	62

one between Stanmore and Flemington, the other between Marickville and Lakemba. More than 50 per cent of females in this area were working, while flats and home units were the predominant type of accommodation close to the railway lines, and private housing increased in importance away from them.

Friendship patterns

The sample data related to about 500 Irish persons since forty of the interviewees had an Irish spouse and 76 per cent of the 484 friends were also Irish. The 484 linkages were cross-tabulated, using thirty-two interviewee variables and ten friend variables. Table 8.6 contains the general characteristics of the interviewees and their friends. A typology of two contrasting friendship patterns was constructed, based on chi-square associations with a significance of 0·05 or less. The main differentiating factor between the two was period of residence, with the first pattern describing friendships of the more established interviewees, and the second describing those of the more recent arrivals (Table 8.7).

Interviewees in the first general friendship pattern had the following characteristics: most of them had been out of Ireland for ten years or more and were settled in Australia. Many came from higher-status occupations and were well established, living in privately owned homes. Few were

Table 8.7 Friendship patterns

Friend variables	Group 1	Group 2	Abroad (years)	Occupation	In job (years)	Work with Irish?	Job location	Journey to work (minutes)	Car(s)	In previous residence (years)	Accommodation	Nature of tenure	Plans to move?	Contact with family?	Contact with kin*	Contact with in-laws*	Naturalization?	Irish centres?	Irish functions?	Irish newspapers?	Australian friends?
Group 1 values	10+		Settled Small bus./profess.		3+	No	Fixed	30+	1+	2+	House	Owned	No	No	Yes	Yes	Yes	No	No	No	Yes
Group 2 values		1–9	Unsettled Unskilled/skilled		3–	Yes	Changeable.	30–	None	2–	Flat	Rented	Yes	Yes	No	No	No	Yes	Yes	Yes	No
Drinking	‹	›	1	1	1	1	1	1							1			1	1	1	1
Family	›	‹	1	1	1	1	1	1					1	1	1			1		1	1
Other	‹	›	1			1	1	0	1				1	1	1			1			1
Hotels	‹	›	1			1	1	1	0	1			0					1			1
Homes	›	‹	1	1		1	1	1	0	1			0								1
Other	‹	›	1	1						1			1					0			1
Unskilled/semi-skilled	‹	›	1	1	1	1	1	1			1	1	1	1	1	1	1	1	1	1	1
	›	‹	0	1	0						0	0	0	1			0				0
Small business/Professional	›	‹	1		1	1	1	1			1	1	1	1	1		1	1	1		1
Irish friends	‹	›	1			1	1				1						1	1	1	1	
Irish spouses	‹	›	1	1	1	1		0			1	1	1	1			1			1	1
Married	›	‹	1	1	1	1				1	1	1	1	1			1	1	1		1
Visited/visit	‹	›				0	0						1			1					
Period of friendship	›	‹	1	1	1	1	1				1	1	1	1	1	1	1	1	1	1	1
Distance	‹	›	1	1			1					1	1					1		1	
Frequency	‹	›	1									1	1					1	1	1	

1, Positive association (significance: 0·05); 0, negative association (significance: 0·05).
* In Sydney.

involved in ethnic circles and they had little contact with relations in Ireland. Some had in-laws in Sydney, most of them had Australian friends, and they were in favour of naturalization. While this first group of interviewees, therefore, were the older established ones, with little involvement in ethnic activities, there were some exceptions to the general rule. In some cases younger migrants shared similar friendship patterns with this older group.

In this first general friendship pattern friends had the following characteristics: they were predominantly family type, most of them were married, and their social life was mainly home-based. Compared with the second general pattern, a higher proportion of friends had higher-status occupations. A smaller proportion of friends were Irish, and fewer of them had an Irish spouse. They had longer periods of friendship than the second group, distances to the homes of friends were shorter, yet frequency of contact was lower. Figures 8.2(a) and (b) illustrate the more restricted spatial spread of established interviewees compared with recent arrivals, many of whom were forced to seek homes in the outer suburbs. The first general pattern, therefore, indicates that the longer-settled migrants had left the 'ethnic community', if they had ever been part of it. In common with previous studies, it suggests that the role of friends in the more advanced stage of the life cycle had declined as family commitments took over.[10]

The second general friendship pattern – the reverse of the first one – reflects friendships of the more recently arrived migrants (Table 8.7). These interviewees had been less than ten years abroad, and many were still unsettled. Many of them were in unskilled or semi-skilled jobs and had been only a short period in their job. They were likely to be involved in Irish construction networks, had lower levels of car ownership, and residentially they were transient. Contact with family members in Ireland was still strong, Irish clubs and social functions were popular among them, while friendships with Australians were less common than among the established migrants. This friendship pattern reflected a less home-based social life, with many friends being single and regarded as drinking rather than family friends. Since working with the Irish was common, they had more Irish friends, and more of their friends had an Irish spouse. Despite the longer distances to their friends' homes, frequency of contact was greater, signifying the more important role of friendship during the early stages in the new environment.

Network composition within the study area

An examination of interconnections between interviewees and friends within the study area provides additional insights into the processes underlying Irish migrant friendship patterns in the mid-western suburbs. The sample was characterized by a considerable degree of interconnectedness, with two sizeable networks emerging which will be examined in detail. One of these, the Concord network, was composed mainly of older established migrants, and the other – the Summerhill–Ashfield network – of more recent arrivals. Other households had only one or two connections with a network, while some had no contact with other Irish persons in the city.

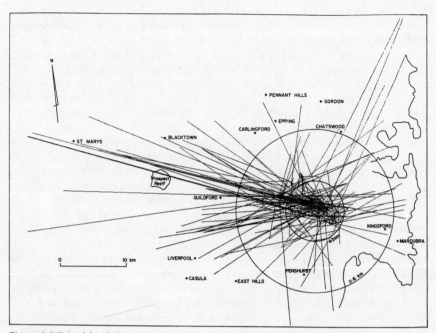

Figure 8.2 Friendship linkages, with period of friendship, (a) one to nine years

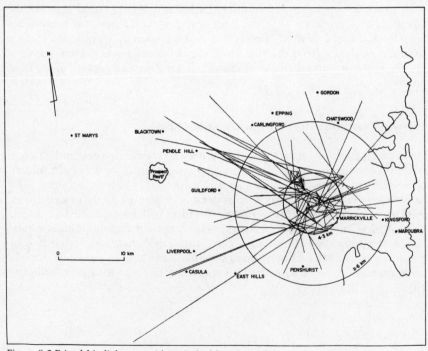

Figure 8.2 Friendship linkages, with period of friendship, (b) nine years and over

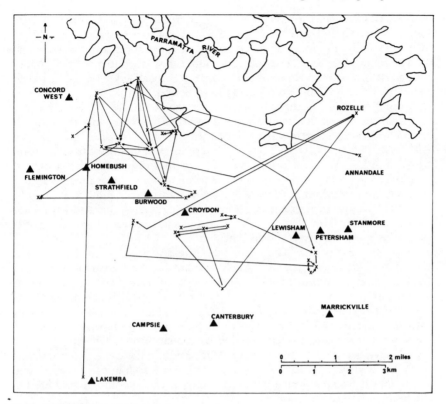

Figure 8.3 The Concord network

The Concord network

This network, composed of linkages between thirty-one Irish households and 138 friends, had a high level of interconnectedness and reciprocity. Yet there were some interviewees who were only tenuously linked, mainly because of a mixture of age groups. Interconnectivity was greatly influenced by distance, with a majority of interconnections occurring locally (Fig. 8.3). Within the metropolitan area this network had a widely dispersed contact pattern, with some longer-distance connections stretching towards the western suburbs.

The highly interconnected knot of contacts in Concord can be explained by the fact that most of these interviewees arrived in Australia in the 1950s, and shared a number of background characteristics. Interconnectedness was not merely the result of spatial determinism, for it was also based on certain social processes. Five of the Concord interviewees shared a west Cork origin, and many of their friendships had been in existence for more than twenty-five years. Some of them had emigrated together from their home area in Ireland.

Some network members had established business partnerships as small construction contractors, thus assuring continuity to friendships despite long distances between their homes. Such contractors frequently employed younger Irish migrants, which resulted in a predominantly Irish work environment. The all-male drinking group, often associated with construction circles, was the main means by which this localized network had been maintained for such an exceptionally long period.

Among the other features associated with the Concord network was the fact that many of its members had worked together on the Snowy Mountain hydro-electric scheme upon arrival in Australia. Many of the Irish who arrived in the 1950s were young single males from a rural background. It was not uncommon for them to 'go bush' in search of employment, and many of this generation spent ten years or more working on camp jobs in different parts of Australia before marrying and settling in the city. Late age at marriage and a low marriage rate – characteristics long associated with Irish demography – also characterized these earlier migrants, as is evident from census data.

Partly because of the male bias in the migrant population of the 1950s, those who did marry were more likely to marry an Australian rather than an Irish wife. Even taking the 'UK and Eire-born' category, 84 per cent of grooms married an Australian wife between 1945 and 1950, compared with about 68 per cent between 1965 and 1982.[11] In many cases, however, Irish migrants married Australian wives of Irish descent. Numerous examples of pairs of interviewees who had married Australian sisters were encountered. Social activities at the Irish National Association in the city – often referred to as 'the marriage bureau' – played an important role in this pattern. The 1950s appear to have been a period of rather inward-looking social life for the Sydney Irish population.

Unlike the highly interconnected interviewees in the Concord area, there were other interviewees from the 1950s who, while sharing many of the same background features, had only tenuous links with the network. After marriage they became dispersed throughout the suburbs, and expansion of the family contributed to a weakening of ties with Irish friends. Unlike the more interconnected migrants, they became involved in the wider labour force, thus ending any connections with close-knit Irish circles.

Migrants of the late 1970s

By the late 1970s three distinct groups of migrants could be identified in the mid-western suburbs. Firstly were those from a rural background, who were involved in some ethnic activities such as Irish construction networks, hotel-based drinking groups or gaelic football or hurling. Secondly were those from an urban background who formed close-knit networks based largely on a local Australian club, and thirdly were migrants unconnected with Irish circles and therefore more integrated into Australian society.

The core of the Irish social world in Sydney in the late 1970s consisted of rural migrants working in construction with Irish contractors. They formed multiplex social networks whose members worked together, who often

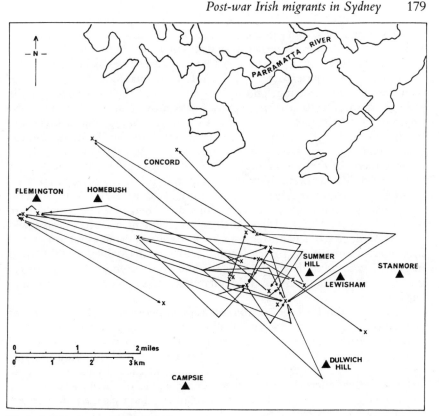

Figure 8.4 The Summerhill–Ashfield network

shared a flat in the case of those who were single, and who socialized together, thereby being encapsulated in an Irish world. Many of them had emigrated together from rural areas and, having served their apprenticeship with the Irish in England, moved to Australia.

The second group of migrants from the 1970s came from an urban background; they were mainly skilled workers who were employed in the wider cosmopolitan society, and they played soccer rather than gaelic football. Like their rural counterparts they also formed an interconnected network, but in this case it was based around a local Australian club. The network consisted of a number of interconnected cliques who had a high level of reciprocity. Spatially its main concentration was in the Summerhill–Ashfield area, and its metropolitan-wide contact pattern had a western suburbs orientation (Fig. 8.4).

A large part of this network was made up of young Dublin couples who, after marriage, took advantage of the assisted passage scheme to come to Australia for a two-year trial period. A small number of Belfast couples of Catholic background, together with a few rural migrants, were also connected by friendship. The Dubliners were mainly working-class, from poor inner-city neighbourhoods, and many of their friendships originated from their residential proximity in the home environment. It was not unusual for these migrants to stay with their friends upon arrival in Sydney.

In many respects these urban migrants saw themselves as being different from their rural counterparts, and the differences manifested themselves in their pattern of socializing, and in the make-up of their networks. While segregated socializing between spouses was more common among rural migrants, the urbanites, who tended to marry younger, had a social life based around married couples meeting together in the Western Suburbs League club.

Since many of these migrants had served their apprenticeship in Ireland and were skilled workers, they were able to bypass the Irish construction networks in Sydney and become more fully involved in the wider society. They also generally avoided Irish clubs and social events which were dominated by the rural Irish, and their involvement in soccer teams was centred on their workplace. Coming from public housing areas in Dublin, they were more likely to seek public housing in Sydney, unlike rural migrants, who were determined to become home owners. In this respect they were more akin to British migrants, who were predominantly urban in background.[12]

Finally, the third group of migrants represented in the data were recent arrivals who had no contact with other Irish persons. A significant proportion of Irish migrants do not become involved in Irish networks, and consequently such persons were less likely to be traced in a study of this nature. The few who were interviewed, some of them living in the same streets as other interviewees, without being aware of them, were mainly from skilled or professional occupations. Among them were a radio officer, a drug company representative, an electrician and a teacher.

Conclusion

Rather than attributing overall measures of assimilation to a migrant population, this chapter suggests the need to examine underlying processes of social interaction to obtain a better insight into both the spatial and the temporal aspects of migrant adaptation to a new environment. On the surface, the post-war Irish migrant population in Sydney manifests many social and cultural characteristics similar to the host population. Yet this detailed examination of friendship patterns among one small part of the migrant population in the mid-western suburbs reveals a more complex process of gradual adaptation, which was reflected by variations in friendship patterns according to length of residence. The general friendship pattern of the longer-settled migrants indicated a rather well assimilated migrant group, whose social interaction was predominantly family-oriented and who were well absorbed in the host society. Yet this more established group also had exceptional networks based on particular background characteristics, which have endured over a long period.

The more recent arrivals had a friendship pattern characteristic of a less settled, transient population, whose social interaction was more involved in the ethnic community. Clearly many members of this younger migrant population were passing through the transition stage of adaptation, and had not fully entered into the wider cosmopolitan society. Again this second general pattern masked exceptions which were more clearly revealed by network analysis. The ethnic community was predominantly composed of rural migrants, yet close-knit networks also emerged among urban migrants, who, because of a contrasting social and cultural background, were involved in the wider society. More difficult to comment on were the larger number of migrants who remained isolated from Irish networks, since they were underrepresented in the data.

The study also revealed that, in the case of these Irish migrants, ethnicity was not so much a question of national identity – although that may be a small part of it – as of more practical considerations such as obtaining employment or accommodation through involvement in particular networks. There was the additional element of a socio-cultural environment for leisure activities in which cultural nuances were better understood, and which provided a buffer mechanism during the early stages of adaptation.

This ethnic community, however, was clearly not a ghetto, nor was it a spatially restricted phenomenon, as evidenced by the far-flung metropolitan-wide friendship patterns associated with these networks. This evidence, therefore, while not based on representative sampling, questions the assumption that a dispersed migrant population is *ipso facto* well assimilated. Residential distribution is more a function of life-cycle stage and of the housing and employment mechanisms of the city. These mechanisms over time make it more difficult to preserve ethnic networks, while the need to do so diminishes with time with increased involvement in the cosmopolitan society.

Notes

1. G. Sherington, *Australia's Immigrants, 1788–1978*, Allen & Unwin, Sydney, 1980.
2. O. D. Duncan and S. Lieberson, 'Ethnic segregation and assimilation', *American Journal of Sociology*, 64, 1959, pp. 364–74.
3. F. L. Jones, 'Ethnic concentration and assimilation: an Australian case study', *Social Forces*, 45, 3, 1967; I. H. Burnley, 'European immigration and settlement patterns in metropolitan Sydney, 1947–1966', *Australian Geographical Studies*, 10, 1972, pp. 341–58.
4. G. C. K. Peach, 'Ethnic segregation in Sydney and intermarriage patterns', *Australian Geographical Studies*, 12, 1974, pp. 219–29.
5. C. A. Price, *Southern Europeans in Australia*, Oxford University Press, Melbourne, 1963; G. Bottomley, 'Community and network in a city', in C. Price, ed., *Greeks in Australia*, Canberra, Australian National University Press, 1975.
6. B. Walter, 'Time–space patterns of second-wave Irish immigration into British towns', *Transactions of the Institute of British Geographers*, new series, 5, 3, 1980, pp. 297–317.

7. A. J. Rose, 'Irish migration to Australia in the twentieth century', *Irish Geography*, 4, 1, 1959, pp. 79–84.
8. S. Grimes, 'Spatial Aspects of Irish Immigrant Friendship Patterns in Sydney', Ph.D.thesis, University of New South Wales, 1979.
9. J. R. Davis and P. Spearritt, *Sydney at the Census: a Social Atlas*, Urban Research Unit, Australian National University, Canberra, 1979.
10. C. S. Fischer *et al.*, *Networks and Places: Social Relations in the Urban Setting*, Free Press, New York, 1977.
11. C. A. Price *et al.*, *Birthplaces of the Australian population, 1861–1981*, Working Papers in Demography, 13, Australian National University, Canberra, 1984.
12. I. H. Burnley, 'British immigration and settlement in Australian cities, 1947–1971', *International Migration Review*, 12, 3, 1979, pp. 341–58.

9 Graduate emigration
A continuation or a break with the past?

Gerard Hanlon

The upsurge in emigration during the 1980s has not gone unnoticed in Ireland. It has generated considerable debate both among academics[1] and in the media.[2] Much of this debate has centred around what could loosely be described as 'middle class' emigration. There is a great concern with the graduate and/or the professional exodus. An image is being implicitly (and, indeed, explicitly) created whereby pre-1960s emigrants are perceived to have been uneducated, unskilled, rural labourers and, in comparison, today's emigrants are highly educated, highly skilled, career-oriented people forming part of a 'European generation'. This latter group have all the features of the quintessential 'yuppie'. The media are particularly guilty of this image-building.

I believe that the picture painted above is a dangerous one. By travelling down this path emigration could be, plausibly at least, viewed as evidence of our economic success over the past thirty years rather than be seen as our failure. It could be construed as proof of our success because people believe emigrants to be in London, for example, working in a financial institution, earning a very considerable salary, gaining invaluable experience, and waiting for the right opportunity to return home. However, such is not the reality. I aim to show in this chapter that graduate/professional emigration is a symptom of our industrial policies. There are similarities between the pre- and post-1960s emigrants. The purpose of this chapter is to highlight them by looking at skilled migrants.

The chapter is based upon thirty-five semi-structured interviews with young senior accountants in various practices. It also makes use of much secondary literature and published sources. It is divided into a number of different sections. The first looks at pre-1958 Ireland, the second at the changes in Ireland after 1958. The chapter then proceeds to look at today's graduate/professional migration, paying particular attention to the accountancy profession, in the light of the fact that it is the key profession within the financial services sector. The latter sector is one which the government is putting increasing emphasis on, the most obvious instance being the building of the Customs House Financial Services Centre. The last section is a brief conclusion.

Pre-1958 Ireland

Ireland had traditionally acted as a peripheral area for Britain before 1958. This meant that in many instances Ireland's economy was shaped by British events to suit British needs.[3] The effect was that Ireland exported primary goods and labour to Britain while at the same time providing a market for British manufactured goods. As has been well documented,[4] this had a disastrous effect upon the Irish economy. I shall comment upon these economic effects only very briefly.

The move from tillage to pasture in post-Famine Ireland led to a decline of some 600,000 people living on the land in the years 1841–71. The move to pasture was precipitated by the high rates of profit that could be gained on the British market for cattle goods. At the same time Irish manufacturing could not create sufficient jobs, as it could not compete with the larger British manufacturers. These twin effects led to a massive exodus of people. The outflow was forced upon the population by economic necessity.[5]

Added to these economic features was the emergence of a new social structure in rural Ireland. This social structure was centred on property ownership and the family farm. The farm was increasingly passed down from the father to the eldest son rather than being subdivided between the sons, as had previously been the tradition. This 'passing down' occurred only when the father was elderly or died. Other members of the family either stayed on as 'relatives assisting' or were forced to emigrate because of the lack of other employment opportunities. These social features compounded and reinforced patterns of severe emigration.[6]

However, it is important to highlight the fact that these occurrences were shaped by international factors largely beyond the control of the Irish population; as already mentioned, British economic domination was one such feature. Another international feature of this process was the fact that the growth of the core facilitated, and one might say greatly encouraged, migration. The core labour markets needed migrants. In the pre-war period the USA was undergoing a massive economic boom except for the 1929–33 period. Thus it is not surprising that between 1876 and 1921 84 per cent of all Irish migrants went to the USA.[7] The booming US core acted as a magnet for Irish migrants.

In the post-war period (and indeed during the war itself) Britain fulfilled this magnetic role. (The United States had introduced restrictions at this stage because the Depression had damaged its economy.[8]) After the war Britain needed labour. This, combined with the fact that the economic and social system in Ireland was stagnant, ensured that Irish migrants fulfilled some of that need. They migrated in search of work and a better standard of living.[9]

During the century or so from 1850 to 1960 Ireland supplied agricultural products to the core, principally Britain, and its manufacturing sector remained weak and internationally uncompetitive. Both the free-trade and the protectionist policies of the post-independence governments had failed to stimulate sustained economic growth or to halt the tide of emigration. This migration was primarily economic in nature, both in the pre-1930 period when the vast majority of migrants went to the USA:

> Rather than a mindless flight from intolerable home conditions, therefore, Irish peasant movement to the New World was a deliberate departure of literate peasants to a society that offered them the opportunity to establish a family and to contribute to the support of their relatives at home.[10]

and in the post-1930 movement to Britain:

> The principle and immediate cause of emigration remains economic.[11]

However, what is perhaps underplayed in the analysis of pre-1958 migration is the migration of the middle class. Skilled or professional people were also leaving in large numbers.[12] Blessing[13] argues that throughout the 1800–1920 epoch an average of 25 per cent of migrants were skilled. This figure fell from a high of 75 per cent in 1820 to a low of 9 per cent in 1900.

> Not at all the Irish came from impoverished backgrounds: at times a significant element departed from the more modern element of the home society where they had worked as artisans, merchants and professionals.[14]

He estimates that in 1920 40 per cent of migrants were skilled. These people had been driven out by the nature of the Irish economy and by the attraction of career opportunities abroad. Thus even in the 1950s when the unskilled, uneducated rural labourer was the typical migrant there was still a notable minority of skilled people leaving. Drudy[15] suggests that the 10 per cent of migrants going to the USA in the 1950s were from the middle classes, and Jackson[16] has shown that the professional, the intermediate and the skilled non-manual workers made up roughly 20 per cent of Irish males in Britain at this time. As stated, however, this process is often underplayed in accounts of pre-1958 emigration.

This section has tried to make two points: one that Irish skilled migration is not a new phenomenon and, two, that Irish migration in general has always been greatly influenced by what takes place within the core.

Post-1958 Ireland

In the post-war era the internationalization of capital took place at an increased rate.[17] This period was different from what had gone before because the production process and the market were made global. The production process was divided up into distinct parts and a particular region of the globe might only be producing one, very specific, component within the total production process. This gave way to the creation of high and low-skilled areas of production and a new international division of labour. This international division of labour was different from what had existed pre-viously in the sense that now exports from the periphery were not necess-arily primary goods; manufactured goods were also exported. This gave rise to dependent industrialization in the periphery.[18]

Alongside this changing international situation Ireland also began to alter. There was a move in 1958 to a policy of export-oriented 'industrialization by invitation'. Ireland sought to attract foreign direct investment at a time when foreign investors were expanding globally anyway. This latter feature of Ireland's developement is also often understressed. It is inaccurate to view the changes taking place within Ireland in isolation or to see them as being rapid alterations of previous policy:

> In reality change was more gradual and again was not unique to Ireland. Thus to emphasise the policy shift as the key factor giving rise to the penetration of the Irish economy by foreign direct investment is to abstract from the more general changes taking place in the structure of the world economy, specifically the post-war conditions of economic growth, industrial concentration and especially the renewed wave and growth of foreign direct investment although the nature of this investment differed from previous forms.[19]

Ireland had not got sufficient control over her economy to enable a policy shift, on its own, to stimulate the most sustained period of growth the country had probably ever seen.

What emerged out of this period of growth contained similarities to before. The nature of Ireland's peripherality has changed and benefits have accrued but nevertheless the Irish economy is outside, to a large extent, the control of the Irish state.[20] This is not to deny that change occurs. As has been well documented, industrial output and employment grew, agricul-tural output grew whilst agricultural employment declined, markets were diversified both geographically and in terms of products, GDP and living standards grew, etc.[21]

However, this success was dependent upon the establishment of factories by foreign multinationals. Ireland's prosperity has become more integrated with foreign capital than had previously been the case. Instead of being dependent upon the British market for agricultural exports, Ireland became dependent upon her ability to attract foreign capital via a policy of granting financial incentives. The financing of such a policy has become increasingly difficult:

> New manufacturing jobs now come almost exclusively from foreign firms. Irish dependence on the metropolitan capitalist economy is clinched by its large and rapidly expanding national debt, which is the inescapable consequence of foster-

ing exports through government deficit financing which has been the hub of Whitakerian–Gerardine policy. Ireland is now so dependent on foreign borrowing that the entire economy would collapse overnight and the polity would disintegrate if foreign credits ceased to be available.[22]

Ireland has merely changed one form of economic marginalization for another. Ireland's fortunes took a downturn in the late 1970s with the rest of the world economy. This recession badly harmed Irish society. A large national debt had been built up and as the world economy slowed down it became harder to export, it became harder to meet debt repayments, and it became harder to attract foreign investors. The market for mobile capital became increasingly competitive as many strong industrial economies also sought investors.[23] As a result of these features unemployment mounted at a time when increased numbers of young people were coming on to the labour market for the first time.[24] The result of all these features was economic hardship for large sections of the population.[25] In such a situation emigration increased.

The bulk of the migrants, in contrast to the past, were urban. They were also, in keeping with the past, non-graduates. Graduates made up a mere 3·6 per cent of all migrants in 1986, down from 7·9 per cent in 1984.[26] However, this figure most likely underestimates middle-class migration, as many professional people leave after working in Ireland for a few years, a fact which the figure does not allow for. Despite this it seems fair to agree with the comment that 'The stress on the "brain drain" character of recent emigration is, however, largely a media construction and should not be allowed to obscure the fact that the majority of emigrants are the urban and rural poor.'[27] Nevertheless, I will concentrate on graduate/professional migration because in many ways it highlights Ireland's continued peripherality in a way that the migration of the 'urban and rural poor' possibly cannot.

Graduate/professional migration

As was mentioned in the section on Ireland's role in the old division of labour, Irish middle-class migration is by no means a new phenomenon in Ireland. It appears safe to say that this form of migration has fluctuated between 10 per cent and 25 per cent of total migrants. In the light of this, Ireland is not experiencing a first 'brain drain' nor a revived one. A 'brain drain' of some form has always been part of Ireland's social structure. (Even in the 1970s when net immigration took place Drudy argues that 60,000 people from the age cohort up to thirty-four years emigrated).[28] It seems safe to assume that many of these would have been professional. Lynn[29] also suggests that professional migration was occurring in the relatively successful 1960s.

Skilled migration did, however, grow during the course of the 1980s. This has been shown by the Higher Education Authority's figures; see

Table 9.1 Pattern of first destinations of Irish graduates 1984–8 (%)

Employment	1984	1985	1986	1987	1988
Seeking employment	6·1	5·3	5·8	3·8	3·1
Gained employment:					
Ireland	34·5	35·9	33·5	32·7	35·6
Overseas	11·4	13·1	16·7	22·8	22·7

Source: Higher Education Authority, *First Destination of Award Recipients in Higher Education 1988*, HEA, Dublin, 1989, p. 14.

Table 9.1. The unemployment rate among graduates has declined but this fact is counterbalanced by the increased migration rate. These migrants were pulled into the UK graduate labour market, where there was a shortage of skilled labour.[30] The graduate labour market is now international and characterized by significant cross-border movement, which is likely to become even more pronounced in 1992.[31] This means that in times of Irish economic recession these graduates, who are educated at considerable expense to the state,[32] will migrate.

However, this alone does not adequately explain graduate migration. Unemployment among graduates is very low; in 1988 it was 3·9 per cent (see Table 9.1), this despite the fact that the number of graduates increased by some 50 per cent between 1982 and 1988.[33] In this rather favourable environment the most noticeable feature of the graduate labour market has been the steep increase in migration. This migration takes place for reasons other than economic necessity:

> . . . given the low levels of graduate unemployment and the relatively attractive starting salaries available to graduates in Ireland, much of this graduate emigration must be deemed to be voluntary.[34]

The voluntary nature of middle–class migration has been noted by a number of other writers.[35] If this is the case – and I shall now go on to argue that it is – then Ireland may well be on its way to becoming a 'human resource warehouse' for Europe.

The reasons for such voluntary migration can be traced back directly to the industrialization process of the past thirty years. The links between the two processes are most noticeable among graduates who have worked in Ireland for a number of years. I will highlight these connections, concentrating mainly on accountants, but other professions will be briefly mentioned.

Before looking at why accountants migrate and how the process has been affected by the recent past it may be helpful to examine what these people do. The interviewees were overwhelmingly young senior accountants in Big Six accountancy practices (these practices dominate global accountancy), and were mainly graduates. The majority of the graduate interviewees had a business degree, although other disciplines such as arts, science, and engineering were represented. The work these people carried out was mainly concerned with auditing, i.e. checking and verifying company accounts for the benefit of the state and shareholders. The purpose is to give a 'true and fair account' of a company's finances. Generally speaking the work was seen as incredibly boring and not what had been expected. As one woman put it to me:

> I thought it'd be exciting and brilliant. Actually when I went in I didn't know what auditing was – I thought I was going to do accountancy. I thought I'd be doing small jobs, I thought I'd be preparing accounts. If I'd known what auditing was I mightn't have been so keen to do it. Having said that, it grows on you a bit. I hated it for the first few years. I actually wanted to get out of it. I realized I couldn't get out of it, and the second year it grew on me a bit, and then the third year I began to actually like it because I started getting my own jobs. [Gerardine O'Kelly, Big Six supervisor]

Because of the nature of work in a large practice many accountants come to view the profession as a means to do other, more enjoyable, work.

> I've never wanted to do auditing . . . like everyone else I saw the ACA as a qualification to move on to what I ultimately wanted to do, which in my case is investment. [Paul McKee, Big Six accountant]

Ultimately many want to go on and join the senior management teams of large non-accountancy organizations, and their ACA qualification allows them to do so. Having taken this brief look at the attitudes these people have to their work and to their future, it is appropriate to examine how changes within the profession impinge upon these attitudes.

Accountancy practices form part of the service sector. The financial services sector grew 37·5 per cent during the 1979–88 period in terms of employment.[36] Cogan[37] has shown how the producer services (which include financial services) have increased as a percentage of the total work force over the 1960–80 time span. They jumped from 2 per cent of the total work force to 6·5 per cent; this required an annual growth rate of some 5 per cent. The IDA's strategic plan 1982–92 anticipated creating 10,000 manufacturing jobs, 25,000 service jobs and 165,000 jobs in spin-off growth. Thus the service sector, despite Ireland's economic difficulties, is buoyant. However, even allowing for this healthy backdrop, accountancy's growth has been remarkable throughout the 1980s. Over the course of the 1980–89 era the Institute of Chartered Accountants in Ireland's membership increased by 69 per cent, up from 4,033 members to 6,817. This compared favourably with the situation in England and Wales, where chartered accountancy increased its membership by 36 per cent.[38] On the surface it would appear safe to presume that Irish accountancy was in a prosperous condition. This, however, would be incorrect. During the years 1984–89 the number of ICAI members abroad went up from 14·3 per cent of all members to 22·3 per cent. These people left voluntarily, as Tansey argues; they did not leave owing to any lack of work. Accountancy employment between 1986 and 1988 grew by 12 per cent and in 1988–90 it was expected to increase by 15 per cent. This rapid growth had led to a shortage of labour and increased poaching of staff among firms.[39]

Why did this migration take place? Migration took place for a number of reasons based upon international factors. The UK accountancy sector and the UK economy generally were booming, which led to a shortage of accountants and rapid salary increases.[40] A number of Irish factors such as taxation and the reluctance of many large accountancy practices to promote staff did help.[41] However, another noticeable feature besides these financial factors was the perception that working abroad was better for one's career and would allow one to move on to the 'better' jobs. This latter feature is directly linked to the policy of industrialization by invitation.

As stated, Irish accountancy is dominated by the multinational firms commonly referred to as the Big Six. These practices, by and large, merged with much smaller indigenous practices. They now employ roughly 70 per cent of chartered accountants in practice[42] and they dominate roughly 80 per cent of fee income within Irish accountancy.[43]

The firms instil high aspirations within their staff. Young senior accountants want to control and manage organizations and they feel that they are well equipped to do so because of their training within the Big Six. This led Sinead O'Driscoll to comment, 'I think people who come here don't have entrepreneurial skills but at the same time we have the aim to be at the top of an established organization.'

However, what is lacking in their training is international exposure, not exposure to any international setting but exposure to a select few core urban areas such as London or New York. The growth in the need for international experience is due primarily to the requirements of multinationals and has come about with the globalization of capital.[44] This is perceived and recognized by the accountants themselves; to quote Sean Collins:

> I think interviewers might have the attitude that you're basically going to say Bermuda because it's tax-free, fantastic social life, but what about the work element? They might view you as a bit of a waster, which mightn't necessarily be true but it has that connotation . . . but places like Hong Kong, an intense hard-working financial centre, along with New York and London, they might view you as more ambitious than if you come back with a sun tan.

The places such as London and New York are where the growth areas in accountancy – for instance, management consultancy – are primarily based. Leyshon[45] has shown how the partnership breakdown in the top UK practices varies according to region. In the south-east 14 per cent of partners are management consultants and only 12 per cent are in the less specialized area of general practice. In comparison with this, peripheral places such as the south-west and Wales fared badly, with 4 per cent and 0 per cent respectively in management consultancy and 54 per cent and 55 per cent in general practice. This is due simply to the concentration of organizational headquarters in south-east England.[46] If one wants to be at the forefront of managerial decision-making, i.e. to get away from auditing and into top management or investment, London, not Wales or Cornwall, is the place to be. Ireland along with these other peripheral regions fares badly, at least in the eyes of Big Six accountants:

> I don't know if too many people abroad would say, 'God, we've got to get to Ireland to work'. I think Ireland is just a spot, really – there's a very small stock exchange here, the whole economy is just so small, a lot of people wouldn't even have heard of Ireland. . . . it is just very, very small and as such is not a major player in banking or stock exchange or international business. [Sean Collins, Big Six accountant]

Why is this the case? Because (1), the whole scale of business in Ireland is very small, and (2), even when the Irish company is part of a multinational corporation it is normally a branch plant without any real responsibility or any key function.[47] Because of this lack of scale and the lack of quality experience accountants tend to look abroad, particularly to the UK, as part of a career move, e.g.:

> They go abroad for the experience of a different level of work. You come here to Ireland, your big firm will be only £100 million turnover; you go abroad and your big company in, say, England is a £100 million profit. It is the level, larger scale, prestige on your c.v. at the end of the day, the fact that in time people will say – you know what I mean – the prophet is never respected in his homeland type thing. You're better to go away and come back, no matter where you are career-wise. [Cathal Murray, Big Six assistant manager]

On top of this is the fact that migration is actively encouraged by the Big Six via intra-firm transfers. This intra-firm transnational movement also lessens the 'newness' of working in a foreign country whilst allowing the Big Six to hold on to their best staff, give them international exposure, and satisfy any wanderlust they may have.[48] The migrants who do not want to stay in practice on a long-term basis can use this Big Six network abroad as a transition or an adjustment period. Added to these advantages is the fact that as Irish Big Six accountants they are well placed for international mobility owing to the high esteem in which the Irish qualification is held.

This feature of looking abroad is not peculiar to accountants; many professions are prone to it, especially if they are dominated by foreign firms. Wickham[49] has shown how many engineers are favourably disposed towards migration. These people see themselves as members of an international labour market. The work they perform in Ireland has low status and less intrinsic value than the work they could carry out abroad. Again this feature of high and low-status work revolves around international firms and the policy of industrialization pursued by the Irish state. Telesis[50] criticized electronics firms in Ireland for having a relatively low skill content because they lacked any significant research facilities. Many graduate engineers wish to carry out research but the transnational corporations that they work for in Ireland have their research institutions abroad, hence the engineers move abroad. Skilled labour moves away from the periphery towards capital's research bases, not vice versa. The work content forms a major part of the reason for migrating among engineers, as Table 9.2 highlights.

Table 9.2 Reasons for considering emigration among Irish electronics staff, 1987 (%)

Reason	Technicians	Engineers
Taxation	50·0	46·8
More interesting work	18·2	25·2
Experience	18·2	10·6
Personal reasons	9·1	8·5
Promotion	4·5	4·3
Life style	–	4·3
Total	100	100

Source: James Wickham, *Technicians and Engineers in Irish Electronics Plants*, NBST Discussion Paper, National Board for Science and Technology, 1987, p. 11.

Other professionals also migrate in large numbers. Sterne[51] has argued that, although in 1986 28.5 per cent of Irish computer graduates migrated, if one returned to the same class two or three years later the figure could be as high as 50 per cent. The reasons for this migration again revolve around the issue of work. Again the computer industry in Ireland, like accountancy and electronics, is dominated by foreign multinationals.

The same feature arises in all three professions, i.e. the careers that people feel they have been trained for and aspire to are not to be found in Ireland. All three professions have really grown since the 1970s and all three are dominated by multinationals. To halt this migration Ireland is relying on foreign multinationals to establish key functions within the country. It has not happened and is not likely to in the near future.[52] Because of this, professional migration will continue.

Conclusion

This chapter has tried to highlight the fact that middle-class emigration is not new to Ireland; there has always been a 'brain drain'. It appears to be more harmful today because so many middle class people are graduates who are educated by the state. What is most interesting about these people is the fact that, although many have work in Ireland and are able to make a 'reasonable' living, they still decide to emigrate. They leave because their career paths are international. To fulfil their professional aspirations they must go to where multinationals have established their headquarters or certain key operations. This leads them to a handful of core regions. Ireland as a small peripheral economy is simply not suitable for such sites.

The changes in capitalism which took place after the war facilitated Irish policies for industrialization. This in turn led to a heavy dependence upon multinationals. The international nature of such firms encouraged their Irish employees to develop international careers. Because of its location and peripherality, Ireland was deemed a poor substitute by these professionals as compared with its core rivals in terms of opportunities for gaining quality experience. The end result is that our industrial policy actively encourages those who have professional jobs to pursue their careers abroad. Whereas the working class emigrate in times of economic hardship, these professionals go in good and bad times because their reasons are not solely economic.

Historically, international changes altered Ireland's economic structure and thus led to emigration. These historical features led to middle-class emigration as many of the managerial and professional jobs were wiped out in the alteration, or simply lost their market in the period after the changes and were subsequently driven out:

> It is impossible to pinpoint the exact areas of origin of these individuals; many were obviously urban artisans, merchants and professionals; others had been employed at managerial level in rural areas, forced out by the same economic and social forces changing the lives of their peasant countrymen.[53]

What is different today is that unlike the middle class of the past (and the working class of today) these professional people are not forced out but choose to go. They could stay and control a rather backward indigenous industrial sector or run a more modern foreign-owned sector, where many of the key decisions would be taken by their superiors abroad. Instead a lot opt to go abroad and hope to take the key decisions themselves. However, for both the pre-1958 and the post-1958 eras the key moulding features are international, not Irish. Ireland's 'brain drain' is not new – it has merely changed its shape.

Notes

1. For a fuller examination of this literature see Ian Shuttleworth and Ulrich Kochel, *Aspects of Irish Emigration in the 1980s*, APRU Paper 90, 3, 1990; Peter Murray and James Wickham, 'Irish graduate emigration and the single European labour market,' *Studies*, spring 1990; Russel King and Ian Shuttleworth, 'Ireland's new wave of emigration in the 1980s', *Irish Geography*, 21, 1988.
2. See Padraig Yeates, 'Emigration USA '88', *Irish Times*, 15–17 June 1988; John Sterne, 'Where do all the computer graduates go?' *Irish Computer*, November 1987; 'Emigration once again', In Brief, *Sunday Tribune*, 1 February 1985.
3. L. M. Cullen, *An Economic History of Ireland since 1660*, Batsford, London, 1972; Raymond Crotty, *Ireland in Crisis: a Case of Capitalist Colonial Underdevelopment*, Brandon, Cork, 1986.
4. Cullen, *Economic History*; James Meenan, *The Irish Economy since 1922*, Liverpool University Press, Liverpool, 1970.
5. Crotty, *Ireland in Crisis*.
6. For further discussion of changes in the rural social structure see John A. O'Brien, *The Vanishing Irish*, W. H. Allen, London, 1954; John A. Jackson, *The Irish in Britain*, Routledge, London, 1963; Damian Hannan, *Rural Exodus*, Chapman, London, 1970; P. J. Drudy, 'Irish population change and emigration since independence', in P. J. Drudy, ed., *The Irish in America: Emigration,*

Assimilation and Impact, Irish Studies 4, Cambridge University Press, Cambridge, 1985

7. Drudy, 'Irish population change', p. 72.
8. Drudy, 'Irish population change'.
9. Hannan, *Rural Exodus*; Jackson, *The Irish in Britain*; John A. Jackson, 'The Irish in Britain', in P. J. Drudy, ed., *Ireland and Britain since 1922*, Irish Studies 5, Cambridge University Press, Cambridge, 1986.
10. Patrick Blessing, 'Irish emigration to the United States, 1800–1920: an overview', in Drudy, *The Irish in America*, p. 16.
11. Jackson, *The Irish in Britain*, p. 27.
12. Drudy, 'Irish population change', p. 2.
13. Blessing, 'Irish emigration'.
14. Blessing, 'Irish emigration', p. 19.
15. P. J. Drudy, 'Migration between Ireland and Britain since independence', in Drudy, *Ireland and Britain since 1922*.
16. Jackson, 'The Irish in Britain', p. 130.
17. Glyn Andrew *et al.*, *Post-war Capitalism*, Fontana, London, 1986.
18. Alain Lipietz, *Mirages and Miracles: the Crisis of Global Fordism*, Verso, London, 1987; Ian Roxborough, *Theories of Underdevelopment*, Macmillan, London, 1979.
19. D. C. Perrons, 'The role of Ireland in the new international division of labour', *Regional Studies*, 15, 2, 1981, p. 86.
20. Richard Breen *et al.*, *Understanding Contemporary Ireland*, Gill & Macmillan, Dublin, 1990.
21. Kieran A. Kennedy and Brendan R. Dowling, *Economic Growth in Ireland since 1947*, Gill & Macmillan, Dublin, 1975; Jim Fitzpatrick and John Kelly, eds., *Perspectives on Irish Industry*, Irish Management Institute, Dublin, 1985; James Wickham, 'The politics of dependent capitalism: international capital and the nation state', in A. Morgan and B. Purdie, eds., *Divided Nation, Divided Class*, Ink Links, Belfast, 1980.
22. Crotty, *Ireland in Crisis*, p. 101.
23. Frances Cairncross, 'Poorest of the rich: a survey of the republic of Ireland', *Economist*, 16–22 January 1988; Guy de Jonqières, 'Europe's quest for foreign investment: a war of diminishing returns', *Financial Times*, 10 November 1986.
24. Paul Tansey, 'Graduating to jobs abroad', *Labour Market Review*, 1, 1990.
25. Breen *et al.*, *Understanding Contemporary Ireland*.
26. Shuttleworth and Kochel, *Aspects of Irish Emigration*, p. 7.
27. King and Shuttleworth, 'Ireland's new wave',
28. Drudy, 'Migration between Ireland and Britain'.
29. Richard Lynn, *The Irish Brain Drain*, ESRI Paper 43, Economic and Social Research Institute, Dublin, 1968.
30. Murray and Wickham, 'Irish graduate emigration'; Brian Elliott, 'Astride the demographic time bomb', *Accountancy*, March 1990.
31. J. Salt, 'International migration: a spatial theoretical approach', in Michael Pacione, ed., *Population Geography: Progress and Prospects*, Croom Helm, Beckenham, 1986; Doreen Massey, 'Uneven development: social change and spatial divisions of labour', in Doreen Massey and John Allen, eds., *Uneven Redevelopment: Cities and Regions in Transition*, Hodder & Stoughton, London, 1988; Tansey, 'Graduating'.
32. Murray and Wickham, 'Irish graduate emigration'.
33. Tansey, 'Graduating'.
34. Tansey, 'Graduating', p. 45.
35. See Shuttleworth and Kochel, *Aspects of Irish Emigration*; King and

Shuttleworth, 'Ireland's new wave'; James Wickham, 'The over-educated engineer? The work, education and careers of Irish electronics engineers', *Journal of Irish Business and Administrative Research*, 10, 1989.

36. Central Statistics Office, *Labour Force Survey*, CSO, Dublin, 1988.
37. D. T. Cogan, 'The service sector revisited: an analysis of job creation potential', *Journal of Irish Business and Administrative Research*, 8, 2, 1986.
38. J. V. Beaverstock, *High-skilled Professional and Managerial Labour Migration: the Case of large Chartered Accountancy Firms*, Working Papers on Producer Services 9, University of Bristol, and Service Industries Research Centre, Portsmouth Polytechnic, 1989.
39. Financial Services Industries Association, *The Financial Services Industry: Manpower and Training Needs. Report of the Focus Group*, FSIA, Dublin, 1988.
40. Giselle Jones, 'Wide variance in growth reshuffles league table', *Accountant*, June 1989; Elliott, 'Astride the timb bomb'.
41. Noeleen Gibson, 'The export market in Irish accountants', *Finance*, December 1987; author's research.
42. Author's research.
43. Kyran Fitzgerald, 'The top accountancy firms', *Finance*, December 1987.
44. Massey, 'Uneven development'; Beaverstock, 'High-skilled labour migration'.
45. A. Leyshon, P. W. Daniels and N. J. Thrift, *Large Accountancy Firms in the UK: Operational Adaptation and Spatial Development*, Working Papers on Producer Services 2, University of Bristol, and Service Industries Research Centre, Portsmouth Polytechnic, 1989.
46. A. E. Gillespie and A. E. Green, 'The changing geography of producer services employment', *Regional Studies*, 21, 5, 1987.
47. Telesis Consultancy Group, *A Review of Industrial Policy*, National Economic and Social Council, NESC Paper 64, Dublin, 1982; Neil Hood and Stephen Young, *Multinational Investment Strategies in the British Isles: a Study of MNEs in the UK Assisted Areas and the Republic of Ireland*, HMSO, London, 1983; S. Nolan, 'Ireland's great leap forward', in Fitzpatrick and Kelly, *Perspectives on Irish Industry*.
48. J. V. Beaverstock, 'New international labour markets: the case of professional and managerial labour migration within large chartered accountancy firms', *Area*, 22, 2, 1990.
49. Wickham, 'The over-educated engineer?'.
50. Telesis, *Review*.
51. Sterne, 'Where do all the computer graduates go?'.
52. Telesis, *Review*.
53. Blessing, 'Irish emigration', p. 19.

10 'And they still haven't found what they're looking for' A survey of the New Irish in New York city

Linda Dowling Almeida

Migration to the United States has been a fact of Irish life for 200 years. Irish men and women have been exiting their homeland for America since the 1700s. By the twentieth century Irish migrants and their descendants had established such a strong and influential ethnic presence in the US that in the 1980 census almost 40 million Americans claimed some Irish ancestry.[1] But during the 1980s the circumstances of Irish migration to the US changed, both at home and in the adopted land. Net out-migration in the 1980s followed a decade of net return migration to Ireland[2] and the majority of 1980s migrants in the US lived and worked as illegal aliens.

The undocumented status of so many late twentieth-century Irish migrants in America makes it difficult to identify who they are, how many they are, and why they leave Ireland for America. As illegal aliens their experience in America during the 1980s and early 1990s is presumably quite different from the experience of previous generations of Irish who entered the country 'legally' and could technically mainstream into the American economy and life style. But because the late twentieth-century migrants often live a 'shadow' existence they are difficult to track and reluctant to talk.

In autumn 1990 the author and the Emerald Isle Immigration Center (EIIC)[3] in Queens, New York, conducted a survey among some of the 'New Irish' (the name the migrants call themselves) for the purpose of obtaining basic biographical details about the migrants as well as some information about their future plans, their reasons for leaving Ireland and their problems, experiences and social habits in New York. Following is a discussion about what the survey revealed and what it can tell us about who the New Irish are and what their future is in New York and the United States.

Background

Before plunging into the survey itself, some background will be necessary to place the phenomenon of the New Irish in context. The 1970s were a period of strong growth and optimism for Ireland. By the end of the decade the country had the fastest economic growth rate of any EC member.[4] Between 1971 and 1979 it experienced a sustained net inflow of population unknown since the republic gained independence in the 1920s.[5] Mary Corcoran, a sociologist who has studied the New Irish and is herself a member of the New Irish generation, calls the 1970s 'heady days'.[6]

The future looked bright for the country. Its young people were arguably the best educated generation it had ever produced. According to Corcoran they were to 'symbolize Ireland's coming of age'.[7] Sean Minihane, a New Irish migrant and founder of the Irish Immigration Reform Movement (IIRM), said that his was to be the generation that did not have to emigrate.[8] But by the end of the 1970s the debt and spending the country had incurred to achieve its ten years of hope and growth caught up on it. The international recession of 1979–80 hit Ireland hard.[9] The country did not recover quickly from the worldwide economic downturn. Persistent inflation and high unemployment plagued Ireland throughout the following decade.[10]

Net out-migration resumed. Between 1981 and 1986 the Central Statistics Office (CSO) in Dublin estimated a total net migration from Ireland of 72,000.[11] From one decade to the next the average annual migration rate changed from 10,389 migrants returning to Ireland between 1971 and 1981 to 14,377 migrants leaving Ireland between 1981 and 1986.[12] As the decade progressed the rate of emigration escalated, so that by 1990 the country had experienced a total net population loss of 208,000 for the 1981–90 period.[13]

It is generally agreed that the majority (probably 70 per cent) of the migrants left for Great Britain.[14] How many found their way to the United States (either directly or by way of Great Britain or other countries) is a matter of dispute. Estimates range from about 40,000 to 150,000-plus.[15] The total number of New Irish is probably not as significant as the fact of their migration, and because of the population's undocumented status and transient existence the true figures may never be known. For the present, logic and the available evidence suggest that the number is probably well under 100,000.

Typically the New Irish entered the United States as tourists or temporary workers and overstayed their visas. Relatively few Irish entered the US with appropriate documentation between 1981 and 1985.[16] The 1965 Immigration and Nationality Act made entry to the US more difficult for the Irish (as well as other Europeans). The 1965 law focused on family reunification rather than the national origins system, which was favourable to Western Europeans.[17] Since Irish migration to the US slowed during the 1960s and 1970s, the family relationships (i.e. immediate family members) required by the 1965 law did not exist. Other visas were available but required planning and qualifications that many Irish did not or could not meet. It was, therefore, quicker, easier and relatively risk-free in the early 1980s for the New Irish to enter the US illegally.[18]

Immigration legislation passed in 1986, 1988 and 1990 contained provisions providing thousands of non-preference visas for the Irish.[19] By early 1991 more than 16,500 Irish, many of them former illegal aliens, obtained green cards as a result of the new laws.[20] Others will join their ranks through the 1990s. This documented population will establish a seed group that could make it possible for their families to enter the US legally and presumably prevent a recurrence of the 'undocumented' phenomenon of the 1980s. However, as will be discussed later in this chapter, many New Irish are uncertain about their future, regardless of their legal status. Why they are uncertain is one of the puzzles of this population and one of the reasons for examining them more thoroughly.

The survey: process and execution

The survey was born as the result of the author's previous study of the New Irish, conducted between September 1988 and March 1989.[21] In the course of that research it became obvious that the New Irish in New York were a population that demanded closer study, both for its place in the continuum of Irish migration to the US and as a reflection of the complexities and struggles of modern Ireland.

Most of the New Irish in the New York area live in the city boroughs of Queens and the Bronx. The presence of so many immigrants in a concentrated area presented an opportunity to gather information that could not be ignored. The experience of conducting oral history interviews with early twentieth-century migrants made the value of reaching recent migrants at the time of or shortly after their arrival, when their feelings and attitudes are fresh and current, apparent to the author. It was necessary to work quickly before the population dispersed, the law changed or networks broke down and the vehicles to organize a study disappeared. The *Irish Voice* conducted a twenty-nine-question survey among 200 New Irish for its premier issue in 1987.[22] Since that time no other survey or research of the kind has been executed in the community.

Having worked with the New Irish community, it was clear to the author that an outsider, particularly an American, would have a difficult time soliciting personal information from the migrants, even though the survey was to be completed anonymously. The population feared detection and tended to socialize and reside with other undocumented Irish. Therefore to establish credibility and co-operation it was necessary to work from within the community.

The EIIC was a natural choice for liaison. The group had trust and visibility among the New Irish and had worked with the author during research for the original study. It had direct access to the population: a membership list of over 1,000 to which it mailed newsletters and various correspondence on a regular basis. It also held public meetings and other service seminars and functions at least once a month throughout the city. The EIIC provided an established, efficient and far-reaching distribution system. A grant from the Irish Institute in New York helped to finance the project.

The survey was mailed to the IIRM membership in October 1990 with the monthly newsletter. It posed forty-two questions (which were to be answered anonymously) plus a request for the respondent's personal impressions of New York and life as an immigrant. The mailing included a stamped addressed envelope for return of the completed questionnaire. The accompanying newsletter urged members to complete and return the survey. A reminder followed in the November newsletter. In the 27 October 1990 issue of the *Irish Voice* the 'Green Card' column, a feature which addresses the visa problems of the New Irish, focused on the survey and encouraged readers to participate. The author was also interviewed on the Next Wave[23] radio programme on WNWK-FM in New York on 5 November 1990 about the survey and its intent and urged the co-operation of the New Irish community.

To supplement the mailing the surveys were made available at the EIIC office in Queens, and at all public meetings and seminars. To ensure that all corners of the community were reached, various local leaders were enlisted to help. Some of the Irish priests living in the parishes of the Bronx, Queens and Brooklyn with the New Irish[24] disseminated the surveys locally or identified New Irish contacts who dispersed the questionnaire among their friends. The execution of the survey relied on the networking system that sustains the undocumented community.

By December 1990 – January 1991 247 completed questionnaires had been returned from an estimated distribution of 1,500–2,000 surveys.

The survey results

The objective of this survey was to reach as many migrants as possible through as many local channels as possible. Therefore the 247 who responded are not a scientifically drawn sample. A base population figure or accurate demographics for this community do not exist. Many in the population simply do not want to be found. The respondents who did participate are probably among the more visible in the community. They deserve attention and more than likely welcome the forum. The information which follows should be considered a snapshot of the New Irish community in New York. It may not provide the whole picture, but it gives some fascinating detail on a population that may never be fully known or understood. And, as will be shown, many of the results are consistent with other observations of the community.

Who are they?

The composite profile of the Irish migrant who completed the survey is that of a single, undocumented Catholic who arrived in America between 1985 and 1987 and is approaching his or her thirtieth birthday. Of the 247 who responded, 45 per cent were male and 54 per cent female. Fifty-eight per cent were undocumented, 22 per cent were Donnelly visa recipients, 6 per cent had a visa through marriage, 4 per cent had a visa through a relative, another 4 per cent had H-1 visa and 2 per cent had sponsorships. Almost two-thirds (64 per cent) were single and 32 per cent married (see survey results, question 7.) The peak year of migration was 1986 – the year the Immigration Reform and Control Act (IRCA) was passed and made jobs for undocumented aliens more difficult to obtain (see survey results, question 4.) Fully two-thirds of those who responded were employed before they left Ireland; 32 per cent had no job.

Through the 1980s, the New Irish were characterized as undocumented university graduates waiting at tables, tending bars, changing nappies or hammering nails. Among this sample the job description was true to type – most of the respondents worked in the areas of construction, child care and bar/restaurant service. About a third were spread among the following categories: professionals (i.e. teachers or accountants), sales and service, nursing, office work and skilled trades (see survey results, question 26.) But a total of only 15 per cent had graduate or undergraduate college experience, while just about half (49 per cent) had leaving certificates or high school diplomas (see survey results, question 19.)

Two of the more surprising (for the author at least) results were the age of the respondents and their place of origin. The average year of birth for males was 1961 and 1962.5 for females, making them twenty-nine and twenty-seven and a half years of age, respectively, at the time of the survey. Previous research (and speculation)[25] suggested that the population was younger, perhaps under twenty-five years of age.

The survey also reveals that the migrants hailed from all over Ireland, with no county in particular dominating. Dublin and Cavan boasted the most migrants, with 9 and 8 per cent, respectively, of all respondents (see survey results, question 3). Historically out-migration has been a phenomenon of the western counties. But the survey results coincide with the National Economic and Social Council's (NESC) 1991 report on emigration suggesting that migration is no longer restricted to the rural population. It has penetrated the middle-class and urban populations as well[26].

The marital status of the respondents is worth noting. The fact that almost one-third of the sample were married is something of a surprise. Through the 1980s the popular media consistently portrayed the New Irish as young single school leavers.[27] But the New Irish who responded to this survey are almost ten years out of secondary school. Almost 60 per cent arrived between 1985 and 1987 (see survey results, question 4), so most had lived in the United States at least three years at the time of the survey.[28] The survey also shows the average age of the respondent upon arrival to be just over twenty-three years. By 1990 these young adults had presumably established relationships, friendships and life styles natural for young independent adults, including marriage.

Significantly, 80 per cent of the married respondents have Irish spouses (see survey results, question 8). This suggests two things – the Irish in the survey did not seek the green card through marriage and, assuming the marriages took place in America, the population does not mix with non-Irish. The 'clannishness' of the community is borne out elsewhere in the survey.

Social habits

The overwhelming majority of the respondents, 83 per cent, identified their friends in New York as Irish. Having the green card apparently had little effect on the social habits of this group – 83 per cent of those who identified themselves as documented[29] also claimed that their friends in New York were Irish, as did 83 per cent of those who claimed to be undocumented. Less than 20 per cent of the entire sample, as well as the documented and undocumented respondents, have American friends. They show a remarkable consistency, no matter what their legal status, in socializing with other Irish migrants (see survey results, question 17).

Consider, for example, how the respondents spend their leisure time (see survey results, question 16.) Sixty-five per cent of them all identified the pub as the place where they spend their spare time, compared with 9 per cent who visit museums or 13 per cent who attend Irish or county organizations, which are the domain of older Irish immigrants (many of whom migrated in the 1950s) and Irish-Americans.

The popularity of the pub can be examined from several perspectives. Traditionally the pub in Ireland is the local meeting place for Irish, so for the New Irish it is a natural destination upon arrival in a strange city or town. But in the context of New York in the 1980s the pubs in the Bronx, Queens and Brooklyn served as sources of job and housing opportunities, places to exchange information about friends and family and news about immigration legislation or community activities. In the early 1980s, the bars also functioned as banks, cashing pay cheques at week's end for undocumented labourers without bank or savings accounts.[30]

While it can be argued that the bar is more than just a drinking establishment for the New Irish, it does have its dark side. Testimony from the the the respondents themselves points to some of the problems: 'The bar scene within the Irish community is a one-track road which is deciding more of the Irish to despair, even more so than being illegal, or being unable to go home.'[31] 'I feel strongly that the young Irish spend too much time in pubs, drinking their money and congregating with their own.'[32] Homesickness, loneliness, an independent income and the long hours of the New York bars undoubtedly contribute to the popularity of the pubs.[33]

On the other hand, a series of articles on emigrant life in New York city boroughs in the *Irish Voice* in the spring and summer of 1991 quotes young migrants who detect a change from the wild days of the 1980s, when money was plentiful and the bars were full from Thursday through the weekend, and often on Monday afternoons. The Irish quoted in the story claim that the community is getting older, settling down, spending more time with boyfriends, girlfriends or spouses – and becoming more serious, generally, about work and the future.[34] Note that 56 per cent of respondents also go to the movies in their leisure time.

In personal interviews with the New Irish, as well as in the popular media, migrants complain about the lack of alternative social and recreational outlets for the population.[35] They cite the absence of dance halls like those at home. Respondents to this survey offered similar observations, citing the need for a 'community centre'[36] or a 'social club with . . . class' because the New Irish miss the 'discos'.[37] During the 1980s and into the 1990s, parish youth groups were organized within the New Irish community, many of which sponsor sports activities and social events. The survey indicates that sports events and exercise are popular with at least a quarter of the respondents.

Clearly, the bar is not the only social outlet for the respondents. But its dominance among the choices is significant as an example of the insularity of the community. In a city like New York it is hard to imagine that a young adult could not find more to do than go to a bar. But the bar is where other Irish like themselves are. It is a safe, known destination – it's what they associate with home.

Fear of detection or mistrust of strangers might be preventing the respondents from venturing beyond their community, but only 11 per cent of the undocumented surveyed listed the Immigration and Naturalization Service (INS) as their greatest fear in New York (see survey results, question 37.) And if INS agents were going to look for illegal Irish aliens, the bars in Queens would probably be their first stop. More significantly 60 per cent of the documented respondents, those who need not fear detection, identified the pub as the place where they spend their leisure time. So with or without the green card, as the answers on friends suggest, the respondents choose to remain among themselves.

Clannishness or reluctance among migrants to assimilate in the host country is not uncommon. But in the case of the New Irish it should be considered in the context of a larger dynamic that involves their reasons for leaving Ireland and their plans for the future.

Education, employment, expectations

The survey indicates that 66 per cent of the respondents had jobs when they left Ireland. This is consistent with previous studies of the community[38] and prevents the automatic conclusion that Ireland's high unemployment rate through the 1980s was the sole factor pushing migrants out of the country. Yet research also suggests that, while migrants may have been employed at the time of their departure, they were probably 'underemployed' or, as the NESC argues, their situation in Ireland was failing to achieve their 'personal and occupational aspirations'.[39] (See survey results, question 25, for the types of jobs held by respondents in Ireland.)

As reported earlier, the Irish who came of age in the 1980s were probably the best educated the country had ever produced, and according to interviews these young people were raised with high expectations. But by the early 1980s Ireland could not fulfil the promise of its young people.[40] The recession was complicated by the fact that almost half (47·8 per cent)[41] of the total population in 1981 were under twenty-five years of age, producing what the CSO calls 'labour supply pressures' that will remain to the end of this century.[42]

Historians have argued that emigration has been among the expected options for generations of Irish young people since at least the 1800s.[43] But this survey suggests, as do other reports,[44] that, despite the economic obstacles, some New Irish explored the job market at home before migrating. The average age of all respondents upon arrival in America was twenty-three and a quarter years. Considered with the fact that the majority of respondents had jobs when they left Ireland, it is apparent that their decision to leave was not a hasty one.[45]

The age upon arrival varies according to the education level of the respondent. The average age upon arrival for respondents with leaving certificates was 24·25 years, for those with some undergraduate experience it was 23·70 years, for those with graduate experience it dropped to 22·70 years. These findings suggest that, for the better-educated respondent, the decision to migrate came soon after or upon entering the labour force. The more years one spent in school the less time one spent pursuing opportunities in Ireland. These results correspond to the NESC findings on the migration and employment experience of second and third-level school leavers between 1980 and 1988.[46] The NESC also argues that for those with higher skill levels the job market in Ireland is very tight, and the opportunities for advancement are limited.[47]

The age of the graduate is also important. While the level of education may correspond to the level of aspiration and ambition of a graduate, those leaving university are older and presumably more mature than those leaving a secondary-level institution or lower, so it may not be surprising that they opt to migrate sooner upon finishing their education.

The impact of expectation and aspiration on migration is considerable, but it is not necessarily defined by the number of years spent in school. The generation which produced the New Irish grew up watching television and therefore had electronic access to the whole world, particularly to the United States. They were exposed to life in the US via television and film, which at the very least may have aroused their curiosity about the country, and very likely introduced them to the opportunities that existed outside Ireland. The United States has been familiar to the Irish for two centuries because of the history of migration between the two countries, but the expansion of the broadcasting industry brought America into the living rooms of the Irish. It arguably made the US a more accessible and more familiar place. The frequency and speed of air travel between the two countries brought them closer together physically and logistically. So for young Irish people of ability and desire New York was not so foreign a destination in the 1980s. Their situation was not unlike that of a young adult from a small town in Maine or Midwestern America who moves to New York city to start a career because his/her home town cannot satisfy his/her ambition.

When asked directly why they left Ireland the answers from the respondents were mixed (see survey results, question 11.) Thirty per cent of the entire sample cited joblessness as the reason for migrating, while 25·5 per cent indicated that a restrictive life style and culture pushed them out. When asked why they came to New York, the response was equally mixed (see survey results, question 12.) One-third came to New York looking for a better future, 25 per cent were looking for work and 14 per cent had a job offer. Twenty-nine per cent migrated because their 'friends are here', 17 per cent because 'family is here' and almost a quarter (24 per cent) came to New York seeking adventure.

Looked at more closely, the results offer additional evidence that the respondents to the survey were not driven from Ireland for economic reasons alone. Despite Ireland's high taxes, only 15 per cent cited taxes as a reason for leaving, and only 25 per cent of the sample came to New York looking for work. The response 'a better future' has financial as well as social or cultural connotations. More specifically, just over a third of the respondents cited a restrictive life style and personal problems as reasons for leaving.

The 'push' factor of social and cultural constrictions deserves attention. Evidence from this study, and from others,[48] suggests that many migrants left Ireland in search of personal as well as financial freedom. One thirty-two-year-old woman in New York since 1985 wrote, 'I like the USA. Am very glad I left Ireland, hated the weather and the way of life.'[49] This is not merely the testimony of youth sowing wild oats. Other commentary suggests that migration was the only route to escape what a migrant in Mary Corcoran's population called the 'cultural straitjacket of Ireland', where personal 'initiative' and creativity are 'scorned'.[50] One thirty-year-old respondent confessed that after living in New York she could never be as 'narrow-minded' as when she left Ireland.[51] A thirty-five-year-old woman from Kilkenny wrote that 'the biggest thing about N.Y. for me is that nobody cares what you do'.[52]

Answers to another question suggest a more subtle form of rebellion. Almost half (49 per cent) the respondents claim to attend church less often in America than at home (see survey results, question 10.) Just under half (45 per cent) admit no difference in their church attendance. Ninety-six per cent of the respondents are Catholic. In Ireland the Catholic Church is a dominant social and political force with conservative positions that are contrary to those held by many young adults. According to the *Irish Voice*, a 1991 poll by the Augustinian Order shows that 'attitudes towards the Catholic Church in Ireland are characterized by a feeling of "anger, frustration and disillusionment" '. The poll results show that many feel the Church's leadership is 'out of touch with what its members need'.[53] Consider the comments of a thirty-year-old woman from Roscommon about life in New York: 'Being able to get a divorce was great. Not being able to get my marriage annulled is horrible. All in all, N.Y. is the best.'[54]

At the very least the decline in church attendance may reflect the absence of social and parental pressure to conform to expected religious behaviour. But it may also reflect more serious dissatisfaction with the Church and its influence on Irish society. In either case it is one example of the exercise of personal freedom these New Irish respondents enjoy in America.

Peer pressure also seemed to have a strong influence on the push and pull factors affecting the respondents' migration. Eighteen per cent replied that they left Ireland because 'friends emigrated', while 29 per cent came to New York because of friends. Migrant interviews and popular newspaper accounts suggest that the out-migration Ireland suffered through the 1980s devastated small towns throughout the Irish countryside. Archbishop Joseph Cassidy of County Galway claims that in the west of Ireland there are villages inhabited only by senior citizens and babies.[55] One migrant interviewed by this author in 1989 said:

> What's the point [of going home to Cavan]? It's changed. You go back looking for people and then you realize they're probably living only 100 miles from you here [New Jersey suburb]. You start looking for them. They're in New York, they're in London, they're in Canada. They're all gone.[56]

The survey respondents are part of a population that emigrated at the point in their life when most young adults begin to explore their independence and go on to build a future. Some in the survey were deliberate in their decision to begin that growth process in New York. But many apparently left because everyone else was going and it seemed the thing to do at the time. Three or four years later, these young people are thirty years of age (or close to it) with no clear direction in their life, and great uncertainty as to where their future lies, at least geographically.

The 1990s and beyond

Almost three-quarters of the respondents live in New York city, the majority (41 per cent) in Queens (see survey results, question 6.) Forty per cent of all the respondents are not sure whether they will stay in the area during the next five years (see survey results, question 5.) Their indecision could be related to uncertainty about their legal status, but 43 per cent of the documented respondents are also not sure where they will be in the next five years. With the green card the migrants' options and opportunities in America are greater. They can leave the New York area for other parts of the United States in pursuit of better jobs or a different life style with greater ease than their illegal peers.

Overall the respondents' uncertainty about the next five years may simply reflect their unhappiness at living in New York city. Crime was identified by 47 per cent of all the respondents as their number one fear in New York (see survey results, question 37). The city was described by various respondents as 'a quagmire'[57] or ridden with drugs. A twenty-six-year-old documented man from Connecticut who had lived in the Bronx for four years wrote that he felt happier, safer and more relaxed in the suburbs. 'I will never – and I mean never – live in New York city again.'[58]

The undocumented respondents, 39 per cent of whom were not sure where they would be in five years, are probably awaiting the distribution of the Morrison visas. Under the programme legislated at the end of 1990, 48,000 visas will be distributed to Irish aliens over a three-year period. They will be assigned by a lottery held the week of 14 October 1991.[59] As one twenty-four-year-old woman wrote, 'It is difficult to plan your future here [New York] when you don't know if you can stay or not.'[60]

The frustration of gaining the green card and the struggles of urban living aside, the respondents' uncertainty about the future may just be ambivalence towards America. The remarks of a documented twenty-seven-year-old man from Offaly reflect other survey results which suggest that the links with home were not entirely severed for all respondents: 'New York is a wonderful city to come and work in and earn money. But New York is not the place to raise a family and grow old in. There is no place like home, after all.'[61]

Sixty-four per cent of all those surveyed, as well as 62 per cent of the documented respondents, said they wanted to vote in Irish elections (see survey results, question 14.) Having the green card does not diminish the New Irish interest in participating in the political process at home. A group called the Irish Emigrant Vote Campaign (IEVC) was formed in 1991 by migrants in the United States who want the Irish government to grant the vote to emigrants, many of whom, according to the *Irish Voice*, 'wish to return home at some time' and therefore have a voice 'in the future direction of the country'.[62]

The personal ties with home are just as strong: more than half (55 per cent) of all respondents phone home more than once a month[63] (see survey results, question 18). Survey results also show that phone contact with Ireland does not diminish over time. Regardless of the year of arrival, a minimum of 50 per cent of all the respondents continue to phone home more than once a month (see survey results, question 18.)

But in spite of the pull towards home the respondents showed a reluctance to leave the United States. For the undocumented the inertia is dictated by their legal status. Forty-four per cent of the undocumented respondents ranked the inability to travel to Ireland as their number one problem (see survey results, question 36.) If undocumented aliens leave the United States they risk being denied re-entry. With the passage of the 1986 immigration legislation the INS enforced tighter screening procedures at points of entry (including Shannon airport in Limerick) to reduce the number of visa overstays. As a result, many undocumented remain in the United States. Much as they miss home, they are not willing to relinquish what they have in America. A twenty-six-year-old woman from Westmeath wrote, '[I] would much prefer to live in Ireland, but only if I could live in comfort with a secure income.'[64]

The documented respondents are free to travel between the two countries. (Only 5 per cent of the documented respondents cite the inability to travel to Ireland as their number one problem in New York.) Almost half (42 per cent) visit Ireland at least once a year, compared to 37 per cent who go home less than once a year (see survey results, question 15). The latter number may include those who cannot return to Ireland because of financial restraints.

It is clear that the majority of respondents want to maintain contact with Ireland. The results show a consistent, conscious attempt by most to hold on to their Irish roots without giving up what they have come to enjoy in America. It is as if they are exploring a binational existence – selecting what they need from both countries but refusing or unable to commit themselves to one or the other.

Conclusion

What does this survey tell us about the New Irish and their future? Anecdotal evidence from community leaders and observers claims the population of New Irish is shrinking in the New York area.[65] The bars and churches appear to be less crowded in 1991 than in the mid-1980s. Many New Irish are believed to have gone home at Christmas 1990 and stayed there. The Emigrant Advice Service in Dublin reported that enquiries about the United States were down in 1990 from the previous year.[66] But by the summer of 1991 the bureau noted that the United States became the most popular or frequently asked about destination for the year, primarily because of interest in the Morrison visa programme.[67]

A look at the survey results shows that few of the respondents arrived after 1987 (see survey results, question 4.) Department of Labour statistics from Ireland show that emigration dropped to 1,000 for the year 1990/1 from 31,000 the previous year.[68] Tougher immigration regulations and a slow economy, particularly in the north-eastern United States, were probable factors in the decline. But as of August 1991 the news at home was not encouraging, either. Ireland faces a serious unemployment crisis.[69] Returning Irish emigrants and school leavers enter an economy that cannot provide jobs for them.

This survey cannot speak for all the migrants in New York, but among those who responded it exposes apparent confusion as to where their future lies. The majority who participated in the survey have lived in the New York area for several years. They entered adulthood in America. Given their age and legal status, it would seem that the majority of the respondents are caught in a limbo. One migrant complained that her 'life is on hold' until her status changes.[70] But documentation does not seem to liberate the respondents in terms of determining their future, either. Uncertainty and indecision persist, with or without the green card.

The survey shows that the respondents have established a way of life – economically and socially – they feel they cannot reproduce in Ireland. Yet while testimony and answers from the survey suggest that they enjoy the social and financial freedom available in America, they resist the notion that their adopted country will be their permanent home. (Other studies and editorial comment in the *Irish Voice* offer the same evidence – that many New Irish ultimately plan to return to Ireland).[71] They insulate themselves within the migrant community. They want a voice politically in Ireland. (And, as discussed earlier, a movement within the community has organized to obtain an emigrant vote for Ireland.) They want the opportunity to travel freely between both countries. They claim they do not want to raise families in New York (although that may just be an objection to a difficult urban environment). On the basis of the respondents' evidence, Ireland seems to be the ideal location for children but not for young adults.

In examining the results, Ireland's poor economy and labour surplus undoubtedly provided the final push that drove the respondents abroad. But as these responses and the NESC report show, except for the best educated respondents, most migrants were not recent school leavers. Most had a job when they left and were a few years out of school at the time of departure, suggesting that they attempted to start a life in Ireland but were dissatisfied with their employment and/or prospects.

Other evidence indicates that dissatisfaction with Irish society may have influenced the respondents' decision to migrate. These factors are hard to quantify and substantiate, but the results and individual testimony reveal a restlessness and personal turmoil that deserve further examination from the point of departure. Apparently Ireland produced a generation it could not support economically or satisfy socially. Some in this generation may have been driven to migration regardless of the recession in the early 1980s.[72] Perhaps Ireland is not big enough – culturally, economically or socially – to manage a population dominated by young adults.

The next decade will be decisive for the New Irish. For many, the future depends on the Morrison visa and how long they are willing to live out of status until the visas are available. But since so many documented migrants in this survey admit to an uncertain future, maybe the green card is not the only answer. The survey shows it may open more career doors, at least in terms of a higher income – documented respondents earned $3,000 to $10,000 more than their undocumented peers. But is that all the New Irish want? Consider one of the population's more visible members. Sean Minihane returned to Ireland in 1990 to accept a job with an engineering firm in Dublin, but he still considers himself chairman of the IIRM in America.[73] The following year he was selected to co-ordinate the emigrant vote campaign in Ireland for the IEVC.[74] Clearly he has not cut the cord between the two countries.

Can the migrants have it both ways? Or will they ultimately have to decide between Ireland and America? Modern communications and air transport offer the opportunities to coexist between the two countries. But as the migrant population grows older and begins to form families a transient life style becomes more complicated. Yet with a green card it would be possible for a migrant to work in the United States and visit Ireland for a period every year. It is conceivable, therefore, that this generation of Irish migrants could lead binational lives.

The 1991 NESC report on emigration notes a change in the character of

Irish emigration over the last century. Since the Second World War its findings show significant simultaneous population flows both in and out of Ireland, suggesting that emigration may not be the final act of severance from the homeland that it was in the last century.[75] Migration to America is not necessarily a one-way trip.

The 1990s, particularly the period of the Morrison visa distribution, will be a crucial phase in the evolution of the New Irish in New York and the United States. The majority will presumably be documented. Their opportunities and options for work and movement within and outside the United States will be greater. But it is unclear how they will respond to these choices and where, or whether, they will settle their families. As the twenty-first century approaches it will be fascinating to observe their experience in the continuum of more than 200 years of Irish migration to the United States.

Appendix 10.1: survey results

All figures per cent unless otherwise indicated.

1 Year of birth:

Males 1961 (average).
Females 1962·5 (average).

2 Sex:

Male 45
Females 54

3 Irish origin:

Dublin	9	Longford	3
Cavan	8	Offaly	3
Cork	6	Sligo	3
Kerry	6	Westmeath	3
Clare	5	Donegal	2
Mayo	5	Kilkenny	2
Tipperary	5	Laois	2
Limerick	4	Roscommon	2
Meath	4	Waterford	2
Monaghan	4	Antrim	1
Galway	3	Derry	1
Leitrim	3	No response	9

Less than 1 per cent: Armagh, Carlow, Down, Kildare, Louth, Tyrone, Wexford, Wicklow.

4 Year of arrival in America:

1990	2	1985	17
1989	6	1984	10
1988	9	1983	5
1987	17	1982	2
1986	25	1980	1

5 Do you plan to spend the next five years in the New York area?

	All	*Undocumented*	*Documented*
Yes	41	42	43
No	16	17	12
Unsure	40	39	43

6 Current local residence:

Boro:	Queens	41	State:	New York	89
	Bronx	22		New Jersey	6
	Brooklyn	4		Connecticut	4
	Manhattan	4			

7 Marital status:

Single	64
Married	32
Divorced	1
Separated	1
Widowed	less than 1

8 If married, is spouse a citizen of:

Ireland?	80
America?	16

9 Number of children: 1·02 average for all those claiming to have children.

10a How would you compare your church attendance in New York with your attendance in Ireland?

The same	45
More often	3
Less often	49

10b Religion:

Catholic	96
Protestant	2

11 Why did you leave Ireland? (Respondents could check [tick] more than one answer.)

No job	30
Restrictive life style, culture	25·5
Career break	22
Friends emigrated	18
Disapointment with government representation	16·5
High taxes	15
Personal problems	10·5
The weather	3

12 Why did you come to New York? (See note to question 11.)

A better future	33
Friends are here	29
To look for work	25
Adventure	24
Family is here	17
Job offer	14
Easiest point of entry	5
Other	3
Education	3

13 What is your current legal status?

Undocumented	58
Donnelly visa recipient	22
Visa through marriage	6
H-1 visa	4
Visa through immediate relative	4
Sponsorship	2

14 Do you want to vote in Irish elections?

	All	*Undocumented*	*Documented*
Yes	64	64	62
No	30	31	32

15 How often do you visit Ireland each year?

	All	*Undocumented*	*Documented*
Less than once	57	73	37
Twice	6	1	12
Once	31	20	42
More often	2	–	3

16 How do you spend your leisure time? (Respondents could check [tick] more than one response if appropriate.)

	All	Undocumented	Documented
Continuing your education	24		
Irish or county organizations	13		
Museums	9		
Sporting events	31		
Exercise	26		
Parish groups	3		
Movies	56		
Pubs	65		60
Dances	15		

17 Are your friends in New York primarily? (See note to question 16.)

	All	Undocumented	Documented
Irish	83	83	83
Documented	26	22	33
American	18	18	17
Irish–American	21	20	18
Undocumented	48	57	39
Other	5	3	

18 How often do you phone home?

Once a month	30
Less than once a month	13
More than once a month	55

Phoning home by year arrived in US:

	Once a month	Less/month	More/month
1990	20	–	60
1989	37.5	–	56
1988	27	4.5	68
1987	23	14	60
1986	33	13	52
1985	35	14	51
1984	25	17	58
1983	25	25	50
1982	50	–	50

19 Please indicate your level of education:

	All	*Undocumented*	*Documented*
Inter cert.	19	23	14
Leaving cert.	49	53	44
A level	2	–	3
Undergraduate	6	4	11
Graduate	9	3	14
Technical cert.	11	13	11
Group cert.	4	6	2
Primary	2	3	2

20 Are you currently continuing your education?

	All	*Undocumented*	*Documented*
Yes	23	19	29
No	74	80	67

22 If you are not in school, would you like to continue your education?

	All	*Undocumented*	*Documented*
Yes	54	61	47
No	21	22	19

23 If you are not in school, which of the following would you be most likely to use in making the decision to return to school?

	All	*Undocumented*	*Documented*
Seminars on the American school system	7	7	7
Literature on the American school system	5	1	12
Listings of schools and degree programmes in the metro-olitan area	16	14	20
Seminars on career opportuni-ties and degree requirements for specific careers	34	31	37
Seminars on opportunities for undocumented aliens in the American school system	31	45	12

24 Were you employed when you left Ireland?

Yes	66
No	32

25 What best describes your last job in Ireland?

Skilled trade	18	Civil service	8
Office work	16	Agriculture	5
Professional	9	Bank position	1
Construction	9	Other	31

The occupations listed under 'other':

Bar/restaurant/hotel	21
Sales/retail	18
Factory	13
Student	12
Blank	12
Management/ business/ self-employed	9
Nurse/health care/ hospital	7
Unemployed	5
Miscellaneous, e.g., welder, fishing	3

26 What kind of work do you do now?

Construction, building, contracting	28
Bar/restaurant	16
Baby-sitting/home care	15
Nursing	10
Office work	8
Blank (no answer)	8
Professional (teacher, accountant, etc.)	6
Miscellaneous	4
Sales/service	3
Skilled trade	2

27 How did you get your first job in New York?

Friend	42
Newspaper ad in US	15
Referral	15
Family	11
Other	10
Newspaper ad in Ireland	5

28 What best describes your experience finding or changing jobs in New York?

Relied on information from friends	72
Good luck in the want ads	13
Connections made in a pub	10
Employment agency	9
I've had trouble finding work because I don't know where to go or who to talk to	4
IIRM office less than	1

29 Do you feel you have ever experienced employment discrimination?

Yes   21

30 Did you file income tax this year?

	All	Undocumented	Documented
Yes	43	25	65
No	56	74	34

31 Have you filed your income tax every year since you came to New York?

	All	Undocumented	Documented
Yes	24	15	32
No	74	84	67

32 Do you have a local savings or chequebook account?

	All	Undocumented	Documented
Yes	83	76	94
No	16	24	5

33 Do you own property in the United State?

	All	Undocumented	Documented
Yes	6	3	9
No	90	94	86

34 What is your current salary level?

	All	Undocumented	Documented
Under $10 000	12	14	9

$10 000–19 999	21	25	17
$20 000–29 999	29	27	28
$30 000–39 999	18	16	21
$40 000–49 999	9	5	16
Over $50 000	3	3	2

	Male	*Female*
Under $10 000	3	19
$10 000–19 999	6	33
$20 000–29 999	31	27
$30 000–39 999	31	7
$40 000–49 999	16	4
Over $50 000	5	–

35 Do you send money back to Ireland, either to family or to a bank account?

Yes	51
No	47

36 What are your biggest problems in New York? (Please rank all choices in order of significance, i.e. 1, 2, 3, etc.) The following show the No. 1 rankings of the respondents:

	All	*Undocumented*	*Documented*
Loneliness	6	6	
Social life	10	6	
Finding work	6	8	
Living arrange-ments	3	2	
Cost of living	13	7	
Insurance	14	14	
Homesickness	6	3	
Inability to tra-vel to Ireland	28	44	5

37 What are your greatest fears in New York? (See notes to question 36.)

	All	*Undocumented*
Crime	47	
Unemployment	17	
Poor health	12	
The INS	7	11
No money	5	

The Internal
Revenue Service   2
Other   2
Alcoholism   1
Loss of housing   –
Drug dependence   –

38 Do you have a local driver's licence?

Yes   72
No   27

39 Do you have medical insurance?

Yes   45
No   55

40 If you are undocumented, have you had difficulty obtaining any of the following?

	Yes	No
Bank account	27	64
Driver's licence	29	60
Admission to education programmes	17	45
Phone	22	67
Credit card	51	31
Loans	25	30
Property	22	29
Mortgage	20	25

41 Which Irish Immigration Reform Movement services or seminars have you used or attended? (Please check as many as appropriate.)

	All	Undocumented	Documented
Hot line	35	36	38
Donnelly visa seminars	28	24	36
Education seminars	22	27	15
Public meetings	32	35	26
Immigration Advice Center	27	34	18
None	23	22	21

42 Do you feel the need for an Irish Immigrant Advice Center?

Yes   96
No   2

Notes

1. *Irish Voice*, 3 December 1988, p. 8.
2. Brendan, Walsh, 'Emigration: an economist's perspective', 14 August 1988, p. 2.
3. The EIIC is the advice and counselling branch of the Irish Immigration Reform Movement (IIRM.) The IIRM is a group founded by illegal Irish aliens to lobby for changes in US immigration laws. The IIRM opened its doors in Queens, a borough of New York city, in 1987. By 1990 it had offices and volunteers in more than seventeen cities around the United States. The EIIC was formally established in July 1988 to conduct the outreach services the IIRM recognized were needed in the New Irish community.
4. *New York Times*, 25 December 1981, p. D1.
5. Walsh, 'Emigration', p. 2.
6. Mary Corcoran, 'Ethnic Boundaries and Legal Barriers: the Labor Market Experience of Undocumented Irish Workers in New York City', paper in possession of the present writer, April 1988, p. 10.
7. Corcoran, 'Ethnic Boundaries', p. 10.
8. Sean Minihane, phone interview, 27 December 1988, notes in the possession of the author.
9. Walsh, 'Emigration', pp. 3–6.
10. Walsh, 'Emigration', p. 5. For a more complete look at the factors leading up to Irish migration during the 1980s see Linda Dowling Almeida, 'The lost generation: the undocumented Irish in New York city in the 1980s', *New York Irish History Roundtable Journal*, 4, 1989, p. 25. Copies available from Irish Books and Graphics, New York.
11. Central Statistics Office, *Ireland Census 86 Summary Population Report*, Stationery Office, Dublin, November 1987, p. ix.
12. National Economic and Social Council (NESC,) *The Economic and Social Implications of Emigration*, 90, National Economic and Social Council, Dublin, March 1991, p. 53.
13. NESC, *Implications*, p. 59.
14. According to a report published by the Higher Education Authority (HEA) in Ireland and reported in the *Irish Voice*, 24–31 December 1988, p. 4, 70 per cent of graduates who emigrate go to Britain, 10·1 per cent to North America and 9·8 percent to the continent. See also Damien Courtney, 'Summary of Recent Trends in Emigration from Ireland', Development Studies Association annual conference, Queen's University of Belfast, September 1989. The author states that most Irish migrants leave for English-speaking countries 'with as many as 70 per cent' going to Britain.
15. The Consul General of Ireland and the US Catholic Conference argue for the lower figures. See Anne Barrington, 'Emigration from Ireland: Why and How Many', May 1991, pp. 5–6, available from press officer in New York; Migration and Refugee Services Staff report, US Catholic Conference unpublished report, 'Undocumented Irish in the US', March 1988 (in possession of author) and Lorcan O'Riada, *Boston Irish News*, 14, 3, April 1989, p. 1 The IIRM, the *Irish Voice* and the Bishop's Episcopal Commission in Ireland advocate the higher numbers. See *Irish Voice*, 5 December 1987; IIRM press kit for releases citing population figures and Corcoran's paper for references to the Bishop's report.
16. According to the Immigration and Naturalization Service, *1987 Statistical Yearbook*, October 1988, p. 6, Irish migration to the US slowed to an average

annual rate of 1,000 between 1981 and 1985, with a low of 902 in 1981.

17. Congressional Research Office, 'US Immigration Law and Policy, 1952–1986', December 1987, pp. 55–7 and Barrington, 'Emigration from Ireland', pp. 7–8.
18. According to a 28 September 1988 interview with James Farrell, New Immigrant Liaison at the Irish Consul General's office in New York (notes in possession of author), prior to 1986 there was no impetus to obtain a green card. According to him the New Irish were afraid of lawyers, and the legal fees ranging from $1,600 to $3,000 at the time (according to discussions with immigration attorneys and New Irish migrants) were too expensive for most of the migrants. Also, according to interviews with New Irish and those with contacts in the community, work was very easy to find for illegal Irish in the early 1980s. It became more difficult with the passage of the 1986 Immigration Reform and Central Act, which imposed sanctions on employers hiring anyone without proper labour certification or proof of citizenship.
19. Known respectively as the Donnelly, Berman and Morrison visa programmes after the legislators who sponsored the Bills, the laws provide non-preference visas for immigrants from specific countries, including Ireland. The most important to the Irish are the Donnelly and Morrison visas. Between 1988 and 1990 Irish nationals received 40 per cent of the 40,000 Donnelly visas made available, and a quota of 48,000 (out of 120,000) Morrison visas has been established for the Irish for distribution over a three-year period beginning in 1992. For a more complete explanation see Barrington, 'Emigration from Ireland', pp. 8–10.
20. Barrington, 'Emigration from Ireland', pp. 9–10.
21. Almeida, 'Lost generation'.
22. *Irish Voice*, 5 December 1987, p. 1.
23. The Next Wave is a programme aimed at the New Irish audience. It combines music, news and interviews of relevance to the New Irish and is hosted by Sean Benson, executive director of the EIIC, and Gary Miley, an officer of the IIRM.
24. The archdiocese of New York and the diocese of Brooklyn working with the Catholic Bishops of Ireland recruit Irish chaplains to live among the New Irish in the boroughs of New York city. Representatives of the first group from Ireland arrived in New York in 1987 to work in the archdiocese of New York and included four priests and a nun.
25. This research and speculation are based on J. J. Sexton, 'Recent changes in the Irish population and in the pattern of emigration', *Irish Banking Review*, Dublin, autumn 1987, p. 37, and on estimates from the IIRM and Irish consulate in New York.
26. NESC, *Implications*, p. 93.
27. See *US News and World Report*, 2 March 1987, p. 15; *Newsweek*, 5 October 1987, p. 35; *New York Times*, 27 November 1988, p. 52; *New York Times Magazine*, 20 November 1988, p. 28.
28. Note that the population can be transient and some migrants may have travelled back and forth between countries since the time of their first arrival. However, since the 1986 Immigration Reform and Control Act such travel has been curtailed because the illegal aliens fear being denied re-entry to America.
29. Documented Irish in the context of this chapter include those respondents who claim to be a Donnelly visa recipient, have a visa through marriage, a visa through a relative, an H-1 visa or a sponsorship.

30. In the early 1980s the New Irish could not open bank accounts because they did not have social security numbers. Since then some banks have begun to offer services specifically for undocumented aliens. The 1 February 1989 IIRM newsletter reported that emigrant savings bank branches offered full services to 'all Irish immigrants'. (Newsletter in possession of author.)

31. Survey questionnaire No. 83, in the possession of the author.

32. Survey questionnaire No. 131, in the possession of the author.

33. Night life in New York city never ends; in Ireland pubs typically close at eleven in the evening.

34. See 'On the Emigrant Trail' series, *Irish Voice*, 8 June 1991, p. 34; 15 June 1991, p. 28; 22 June 1991, p. 20.

35. Good examples of migrant testimony include Higgins, Connie, Astoria, New York, letter to editor, *Irish Voice*, 17 November 1990, p. 9, and taped interviews with migrants Ted and Tom on 23 March 1989, Ellen and Siobhan on 27 September 1987, and Avril, Ellen and Ted on 12 October 1988. All migrant names are aliases and the tapes are in the possession of the author.

36. Survey questionnaire No. 210, in the possession of the author.

37. Survey questionnaire No. 37, in the possession of the author. Regarding the demand for discos, in Ireland socializing among young people continues in the discos after the pubs close at 11 p.m.

38. Mary Corcoran argues in her paper (p. 11) that the migrants in her study were underemployed and overtaxed in Ireland. All the migrants interviewed by the author of this chapter for her initial research were employed at the time of their migration. Eighty-two per cent of the respondents interviewed for the *Irish Voice* survey in 1987 were employed at the time they left Ireland. See *Irish Voice*, 6 December 1987, p. 1.

39. See NESC, *Implications*, chapter 6, in particular p. 159.

40. See NESC, *Implications*, chapter 6, pp. 142 and 158 in particular.

41. CSO, *Census*, p. vii.

42. CSO, *Population and Labour Force Projections, 1991–2021*, Stationery Office, Dublin, April 1988, p. 15.

43. See Kerby Miller, *Emigrants and Exiles: Ireland and the Irish Exodus to North America*, Oxford University Press, New York, 1985. The author argues that Ireland suffers from a culture of exile.

44. NESC, *Implications* pp. 88, 160; Sexton, 'Recent changes', pp. 38–9.

45. It should be noted here that the United States may not be the first destination of the migrants upon leaving Ireland. As mentioned previously, most migrants go to Britain, and it is not unusual for them to then move on to the US.

46. NESC, *Implications*, p. 88.

47. See NESC, *Implications*, chapter 6, particularly pp. 88, 123, 144, 145, 159.

48. See Almeida, 'The lost generation'; Corcoran, 'Ethnic boundaries'; Ide O'Carroll, *Models for Movers: Irish Women's Emigration to America*, Attic Press, Dublin, 1990.

49. Survey questionnaire No. 143, in the possession of the author.

50. Corcoran, 'Ethnic boundaries', p. 12.

51. Survey questionnaire No. 33, in the possession of the author.

52. Survey questionnaire No. 201, in the possession of the author.

53. *Irish Voice*, 22 June 1991, p. 7.

54. Survey questionnaire No. 139, in the possession of the author.

55. *Irish Voice*, 16 February 1991, p. 7.

56. Tape interview with Ted (alias), 23 March 1989. Tape in the possession of the author.

57. Survey questionnaire No. 24, in the possession of the author.
58. Survey questionnaire No. 46, in the possession of the author.
59. Barrington, 'Emigration from Ireland', pp. 8–9. See *New York Times*, 12 October 1991, Metropolitan section, for more on lottery.
60. Survey questionnaire No. 30, in the possession of the author.
61. Survey questionnaire No. 36, in the possession of the author.
62. See *Irish Voice*, 1 October 1991, p. 4, for the story on IEVC. Also, the 29 October 1991 *Irish Voice* editorial called on the New Irish to fight for the emigrant vote, since the Morrison visa effort was over 'for now'. See p. 10.
63. AT&T reported that in 1988 5·1 million calls were made to Ireland, an increase of 3·1 million since 1982. See *Irish Voice*, 7 January 1989, p. 1. This does not include calls made on other overseas carriers.
64. Survey questionnaire No. 51, in the possession of the author.
65. *An Gael*, VII, 41, September 1991, p. 4.
66. Emigrant Advice, *Annual Report 1990*, Dublin, p. 5. Copies available from Emigrant Advice Service.
67. Nic Giolla Choille, Triona, Emigrant Advice Information and Counselling Service, Dublin, 19 August 1991. Letter to Linda Dowling Almeida, in the possession of the author.
68. Freda Nolan, Secretary, Office of the Minister for Labour. Letter to Linda Dowling Almeida, 30 July 1991.
69. The *Irish Voice*, 13 August 1991, p. 3, and 20 August p. 3, reported that Ireland recorded its highest unemployment rate in the history of the republic.
70. Survey questionnaire No. 27, in the possession of the author.
71. Both O'Carroll and Corcoran argue that the New Irish interviewed for their studies do not believe that the United States is their final home. See also *Irish Voice*, 22 October 1991, p. 7 and 29 October 1991, p. 18.
72. The NESC report (p. 73) shows that even during the 1971–81 intercensal period a net out-migration of persons in the fifteen-to-thirty-four-year-old age group continued, albeit much lower than previous decades, despite a net inflow of population to Ireland in that decade.
73. See *Irish Voice*, 5 January 1991, p. 2; 2 March 1991, p. 1; 9 March 1991, pp. 3, 32. Minihane's claim to the title is disputed by IIRM co-founder Pat Hurley, who claims he was elected national co-chairman on 26 January 1991.
74. *Irish Voice*, 22 October 1991, p. 7.
75. NESC, p. 59.

Index

Introductory note

The six volumes of *The Irish World Wide* bring together material to begin the inter-disciplinary, world-wide study of the Irish and their migrations. The aim of this index to Volume 1, *Patterns of Migration*, is to provide a useful guide to the contents of this volume, while bearing in mind the contents of later volumes – all building, of course, towards the cumulative index at the end of the series.

The words 'Irish', 'Ireland', 'migration', and so on, appear, as you would expect, regularly throughout the pages of the series, and there is little point in exhaustively indexing such words. In the same way, since this is a series about the Irish and their migrations, there would be little point in putting the word 'Irish' in front of every appropriate main heading. Thus 'family names' refers to 'Irish family names', 'women' refers to 'Irish women', and so on. The index aims at guidance to key themes and debates under such headings.

Irish family names are often used as evidence by researchers – knowledge of the patterns of Irish family names is in itself a research tool. Names of places, within Ireland and outside, appear repeatedly throughout these pages. If we indexed every mention of every Irish family name, and every mention of every place, the index would become prohibitively long.

Chapters are thoroughly indexed under their main headings, to do justice to the work and thought of contributors. Names of people and places and keywords are indexed if there is a substantial section in the text about that person, place or theme, *or* if such indexing helps specialists to find material of interest, *or* if those names or words cumulatively link with important areas of discussion within Irish Migration Studies.